KINSHIP, AFFINITY AND DOMESTIC GROUP
A Study among the Mishing of the Brahmaputra Valley

Kinship, Affinity and Domestic Group

A study among the Mishing of the Brahmaputra Valley

J.S. BHANDARI

GYAN

GYAN PUBLISHING HOUSE

NEW DELHI-110 002

GYAN PUBLISHING HOUSE
5, Ansari Road, Daryaganj,
New Delhi-110002

ISBN **81-212-0388-0**

PRINTED IN INDIA

Published by Mrs. Gayatri Garg for Gyan Publishing House,
New Delhi-110002. Printed at Goyal Offset Printer, Delhi
Laser Typesetting by Mr. B. L. Chhabra & Sangita

PREFACE

The study of kinship has been considered an essential part of social anthropological study. The preeminent place of kinship studies was based on the assumption that kinship systems provide the basis for social formation of nonliterate societies. These studies emphasized the content of human social relations in extremely diverse forms of social systems on the basis of the lowest common denominator of culturally conceptualized biological relatedness, viz. kinship.

The study of tribal societies in India have a very long history and we have many outstanding monographs about several tribes many of which have been studied with kinship systems as their focus. With the country achieving independence, anthropological studies underwent a change engendered by priorities that were envisaged for the new nation were largely centered around problems of integration and development. Caste and peasantry played a pre-dominant role in this respect. The village and the village societies thus became the focus of all attention. Consequently anthropological studies moved from the tribal to rural. Kinship studies did remain within the frame of anthropological enquiry but the focus shifted. Thus, despite a very significant number of distinct tribal societies in India, we have very few analytical studies of their social structures in the past 2-3 decades. The theoretical advance in anthropology were not adequately reflected in Indian tribal ethnographies as few of them were conducted in recent times. The scholarly attention remaining confined to caste and Sanskritic traditions which encapsulated most of the current theoretical debates. Such attention was denied to tribal studies which were represented largely by the classical ethnographic traditions and later by some focus on development.

The present study is aimed at providing an analytical study of the kinship system of one of the largest tribal communities of the plains of Assam, and thus fills in a much felt gap by providing a theoretically oriented tribal study. The main emphasis in this work has been reiteration of the views that kinship system forms the basis of social relationships, descent, filiation, consanguineal ties, and affinity. The reality of kinship is understood in terms of kinship per se and not as a reflection or epiphenomenon. In other words this study intends to restore kinship to its rightful status which was getting lost in a plethora of materialistic explanations.

The study has passed through many phases of introspection to be finally presented in its present form. I should like to express my grateful thanks to a number of friends and scholars who have commented upon the work. My sincere thanks are due to Dr. Subhadra Channa, Mr. Soumendra Patnaik and Mr. Sukant Chaudhury for their sincere and ungrudging help in giving the present work its final shape.

Delhi February 29, 1992 **J.S. BHANDARI**

List of Maps and Figures

List of Tables

Contents

Introduction

The Study of Kinship has occupied the centre stage of anthropological research for a long time and has provided not only the major field of enquiry but also the central concept to generations of anthropologists for writing and analysing the behavioural and organizational dimensions of human society. But even after more than a century of research and discussions, many issues remain unresolved and continue to attract academic interest.

Of late, the two major questions that have engaged the attention of anthropologists revolve round (i) the question of whether Kinship is rooted in biology/ nature or is it purely social/cultural and (ii) what exactly is the nature of kinship; is it be explained as a "thing-in-itself" or is it an epiphenomenon of a deeper more fundamental structural reality.

The nature/culture dichotomy has formed the focus of debate, which includes among others, Needham (1971) ,Barnes (1973) and Gellner (1987). Needham (1971) is of the strong opinion that kinship is purely social, in fact for him there does not exist anything as kinship in the sense of a blood relationship or any kind of relationship. It is simply a transference of rights and duties from one generation to the other.

"Let me simply adopt the minimal premise that kinship has to do with the allocation of rights and their transmission from one generation to the next. These rights are not of any specific kind but are exceedingly various : They include most prominently rights of group membership, succession to office, inheritance of property, locality of residence, type of occupation, and a great deal else. They are all, however, transmissible by modes which have nothing to do with the sex or genealogical status of transmitter or recipient. Certainly they have no intrinsic connexion with the facts, or the cultural idioms, of procreation" (Needham 1971 : 4).

Further he writes : "These jural systems and their component statuses can be genealogically defined. Why this should be so is a fundamental question that has never been properly resolved, and *I cannot take it up here* " (op.cit.) (emphasis added). It is this fundamental question unanswered by Needham that underlies the crux of the debate regarding the true nature of kinship. Needham evades all responsibility by conveniently sidestepping the issue.

In a strong criticism of Needham, Gellner upholds the merits of studying kinship as a set of relations derived primarily from biology. There need not be a one-to-one correspondence, but the ultimate referent remains biological. "There is of course an element of truth in the view Needham stresses...... : namely the fact that social kinship systems are not identical with the reality of physical kinship, but on the contrary, systematically add to it, omit from it, and distort it" (Gellner 1987 : 168). The use of clan names, for instance which after a few generations do not correspond to real genealogical connections may be taken as an example of what Gellner has said "Makes anthropologists insist on not equating kinship beliefs with kinship reality"(op.cit.).

But here the social relationship has as its referent, a physical relation, even if indirectly. An adopted son for instance, is recognized as not having a physical relationship as against biological relationship son, but the social relationship is understood only with reference to the biological relationship, as being established parallel to it. Kinship is a 'function' of biology bearing in mind "that function is not identity" (op. cit.)

Barnes (1973) is concerned with physical kinship in the sense of the beliefs of members of the society about the physical processes involved. Paternity in the physical sense is not in any society a scientifically established fact but a social one in the sense that physical kinship is physical to the extent that it is socially recognised as such, "physical motherhood to physical fatherhood is as nature is to culture" (Barnes 1973 :72). However, according to Gellner, whatever may be the reasons, biological paternity is rarely questioned. In a society where biological paternity is known , very few persons ever have any doubts about the identity of the biological fathers.

Without any reference at all to genetic fatherhood one could not be talking of a father at all. If simply one were to deal with a role of provider/protector without any reference to biological paternity, then why use the term 'father' -with its implication of paternity, either biological or social or both. What Gellner has tried to point out is that ultimately the referent will be biological. This has nothing really to do with Barnes' distinction between a 'physical-physical' relationship or a 'socially recognized physical relationship'.As long as the basic relationship is biological - the social interpretation of it can then be understood only as an interpretation. "If a term is to be classified as a kin term, it must refer to a type of biological relationship , and if a type of relationship is to be held to be a kin relationship , it must be built upon a type of biological relationship. If this logical condition is waived, kinship simply disappears " (Harris 1990 : 38).

Since the Pagro-Mishing are a classical example of what the Neo-Marxist School has defined as a lineage mode of production I would like to give a brief resume of this debate to show that ultimately, no matter how we approach kinship, its reality can only become apparent by the biological referent and ideology of cooperation and amity.

The Neo-Marxist School of thought represented largely by the French Marxist school, struggled hard to rise above vulgar materialistic determination while subscribing to the tenet of determination by the economy in the last instance. Kinship was not to be seen directly determined by productive forces, yet there are differences of opinion as to what exactly is its relation to the economy. One major debate centered around what was widely known as the lineage mode of production, which was concerned with pre-capitalist societies of the non-state type, whose social organisation was based on the patrilineal ideology, where there was a clear cut distinction between elders and youngers, men and women, dead and living, elder sibling and younger sibling etc. These differences led to relations of mutual dependence, not necessarily of exploitation. Women, except in their relationship to men were not accorded independent social and ritual status. They even had to worship their husbands'ancestors and not their own.

An attempt to explain these societies through historical materialism gave rise to a crucial theoretical problem because Marx was not aware of these types of society and had not given his own analysis of them. So the questions were, whether or not and in what way Marxism could be used to explain these societies. One school of thought believed that they represented groups of exploitative classes and thus evolved through their own contradictions. Other school of thought believed that classes as classes existed only in a state society and to talk of classes in a stateless society is itself contrary to classical Marxism. With reference to the concept of kinship, this debate raised questions about the ideology of kinship: whether it was genuinely based on cooperation and amity or did it serve to mask relations of exploitation between different classes of people.

The debate has been summarized very well by Kahn (1981) and Clammer (1985). I shall reproduce only a brief sketch of it. Apart from the questions of exploitation and classes, the other question was of the primacy of kinship in pre-capitalist (or specifically lineage) type of societies.

Meillasoux (1986), who through his classical study of the Guros was the father of the debate, talked of the determining role of a certain level of development of productive forces. Lineage, as a type of social organisation occurs in conjunction with a level of development of productive forces which he calls the Agricultural Domestic Community. Though he talks of the authority of the elders, he does not speak of a class based exploitation. The exploitation he speaks of is of a more fundamental nature based on men's appropriation of the fertility of woman. Patriarchy, according to him, is a control of a female womb, socially necessary for the men who cannot procreate. This is, however not directly related to the Marxian concept of class exploitation neither are the women 'conscious' of themselves as classes.

Terray (1972) has taken Althusser's conceptualization of the social formation as relatively independent levels of economic, juridico-political and ideological structures. He has adopted Althusser's distinction between determination and domination to say that kinship becomes the dominant element when society is self sustaining and there is no exploitation of labour. Thus the lineage mode with its dominance of kinship is seen to have no exploitation. According to him class antagonism gains strength as a concept by distinguishing between societies that have classes and that do not have classes, and would lose all meaning if imputed to lineage societies.

At a later stage Terray (1979) slightly modifies his stance to speak of classes, at least classes-in-themselves, based on pre-existing categories, but not 'self-conscious' classes-for-themselves.

For Godelier (1972) kinship is dominant in pre-capitalist societies but determined in the last instance by the economy. Kinship becomes the dominant principle of social organisation when it performs the 'functions' of both superstructure and infrastructure, i.e. kinship itself functions as relations of production. The unanswered question remains as to why kinship forms the relation of production and not any other superstructural element?

Clammer (1985) has extended Meillasoux's analysis to traditional Chinese society and finds it inadequate. The relatively undifferentiated egalitarian lineages of the Guros (similar to that of the Mishing), are not present in China where there is lineage segmentation, feuds and oppression of the poor and exploitation by an extension of the kinship idiom of lineages, yet determined by conditions outside of it. It is the existence of class differences in society at large that is associated with class difference within lineages.

In view of the great difference in structure of the Guros and the Chinese, Clammer raised the doubt that if it is possible to talk of a lineage mode of production at all? Earlier Hindess and Hirst (1954) had also talked of a uniform stage of Primitive Communism based on collective appropriation marked by a division into simple (hunters and food gatherers) and complex (horticulture, pastoralists) redistribution. The dominant instance here is ideology. They had also denied the existence of a separate lineage mode of production.

According to Clammer (1985:108), " The lineage itself forms a sociological and ideational framework within which different labour processes--farming, fishing etc. are organized; but it itself is not a mode of production ... it is also a kinship system *per se* "

Further as a reversal of Meillasoux's contention he says that "Control over the processes of production allows the elders to exercise in practice, the control over reproduction *already assigned* to them by kinship ideology" (*ibid*.:109) (Emphasis added).

Godelier (1979) too, is skeptical about the concept of the 'lineage mode of production' and also points to the Marxist anthropologists' failure to answer the central question of kinship analysis.

One moot theoretical point raised by Clammer (1985:113) is "that structurally similar kinship systems (in this case the patrilineage) can be found in conjunction with different systems of production and in different ecological settings .... what it does suggest is that there are only a relatively limited number of structural permutations which kinship system can take *given the unchangeable biological factors which underlie all such systems* and that the specific choice of system is a product of history and cultural decisions, as much as it is ecology or of a particular mode of production (which, as we have stressed, is analytically independent of the kinship organisation)". Further he writes, "Kinship does not merely have a function in production, nor does it actually 'mask'actual relations of production. It may do both these things, while still retaining its status as a system of *social organisation* in and for itself" (*ibid* :114) (emphasis added).

Ultimately there appears no consensus to treat any form of kinship organization as mode of production and to believe that any type of kinship structure corresponds to any specific invariant relationship to productive forces. That in certain types of societies at certain historical points of development of productive forces, kinship may function as relations of production, does not justify talking of any form of kinship structure such as lineage as a mode of production.

Further, except for Dupre and Rey none of the other Neo-Marxist scholars agree that there exist relations of real exploitation in the lineage. None of the theories can satisfactorily explain why kinship is the primary form of social relationship in pre-capitalist societies. We have to look towards what Clammer has mentioned as the unchangeable biological factors that make kinship relations the primary form of relationship in all societies whether capitalist or pre-capitalist. As Clammer has rightly pointed out, the variations in kinship structure are only a few and these occur in conjunction with a large number of political and economic organisations. In each society the relations external to kinship may be reflected to some extent in kinship structures. In the hierarchical state society of traditional China, the lineages show a degree of stratification not exhibited, for example, among the Pagro-Mishing. In an egalitarian society like the Pagro - Mishing the relationships within the lineage are guided by the ideology of kinship i.e. of amity. It then depends upon the level of stratification of the society whether or not the lineage is used as mode of exploitation.

Classes actually occur when there is a breakdown of kinship ideology, when groups formed on the basis of appropriation and accumulation actually tend to separate out from the kin-groupings. Kinship in itself is not based on exploitation nor does it have a class character determined by the economy. The kinship idiom may be widely used, however, to perpetuate any other type of structure, even classes.

Thus the basic character of kinship remain rooted in biology and it is this that gives it primacy of importance in almost all social organisations. With capitalism, there is a separation of kinship from economy; whereas in pre-capitalist societies they remain embedded in each other. Till such time as it is superseded by ideologies of exploiation and conflict mainly arising in the extra-kinship domain, kinship ideology is based on affective, emotional ties which to some extent are retained even under highly capitalist conditions. Irrespective of the functions performed by kinship, amity is the principle that is invoked even in the performance of the most pragmatic tasks.

The Pagro-Mishing, who are the subject of the present study, show an overwhelming concern with biological fatherhood at the level of the functioning domestic group. This is somewhat inexplicable in a society otherwise based on a strong principle of unilineal descent. Membership into the patrilineage is strictly on the basis of what is socially recognized as biological paternity. At this point it is valid to stress that the Pagro-Mishing do recognize a biological father established through the act of coitus. Unlike other patrilineal societies like the Nuers, the social factors are not responsible for the incorporation of the child into the lineage; it is not the sociological husband of the mother i.e. the pater, but the actual genitor who is responsible for incorporating the child into the lineage.

This is not in tune with the existing theories of descent groups. Actual biological paternity does not affect the corporate nature of the descent groups (Fortes:1969) neither does it affect the status of descent groups as units of exchange (Levi-Strauss:1969).

Among the Pagro-Mishing, the concept of biological paternity is strongly linked with the ritual of ancestor worship which is the central organizing principle of their society. According to Meillasoux (1986) agricultural domestic community have ancestor worship because it is the ancestors who are ultimately responsible for passing on the seeds (for agriculture) to the descending generation. The Pagro-Mishing society is characterized by a patrilineal clan based organization which is strongly marked by the rituals of ancestor worship. Economically they approximate quite well to what Meillasoux has called an agricultural domestic community. In such communities the lineage elders maintain their authority over the youngers through the institutions of bridewealth. For the Mishing the bridewealth has a ritual significance in that it makes the ancestors of the groom accept the woman as an affine. A woman is not considered to be fully integrated into her husband's patri-clan unless at least a token bride-price has been paid for her at the time of marriage. In this society, it must be mentioned, the incorporation of a woman into her husband's group is total.

On the lines of the characters given by Meillasoux, the Pagro-Mishing can also be identified as an agricultural domestic community. The economy is largely agricultural supplemented with fishing. They are self-sufficient in terms of production and consumption, there is a definite predominance of 'use-value'over 'exchange-value' although market relations are not totally absent. Technologically, they are dependent on human and animal energy. They weave their own cloth and the cash cropping is only sufficient to provide for their subsistence. It is not as much technology, but the "socially accepted effects of its uses" (Meillasoux:38) that determine a particular type of economy. The Pagro-Mishing society is definitely organised around agriculture and all other activities are subservient to it.

"The social organization of the domestic agricultural community is built (simultaneously and indissolubly) both upon the relations of production in so far as these emerge from the economic constraints imposed by agricultural activity undertaken under conditions defined by the level of productive forces and upon the relations of reproduction necessary to perpetuate the productive cells"? (op.cit). And because the productive cell is composed of kinship relations, society emphasizes kinship.

In such a society the ancestor becomes the object of worship because ultimately it is he who is the provider of seed. Agriculture is a cyclically repetitive activity in which seeds of one season are passed on to the next and in this cycle of 'advances and returns' ultimately one generation is beholden to an earlier one for the seeds which it requires for agricultural production. It is this 'gratitude' that leads to the ancestors to be worshipped according to Meillasoux's reasoning.

Bride wealth here serves as a token of respect to the ancestors who are ideologically viewed as commanding respect and even after death to be an integral part of society. The ancestors are not simply worshipped; they appear at various levels of integration of Mishing society. The lineages are united at higher and higher levels through the worship of common ancestors. All those who can worship a common ancestor, even at the highest level of inclusion, are regarded as kin, and marriage to any one belonging to a kin category is incest. The affines can never worship the same ancestor as a kin. A woman after marriage is totally a part of her husband's patrilineage and will worship only his ancestors and not those of her natal lineage.

It is the ideological and structural aspects of ancestor worship that has been viewed as the organizational basis of the Pagro- Mishing society. It is through the institution of ancestor worship that 'descent' and 'alliance' can be seen as theoretically integrated and at the empirical level it provides the structuration of Mishing society. The relevance of 'biological paternity' is visible in this context. The ancestors are worshipped at several levels, the nearest one being worshipped at the level of the 'minimal lineage' which is of three generations depth.

The persons who enter into ancestor worship must be the direct descendants in the male line of the ancestor being worshipped and the link must be real (biological) and not social. The ritual significance of kinship is here related to the biological link and not the social, or what is socially recognized to be 'biological'. The cultural explanation is that the ancestors will not tolerate anyone who is not actually linked to them by blood and obviously one may fool living persons but one cannot fool the dead. The emphasis on biological paternity is thus not explicable in itself by reference to any particular material or structural condition, but is part of a 'holistic explanation' which takes 'ancestor worship' as the integrating variable for the entire Mishing social organisation.

The existence and influence of the supernatural ancestors here assumes the form of an ideology that has its own independent existence. Both 'descent' and 'affinity' are linked together in this ideology. Structural points of differentiation in the Mishing society arise out of who can or who cannot sit together to worship a common ancestor and this occurs at several levels, finally separating the kin from the affines. Every social division of Mishing society is symbolically represented and acted out ritually in ancestor worship. 'Ancestor worship' looked at from inside gives us the people's own rationale for organizing their society. It gives the rationale for bridewealth, for integration of the domestic group, marriage and other aspects of society. At the etic level it gives the structural rules for organisation of Mishing society. In the absence of any other visible regulating mechanism, such as war (as in the Nuer), the cult of ancestor worship provides a model for analyzing this society.

The link between biological fatherhood and ancestor worship becomes clear further, when we look into the practice of adoption. In case there is no child after a few years of marriage, the young couple resort to adoption. Invariably, the child adopted is that of a brother. The significance of this becomes apparent when we see that the minimal unit, which worships a common ancestor, is the minimal lineage which is of three generations depth.

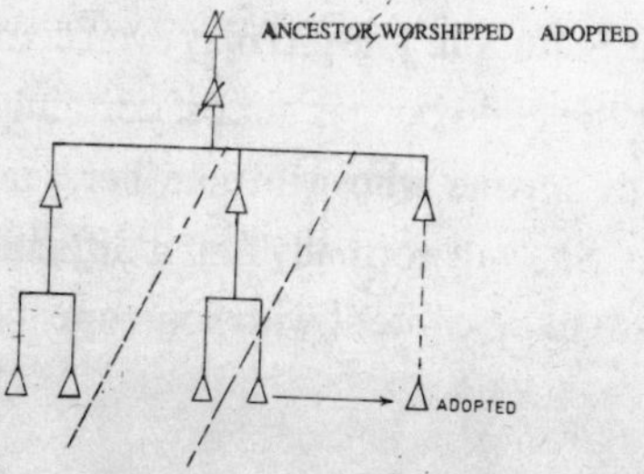

Fig 1.1 Adoption and Ancestor Worship

Figure 1.1 shows that the fact of adoption does not change the position of the child in the minimal lineage. His position does not change with respect to the ancestor which he would be worshipping by virtue of being the natural son of his father. In other words, it is ensured that the person remains in a social position to worship the common ancestor whom he would have worshipped by fact of biological paternity. Thus adoption is always done in such a way that the structural relationship within the lineage does not change.

Socially and culturally, adoption is then done to ensure emotional and economic support during one's life-time by someone who is in the category of a classificatory son. If at any point of time the lineage undergoes fission, as indicated, the adoptive father would have a son to look after him in his old age and to perform his last rites. If after adopting a son, the parents have children of their own, the status of the adopted son remains the same as the eldest child. Blood parenthood is seen as directly linked to the concept of ancestor worship, than to merely the physical relationship between father and son. The biological paternity here acts as a link between the child and his ancestors and adoption, whenever it takes place, ensures that this link is not disturbed.

Since pre-marital sex is prevalent in the community, one may well ask -- what is the status of illegitimate children in society? A boy and a girl would almost never enter into intimate relationship if they are not already in the marriageable categories. Sexual relationship with a girl of a prohibitive kin category is regarded as incest and severely sanctioned against in society. If found out, the boy and his entire family is subjected to severe pollution. The girl may even commit suicide out of shame. Otherwise the child born is almost certainly killed and the girl is married off to anyone who will take her, again within the prescribed categories. She will normally find it difficult to get a proper husband and may have to be content with someone old or very poor.

In case a boy and girl who are in the proper marriageable category do have intimate pre-marital relations which result in pregnancy, they would normally get married; such marriages are not infrequent in this society. However, due to certain personal or socio-economic reasons, the boy may not want to marry the girl he has impregnated. Under these circumstances it is imperative that the girl declares the name of the child's father. She cannot deliver this child in her father's house because no child can be born into a house where its own (that is genitor's ancestors) are not present. The girl then has to deliver in an especially constructed place outside her house. After birth the child may remain with mother for its nurturance. When the unwed mother eventually gets married, the child may be handed over to its natural father to be brought up in his family. Otherwise the mother may also carry the child to her affinal household where it will only have right of nurturance. If the child is a girl, she poses no problem for she is incorporated into the lineage of her husband as soon as she is married. If the child is a boy then he must on maturity leave his mother's house and set up his own house because he cannot worship his own ancestors (through his natural father) in some one else's house, which is the abode of their ancestors. Under no circumstances can he worship the ancestors of his mother's affinal household.

An interesting case arose when a girl had eloped with a boy of her choice but since the parents on either side disapproved of the marriage, the couple were brought back after they had lived together for 6-7 days and the girl was almost immediately married off to another boy. The question which came to my mind here and which I also put to the parties concerned, was that how was anyone to know, in case of an early pregnancy, whether the child was of the legal husband or of the boy she had cohabited with for a week? After much pondering, the reply was that a child, if born, would be treated as the child of the legal husband. In case of a girl there is no problem. In case of a boy, he would worship the ancestors of his legal father. In case no calamity befell the household he would continue to do so. However if repeated misfortunes made it apparent that the household had invoked the displeasure of its ancestors, then a *mebo* (Shaman) would be brought in to determine the real parentage of the boy. The ancestors as we know are never fooled.

In the agricultural domestic community, access to land is through affiliation into a community, either through kinship or affinity. Access to resources is through one's previously existing social relationships, quite often, as in the case of the Mishing, through membership into a descent group. Land and resources are hence seen as integrally tied up with one's ancestors. Just as a man is incorporated into his descent group through the physical links with his ancestors, it is through these links that he reproduces himself and his progeny forming an unbroken chain of association of land and human beings. Ancestors are then responsible for providing him with both the means of production and reproduction and hence worshipped.

What exists in such a society in terms of ownership and transference of goods is not a concept of 'property' but of 'patrimony'. Reproduction is the central concern of such societies and relations of affinity which establishes the marital unit responsible for reproduction are important. To this are associated elaborate social and ritual institutions as well as prestations.

Interestingly enough Meillasoux writes, "Father does not in fact mean genitor but he who nourishes and protects you, and who claims your produce and labour in return. In fulfilling his functions of regulating social reproduction, the 'father' is also he who marries you" (Meillasoux 1981:47).

Amongst the Mishing, the father is precisely the genitor. The significance of ancestor worship among the Mishing lies not only in the functions mentioned above but in regulating the fission and fusion of lineages in a manner in which it is regulated by 'complementary opposition' in the lineages of the Nuer.

It is Meillasoux's contention that at the level of development of productive forces at which the domestic agricultural community exists, the relations of production are determinant of the relations of re-production. However historical materialism here does not signify the control over material means of production but human reproduction. It is with reference to this analysis that we can understand the significance of physiological genitor in this society. The elders control the means of production, that is the seeds and the land and the means of reproduction i.e. the female wombs (that are transferred from another group) and the progeny that is born of them. The ancestors transfer not only agricultural seed but their own biological seed (or blood) as well. Ancestor worship symbolises not only continuity of land and material resources but continuity of blood as well and hence the emphasis on biological paternity. In this way I would differ from Meillasoux's concept of 'father' as sociological, it is biological as well, especially in a society where the role of father in conception is known.

If kinship was only the juridico-ideological representations of the relations of reproduction which in turn are determined in the first instance by the relations of production, then social paternity established by marriage should have been a sufficient condition for the reproduction of such a society.

The importance of biological paternity can be understood if we extend the concept of continuity from production to reproduction. Not only the agricultural 'seeds' but the reproductive 'seed' also is handed down. The significance of this is apparent. According to Meillasoux the authority of elders is established by two factors. 1. The passing on the agricultural seed, established as a factor of the productive forces. 2. The control of pubescent women of their own group which is a correlate of the need to reproduce the productive cell, which cannot reproduce itself at least at the initial level, when the size of the cell is small or only geared to requirements of production. The need to reproduce this cell required the exchange of women and the elders who by their position in the relation of production hold a higher position as providers of seed as an extension of this position become the controllers of women also. The rules of exogamy extend over wider groups as the elders extended their power. When the group becomes large enough to be able to reproduce itself demographically, the power of the elders is established through ideological means such as the rules of incest in which clan exogamy is akin to incest.

However, if the ideological basis of ancestor worship lies in the passing on of blood or biological 'seed' from the ancestor, then the fact of kinship based on biology becomes anterior to or independent of the forces of production. If it is the biological link that is most important then this biological link is independent of the relations of production or at least not determined by it. This is what Meillasoux was specifically trying to deny when he said that 'father' is not who gives birth to you but one who marries you.

This is further made significant by the fact that among the Mishing, large number of marriages are established by the young people themselves. Since there is no curb on the sexual activity of unmarried boys and girls, a number of them enter into matrimony on their own and the role of the elders is minimal. It is the same with bridewealth. More often than not the bridewealth does not consist of any real gifts or does not represent the material accumulative power of the elders. On the contrary the bridewealth is only a token payment towards recognizing an already existing ideological superiority of the ancestor. This ideological superiority is a fact of kinship derived from biology and not a reflection of any juridico-political epiphenomena of production relations.

Here I once again want to emphasize that kinship should be understood as a phenomenon in itself rather than as epiphenomenon of underlying structures.

Fortes has criticised the approach of Worsley and Leach,specifically on their overemphasis on economic determinism or as Fortes has put it "to find the hidden hand of economic compulsion everywhere" (1969 : 220).

The major criticism of all such advocates of the theory that kinship is only an expression of some other fundamental feature of social structure, is that in that case, why relate it to some real or stipulated blood ties---called kinship? In every society the biological link of mother and child and between siblings is recognized as some basis of kinship. Moreover, and importantly kinship is not merely a bundle of rights and duties---it is also emotional and affective. They are relationships of cooperation and sharing of emotional and physical security. The cultural content of kinship is an important aspect and it is recognized that few relationships can replace kinship relationships in this respect in any society. "Kinship predicates the axiom of amity, the prescriptive altruism exhibited in the ethic of generosity" (Fortes 1969 : 237).

2

The Land and the People

The north-east region of India is the home of a number of tribes. It comprises seven states, all carved out of the former Assam province, and the princely states of Manipur and Tripura. Today, these seven states are Assam, Meghalaya, Nagaland, Manipur, Tripura, Mizoram and Arunachal Pradesh. The entire north-east region is multiethnic and multilingual and it is noted for an assemblage of a large number of tribal communities which form the bulk of its population. The anthropological study of the peoples of this region began with the occupation of the area by the British in the first half of the nineteenth century[1]

This is a study of the Pagro-Mishing of Assam (see Map 2.1) who belong to congeries of sub-tribes that comprise the Mishing people. The Mishing constitute one of the largest tribal groups in Assam but so far, they have not been studied anthropologically, though some brief accounts about them are available in the form of administrative reports or as travelogues of the explorers.

The present study was mainly conducted in and around Kumarbari village situated in Majuli, an island in the Brahmaputra river. The village is about 35 miles from the town of Jorhat, the district headquarters of Sibsagar district, within which Majuli constitutes an administrative unit. I first came in contact with the Pagro-Mishing in the course of my anthropological researches in 1960 and have maintained my relationships with them ever since. The data of the present study were collected through an intensive fieldwork. Most of the information for the study was collected for a long period over several years stretching upto 1973. Over the years 1974-1975, I once again visited them and refurbished my information.

The anthropological fieldwork presupposes a degree of mutual understanding between the anthropologist and his subjects, which can be built up only gradually by creating trust and respect between them.

For me, the study of the Pagro-Mishing, was, in fact, a study of the 'other culture'. Linguistically, ethnically and culturally the Pagro-Mishing had nothing in common with me. It was, so to say, an adventure into the unknown. This great cultural difference, between their society and my own, had a positive impact on my perception and cognition of even those aspects of their social-cultural nuances which might have gone unnoticed had I been studying a familiar socio-cultural system. Initially it is true, I had to face a handicap due to the lack of my knowledge of either their language (i.e. the Mishing) or the Assamese, which is used by them almost like a second language, especially by the menfolk. The necessity to communicate with them effectively accelerated my learning of their languages. It was, as I found, not difficult to learn the Assamese language, since the basic content of the language is similar to the Sanskritic Hindi. Though I could not master the Mishing language, but gradually I could communicate and was able to understand them. The people, however, used the Assamese language more frequently and therefore communication was easy and extempore.

I was introduced to the people by the local administrative officer. I was also fortunate to have been introduced to a Pagro-Mishing student who became my friend. He introduced me to his people, and to his culture; and he also explained to his people the purpose of my visit to their community.

The Pagro-Mishing have quiet dignity, and in their deportment they conduct themselves with restrain and equanimity. They, therefore, never expected anything from me in terms of gift, either in cash or kind. In fact, with the passage of time, they thought it was their concern to look after my welfare in their midst. This is an important point because the entire data presented in the study was thus collected through voluntary and free and frank communication, and unhindered observation. The information was always provided with trust and good faith and never in return for any reward. In the beginning although the people were little taciturn, but gradually they accepted me as part of the local social set up. The change in their attitude was due to their own evaluation of my person in terms of my values and attitude which they compared with those of the Assamese Hindus, their closest neighbours. The Assamese Hindus regard the Pagro-Mishing equivalent to "untouchables" and, therefore, there is virtually no communication between them. I, as an individual, was never imbued with any caste prejudice and therefore acted as a normal participant in any social situation. I accepted their food and drink whenever proferred. It was spontaneous and this made my position clear to them that I treat them as equal. I was thus most welcome to enter their houses which is normally kept out of bounds for the strangers. When I was accepted by them as a persona grata in their midst, it defined my position and status in the neighbouring areas as well. The contacts of Kumarbari villagers with other villages greatly facilitated my work in the area. I was already known even in those villages which I had not visited earlier.

Until I was fairly conversant with their language, I collected data mostly by observation - observation of the activities both inside the houses and outside in the village environs. I could generally observe the economic activities of the men, women, and children and the type of social interaction in the small work groups, or the behaviour pattern of gossip groups or the interpersonal behaviour in peer groups of the boys and girls etc. However, the image that I had formulated as an abstract reality of social activities in the beginning due to the lack of understanding the meaning involved in many of their acts, became meaningful only when I also began to understand their language. The same interactions were repeated again and again in different houses and at different places. Thus repetitiveness of the act reflected the generality of the situation from which one could infer the accepted pattern of behaviour between individuals in their respective positions. Observation, both participant as well as non-participant, however, was utilised throughout my fieldwork. It assumes all the more importance when the field worker has become familiar with the meaning of the acts and is also able to place the individuals in their proper statuses - social as well as kinship. Thus the relationship between the members of a domestic group - between father and son, husband and wife, brother and sister, and other dyads within the kinship universe were observed in different situations from which the invariant pattern was abstracted. The verbal and non-verbal actions became meaningful even when I was merely observing them. The observation was also useful in serious situation like the village *kebang* where some cases of elopement were decided. I was invited to various weddings, rituals and social gatherings where I was treated almost like one of the villager. My presence in the rituals and ceremonies was treated to be almost a normal phenomenon. As an invitee to a wedding, I was expected to act as other Pagro-Mishing invitees were expected to do.

The other techniques used for data collection include interviews, discussions[2], case histories of the families, and the use of genealogies.

The interviews were used for collection of specific data and also for clarification of the information that was gathered by observation.

The interviews were seldom prearranged and focussed. The interviews were carried on in a natural conversational style, the conversation moving according to the topic we happened to be talking - whether it was politics, or the elopement of a girl or regarding the availability of fish or the nocturnal exploits of the boys! In short, I believed that the relevant information could not be gathered in one or two prolonged focussed interviews. An anthropological work, which has to have depth and meaningfulness must be done in an unhurried fashion and the relevant data may then to be sifted from the mass of information that one might collect in this manner.

The information that was gathered through conversation was later on, when the opportunity came, was fully documented by the actual concrete situation. Thus, for instance, the rules and norms regarding marriage by elopement were subsequently checked against the actual cases of elopement, as and when they happened. The ideal pattern, the conscious notion of their customs and institutions, the images that they had conjured up of their values and pattern of relationship, were all observed in the actual situations.

The genealogical method was of great use in the field. As we shall see in the discussion later, the domestic group and the kinship relations among them have great ramifications. Through the genealogies, I was not only able to find out the composition of the household but also the interlinkages of persons in various situations like ancestor worship, worship of the heavenly bodies and also of the work groups. The genealogies also gave the basic information pertaining to network of relationships based on affinity. Besides these, case studies and biographies of the families were also collected to see the role of kinship and affinity in the lives of the families and individuals.

In my fieldwork, then, the data on conceptions of kinship and kinship norms was obtained from the informants who were also the

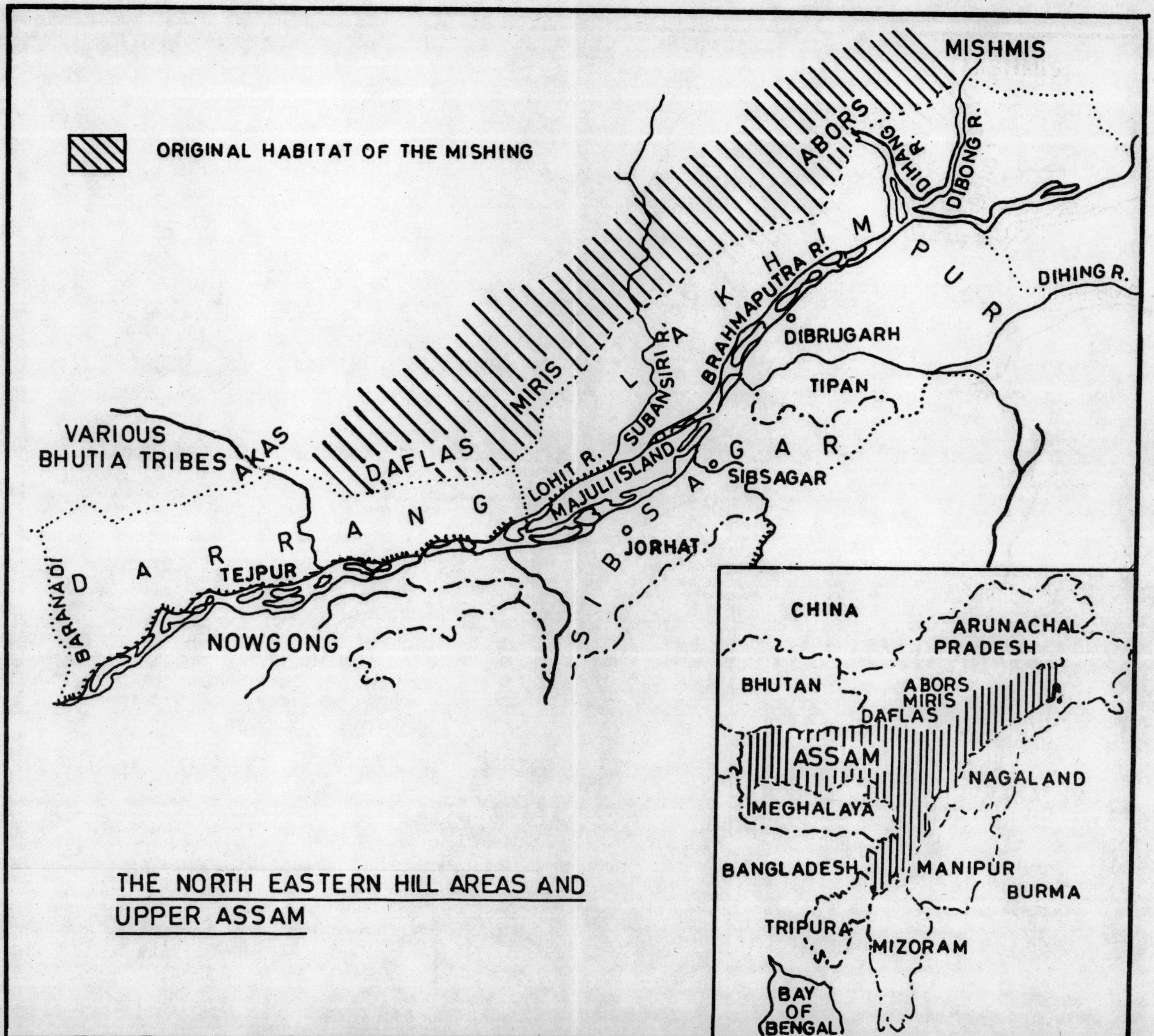

Map.2.1. The North Eastern Hill areas and Upper Assam

actors. Thus the data presented in my study are not merely generalized cultural statements about kinship but have an existential reality.

The Mishing and the Miri

The Mishing constitute one of the major tribal groups of Assam inhabiting large parts of Lakhimpur, Dibrugarh, Sibsagar, and Jorhat districts. Originally they inhabited the hills lying north of the upper Brahmaputra Valley in the Siang and Lohit districts of Arunachal Pradesh. Although they identify themselves as Mishing and regard it to be the correct name of their community, they have been identified by the term Miri by the people of Assam. The term Miri has been used for the Mishing by the Assamese ever since they came in contact with them in the remote past. Owing to its widespread use the term Miri eclipsed the original name 'Mishing' and was officially listed as Miri in the list of the Scheduled Tribes (Refer Appendix).

The Original Home of Mishing

The Mishing originally lived in the hills situated on the north of the district Lakhimpur of upper Assam. This hill tract has been referred to as the Miri Hills and is situated between what was once referred to as the Aka-Dafla and the Abor Hills. This region covers the entire territory to the north of the Brahmaputra valley in the upper Assam - roughly the area lying between gorge of the Subansiri in the west to the Dibong river in the east. At present, this region forms the major portion of the Subansiri and Siang districts of Arunachal Pradesh (See Map No. 2.1).

The Siang - Subansiri region of Arunachal Pradesh at present is the home of many tribes among which the more prominent are the Padam, Minyong,[3] (Adi) Galong, Daphla, Mishmi and the Apa Tani.

The Mishing and Their Relationship with the Padam- Minyong

The Mishing claim a close affinity with the people inhabiting the Siang-Subansiri region, especially with the Adis i.e.the Padam - Minyong people and believe that they had a common origin. Culturally, linguistically and ethnically, the Mishing and the Padam - Minyong do have great similarities as will be clear from the following discussion.

Common Myths

The Mishing and the Padam-Minyong cosmogony share the same myth. The Padam and Minyong claim to be the direct descendants of Abo Tani or simply Tani and identify themselves as such (Dunbar:1916). The Mishing also claim to be the progeny of Abo Tani and refer to themselves as Tani.

The Mishing myth of creation describes a common origin of the three groups viz. the Mishing, Padam and Minyong from the creator of the universe itself. The myth is as follows :

'Sedi Babu' (father Sedi); the Supreme Being is the creator of all the animate and the inanimate in the universe. *Sedi Babu* first created *Melo-Nane* (mother Melo). *Sedi Babu* and *Melo Nane* then, together created *Ditem* (the earth), *Adi-Ditem* (the mountain), *Nei-Nougan* (the trees with green leaves), *Rukji-Meran* (the ants and insects), and *Pevi-Peltang* (the birds and animals). At the same time they created the Sun *(Donyi)* and the moon *(Polo)*, wind *(echar)*, water *(asi)*, fire *(enic)* and other natural objects. *Sedi* then created Diling who was survived by Litung, Litung was survived by Tuye, Tuye by Yope and Yope by Padong. Padong gave birth to Dopang, Domi and Doshing. The son of Dopang was Padam and his off-spring are the Padams of today. The son of Domi was Minyong whose descendants are known as the Minyong and the son of Doshing was Mishing whose descendents are the Mishing'. (Pegu : 1956)

Thus according to this myth, the Mishing, the Padam and the Minyong are the descendants of Pedong-*ane* and *Sedi babu*. A similar myth with some variation is also prevalent among the Padam and Minyong. They also believe that *Sedi* is the creator of the universe. The animate and the inanimate and the cosmos were created by him. *Sedi* created the sun and the moon which act as the two eyes of the Supreme Being through which he watches the people of the earth and no man can hide or escape from him. Both the Mishing and the Padam-Minyong (Adis) share this common belief and regard the Sun and the Moon as the manifestation of the Supreme Being. The *Donyi-Polo* (Sun and Moon) are venerated by the Mishing although they are not worshipped exclusively. However, the cult of *Donyi-Polo* has a great influence on this Mishing as well as on the Padam and Minyong. No ceremony among them, either secular or ritual, ever begins without addressing *Donyi-Polo* for their blessings.

The social and political relationship between the Mishing and their neighbours the Padam and Minyong were, however, far from cordial notwithstanding a common mythical origin and sharing the cult of *Donyi-Polo*. The Mishing who migrated to the plains of Assam from the vicinity of the Adi people did so because of the socio-political conditions that overtook them in the hills (Refer Appendix II).

THE MISHING SUB-TRIBES

Although the Mishing of Assam are regarded as one single homogeneous tribal group by the layman as well as the administrators, they are in reality, composed of many small sub-tribes which are named and form distinct endogamous groups. The members belonging to one sub-tribe are by and large settled in one contiguous region in a number of villages. The Mishing sub-tribes are conscious of their identity and each one has its distinctive traditions, myths and folklore. Their identity is an acknowledged reality for other sub-tribes. Thus the term Mishing refers to a number of distinct autonomous ethnic units which have, however, a common historical tradition of migrating to the plains from the same regions in the north-eastern hills. Although these sub-tribes have distinct identities, nonetheless, all of them share the same cultural and structural characteristics. They speak the same language with a slight regional variation, their economy is the same and all of them have a common belief and ritual complex. The similarity between various sub-tribes of the Mishing is quite conspicuous which creates an impression about them that they constitute one single community.

At the cultural and structural level, one does not find much difference between the various groups of the Mishing. In fact, the various sub-tribes of the Mishing are aware of their common heritage and culture. As early as 1924, some of the educated Mishing belonging to different tribes conferred and decided to form a socio-political organization of the entire Mishing people. This association was named as the *Mishing Bane Kebang* (Great Assembly of the Mishing). This is now an important socio-political organization of the Mishing of Assam and holds its annual sessions in different parts of Mishing dominated areas. The emphasis on the homogeneity of all the Mishing sub-tribes is laid more for political reasons subordinating the sociological facts.

It is also important to reiterate that the various Mishing sub-tribes that are now settled in Assam did not emigrate simultaneously. The emigration of the Mishing was spread over a long period of time, approximately from the seventeenth century to the beginning of the twentieth century. It is, therefore, obvious that the various groups have undergone differential degree of culture change depending upon the duration of interaction with the people of the plains of Assam.

Barogam and Dobgam Mishing : The Two Sections of the Mishing

The Mishing sub-tribes are notionally grouped into two mutually exclusive sections known as Barogam and the Dohgam, meaning 'twelve-chiefs' and 'ten-chiefs'. These names are of Assamese origin. Many folk theories have been current to explain why these names were adopted but historically, no authentic record is available to substantiate them. In spite of a lack of a clear knowledge as to why these names were adopted, the two sections of the Mishing sub-tribes are a living reality having cultural and structural variation between them. According to one legend, when the Mishing settled on the plains in the days of the Ahom king, they established two villages. In one village there were ten score households and in another village there were twelve score households. In each village one score households were under one *Gam*[4] (chief). Thus in one village there were twelve *Gams* and in another there were only ten *Gams*. Thus the sections Barogam and Dohgam were created due to socio-political necessity and today the Mishing are divided into these two sections. Yet, according to another folk theory, the Ahom[5] kings of Sibsagar covenented with the Mishing to ensure order and maintain peace on the borders of their kingdom. The Ahom kings recognized twelve *Gams* from one cluster of the villages and ten from other. These clan chiefs were paid an annual retainer. Since then the Ahom, it is said, propagated the term Barogam and Dohgam for different clans of the Mishing. It may be presumed that a *Gam* was not actually the head of the village, but chief of a clan, as was the practice among the Mishing. Thus a cluster of clans was represented by twelve chiefs and the other cluster was represented by only ten chiefs. This recognition also created a political hierarchy between the two sections on the basis of their respective strength. Although, this conclusion is not historically verifiable, it is a fact that Barogam Mishing regard themselves superior to the Mishing belonging to Dohgam section. The Barogam Mishing are also called Pagro-Mishing and occasionally as

Chutia Miri[6] as well.This has certain historical reasons as discussed subsequently. The Dohgam Mishing are also known as Oringam; *Orin* being the Mishing term for ten.

THE DOHGAM MISHING SUB-TRIBES AND THEIR DISTRIBUTION

The Dohgam Mishing comprise six autonomous sub-tribes Each sub-tribe is a named endogamous community and is composed of a number of exogamous clans which are patrilineal. A brief account of each sub-tribe follows:

Oying : The Oying Mishing, according to their tradition , are said to have migrated to the plains of Assam only after the invading Burmese had been expelled from Assam by the British and peace had prevailed once again in the plains. This would place the time of their migration after 1826. They migrated due to increasing oppression of the Minyong Abors while they were living in the hills. The Oyingia, as they are called, inhabit the banks of the Ghunasuti river, a tributary of the Subansiri in Lakhimpur District. The Oyingia are a small group and have only a few villages. The Oying Mishing have the following main clans: (1) Mili (2) Payang (3) Merang and (4) Pertin.

Shayang: The Shayang, on the basis of the legends, are believed to have originally inhabited in the Pesang hills. Shayang was the name of their main village in the hills and now they identify themselves as Shayangia. At present, they live on the banks of the Subansiri river in Lakhimpur and Sadiya. A few Shayang villages are also situated on the Dibong river. They have eleven clans: (1) Pame (2) Payang (3) Sangkang (4) Noro (5) Pogag (6) Taoni (7) Koman (8) Yogate (9) Shinte (10) Basing and (11) Madok.

Dambok : In the Mishing legends, it is mentioned that the Dambok Mishing have migrated to the plains of Assam relatively recently. They claim to be related to Damro people who are regarded as a cognate section of the Minyong Abors. This group is referred to as Dambok or Dambokial. At present they are settled in north-Lakhimpur. They have one village in Majuli island also. The Dambokial have four clans : (1) Tayang (2) Mili (3) Parme (4) Taond.

Delo : The Delo sub-tribe migrated to the plains from the south bank of the Brahmaputra and are, therefore, known as Delo which means 'South' in the Mishing language. They have settled mainly on the banks of the Disang river in Sibsagar district. Their main clans are (1) Taye (2) Mili (3) Panging (4) Pagag (5) Nara (6) Shinte (7) Payang (8) Pame and (9) Bori.

Moying: The original home of these people was the Moying village after which they are now called Moyingia. The Moying villages are mainly situated on the banks of the Bhoroli river in Tezpur district. Some of their villages are also situated on the banks of the Rangamati in Lakhimpur district. The Moyingia are relatively a bigger sub-tribe. They have a number of clans of which the following are the main ones :(1) Paing (2) Pame (3) Noro (4) Mili (5) Shinto (6) Kardong (7) Daong (8) Lagong (9) Pagag (10) Paging (11) Payung (12) Padam (13) Tayo (14) Yagate (15) Koman (16) Suring (17) Pabo (18) Gotag (19) Boral and (20) Palong *etc.*

Samuguria or Mirang : The Samuguria Mishing constitute a distinct subtribe of the Dohgam section. They have a unique position in the Mishing society as they speak only Assamese language and not the Mishing language as is the case with other sub-tribes. They can however, understand it.

The folk history of the Samuguria Mishing tells us about the migration of this subdivision. The Samuguria are regarded an offshoot of the Damro Minyong of the hills. According to traditions, they had developed animosity with their neighbours who lived across the river. One day they decided to attack them at night. Before attacking the enemies, they propitiated the guardian spirits, and as part of the ceremony, drank '*apong*' which made them intoxicated. Under the influence of intoxication they forgot to cross the river, and instead, mounted an attack on their own village, mistaking it to be the enemy village. The result of this mistake was that they killed all the women, children and the old men who were left behind in the village by the attacking party.

On the following morning, when they regained their normal sense, they realized the terrible mistake they had committed. In sheer disgust they left the place and started moving down hill. As they had neither women, nor children, nor any personal belongings with them, they were called *Mirang* i.e. the celibates, the name still used to designate them. When they reached near Sibsagar, they stayed at a place called Samuguri. At that time an Ahom king was the ruler of the area. The legend further mentions that these emigrants from the hills killed a python who had terrorized the people of Samuguri. This act was commended by the king. He also came to know of their tragedy and offered them women from amongst his subjects. Subsequently the descendants of the Samuguria Mishing forgot their language and adopted the Assamese language. The Samuguria Mishing are composed of three sections : (1) Shabruganya (2) Tomarganya and (3) Bongkoyal. At present, the Samuguria are settled on the banks of the Ranganadi in Lakhimpur district and on the banks of the Dikrang and Dhansiri rivers in Sibsagar district.

The Barogam Mishing and Dohgam Mishing : Their Distinctive Features

The other section of the Mishing people namely the Barogam or the Pagro comprise three phratries and a few unattached clans.

These phratries are named as Pagro, Bomi and Tayo-Taye. Since the Pagro are the most numerous of the three phratries, this entire division of the Mishing is generally referred to as Pagro.

The most significant feature of the Dohgam Mishing is that it is a collective name of six sub-tribes each of which is autonomous social unit. In contradistinction to the composition of the Dohgam, the Pagro-Mishing section is a single structural system having an exogamous dual organization. The dual organization has formed an organic solidarity among its constituent clans which belong to the three phratries by placing them into two intermarrying moieties. The Dohgam tribes, on the other hand, maintain distinct identities though the Mishing people as a whole share a common body of myths and traditions; subscribe to a common religious system; speak the same language and have migrated to the plains of Assam from the same region, albeit at different times. The Dohgam and the Pagro-Mishing are structurally very similar though not the mirror images of each other. Though they have no moieties, they also practice bilateral cross-cousine marriage. The two sections of the Mishing are neither complementary nor interdependent on each other. The social interaction between different sub-tribes of the Mishing is almost non-existent although there are no formal restrictions either on commensal relations or social intercourse. Intermarriage between persons belonging to different sub-tribes is considered irregular and deviation from the norm. The villages of each sub-tribe are inhabited exclusively by its own members.

It is, thus, clear from the above discussion that the Mishing people are composed of many sub-tribes which migrated to the plains of Assam from the hills in the past. Although they are considered one single homogeneous tribal group by the non Mishing, the term Mishing refers to a number of sub-tribes; each of which has a separate social boundary defined by its social system, though sharing to a great extent, a common cultural milieu.

Distribution and Population

The Mishing is one of the largest tribal group of north-east India and constitute the second largest tribal community in the state of Assam (The largest being the Boro-Borokachari group). The Mishing are settled mainly in Assam although a small number is found in the lower hills of Arunachal Pradesh as well.

According to Capt. Nuefville who was the first British officer to have reported about the plains Mishing in 1825, they inhabited only the north bank of the river Brahmaputra from the Sisi in Lakhimpur as far as the Dihong river (Mackenzie, 1884). At present the Mishing are settled in a much wider region of upper Assam inhabiting mainly the banks of various rivers. The maximum concentration of the Mishing population is in 4 districts of upper Assam, namely Lakhimpur, Jorhat, Sibsagar and Dibrugarh. In smaller number, they are also settled in Sonipur, Darrang, Nowgong, Goalpara and Kamrup districts of Assam as shown in the Table 2.1.

TABLE 2.1
Districtwise Distribution of the Mishing in Assam 1971

District	Mishing Population	Per cent of the Total Mishing Population
Dibrugarh Lakhimpur	1,55,038	59.73
Sibsagar Jorhat	84,752	32.66
Darrang Sonilpur	14,948	5.76
Kamrup Goalpara Nowgong	4,808	1.85
Total	2,59,546	100

Source : Census of India 1971, Assam Part V-A.

Since the Mishing emigration of the plains of Assam was spread over a long period of time, commencing approximately in the 16th century and ending only in the early decades of this century, they settled wherever the virgin areas existed in the Brahmaputra valley. Due to the staggered nature of their emigration, it was not possible for the Mishing to occupy one compact region, consequently they are settled in a wide area. They have, however,invariably settled on the banks of the major rivers of upper Assam including the Brahmaputra. The main rivers of the region are the Subansiri, Digaru, Diphu, Bharali and Dikrang, besides many other smaller rivers. The Mishing villages are situated on the banks of these rivers. One of the most important area that is inhabited by the Mishing is, however, Majuli, a river island in the Brahmaputra in district Sibsagar.

Decennial Variation in Mishing Population : 1871-1971

The population of the Mishing was enumerated for the first time in 1871 and subsequently each decennial census recorded the Mishing population, the latest available data is from 1971. One hundred years of census records give us valuable information regarding the distribution and variation of the Mishing population in different districts of Assam as shown in Table 1. In 1871, as the table shows, the total Mishing population was only 13,786 and was distributed in the districts of Lakhimpur, Sibsagar and Darrang. The significant point in 1871 census figures is that Sibsagar district has 49.70% of the total Mishing population whereas Lakhimpur district has only 35.45% of their population. This ratio is reversed in the subsequent decennial records. From 1881 to 1971, Lakhimpur district shows a higher percentage of their population. Since 1901, in fact, their population in Lakhimpur has been always more than 50% of the total Mishing population of Assam, and there is a corresponding decline in the percentage of the Mishing population in Sibsagar district. In 1971, we find that district Lakhimpur has 59.73% of the total Mishing population and district Sibsagar has only 32.62% of the Mishing population of Assam. The higher concentration of the Mishing in Sibsagar in 1871 is attributed to the fact that it provided a more peaceful and safer haven to the emigrant Mishing as compared to the more turbulent Lakhimpur region which was prone to the marauding raids of the hill tribes. But with the establishment of the effective British administration the emigrant Mishing began to settle in the hitherto uninhabited areas of Lakhimpur district. This is clearly evident from the fact that in 1881, Lakhimpur district shows a tremendous increase in the Mishing population. In ten yeas, their population rose from 4886 to 11,687, an increase of 130.9%. In Sibsagar district on the other hand the population rise was only 58.2%. The distribution of the Mishing is confined to only these three districts until 1891, when for the first time they were reported in Nowgong district as well, though their number (462) was quite insignificant. The Mishing are also now settled in two other non-traditional Mishing areas namely Kamrup and Goalpara districts. However, the total number of the Mishing in Nowgong, Kamrup and Goalpara districts in 1971 is only 4,808 which amounts to 1.85% of the total Mishing population in Assam.

The Mishing population in Assam has increased substantially during the last one hundred years as will be observed from the following table (Table 2.2).

TABLE 2.2
Growth of Mishing Population 1871-1971

Year	Population	Percentage of increase	Year	Population	Percentage of increase
1871	13, 786	------	1931	84,976	23.68
1881	25, 636	85.96	1941	N.A.	-----
1891	38,430	49.91	1951	108,736	27.96
1911	47,719	21.57	1961	163,453	50.32
1921	68,706	23.03	1971	259,351	58.79

It is clear from the above table (Table 2.2) that there has been a steady growth of the Mishing population in Assam. We find a significant growth of their population in the twenty years span between 1871 to 1891. In the first decade it increased by 85.96% and in the next decade by 49.91%. This period is characterized by the consolidation of British administration in upper Assam which induced more and more Mishing from the hills to settle in the plains of Assam. So the increase in their population may not be merely due to the natural growth factors but may also be attributed to emigration of the Mishing from the hills. During the period between 1901 to 1951 the population of the Mishing had a steady growth which is more or less uniform for each decennial period. However, in 1961 their population increased by 50.32% and in 1971, it increased by 58.79%. During this period emigration of the Mishing from Arunachal Pradesh is not reported. The reason for this enormous increase, therefore, lies in the fact that perhaps some communities which did not return as Mishing earlier, identified themselves as Mishing in the later censuses thus causing an apparent influx in the total Mishing population.

The Mishing are exclusively a rural people. According to 1961 census the total number of urban Mishing was only 242 (0.15%) and the rural Mishing constituted 99.85% of the population. In 1971, the number of urban Mishing rose to 720 (0.27%) whereas the rural Mishing constituted 99.73% of their total population.

3

Habitat and Social Setting of the Pagro-Mishing

The Pagro-Mishing who constitute the Barogam division of the Mishing people are composed of three phratries, namely (1) Pagro (2) Bomi and (3) Tayo-Taye, and a number of individual unattached clans. The Pagro phratry is numerically the largest of the three phratries and is also believed to be the earliest emigrant to the plains of Assam from the hills. The other clans and phratries, which are numerically smaller in size, are believed to have emigrated later and were gradually incorporated in the Pagro -Mishing society. For this reason, the Barogam Mishing are also identified as the Pagro-Mishing, and as such, the term Pagro-Mishing encompasses the other two phratries and the independent clans as well, which together form the Barogam Mishing.

The term *pagro* is a Mishing word which means "one who has lost purity". It is not a complimentary term. The reason for the use of this uncomplimentary term for the entire community has allegedly a historical basis. When the Ahoms entered Assam in 1228 A.D., the area which comprises the greater part of the present districts of Sibsagar, Jorhat, Dibrugarh and Lakhimpur were ruled by a Chutiya King. The Ahoms conquered the Chutiya kingdom in 1503 A.D. (Gait 1905 : 87). During the war, it is said, many Chutiya took shelter in the Mishing villages and were finally assimilated in the Mishing tribe. The close relationship between the Chutiya and the Mishing was noticed by many other Mishing clans who were still living in their hill abode. These Mishing clans started calling those Mishing clans as *Pagro* which had established close contacts with the Chutiya people. Though initially the term denoted a derogatory status for the community, gradually the term lost its derogatory connotation and the people also began to identify themselves as Pagro-Mishing. In fact, later on they seldom referred to themselves as Barogam Mishing. The Pagro-Mishing, however, do not agree with the theory of intermarriage between them and the Chutiya, but suggest that since they were living within the Chutiya kingdom for a long time, they were given this name. There is, however, no historical evidence to prove or disprove any one of these theories. But the name *Pagro* is definitely an acceptable term today. A significant point that emerges from this controversy is that the Pagro-Mishing had been settled in the vicinity of the people of the plains of Assam, namely the Chutiya, since long in the past which must have influenced their society to a great extent, and hence the term 'Pagro', implying "not pure" in their norms.

The Pagro-Mishing Territorial Distribution

The Pagro-Mishing do not inhabit one compact region of upper Assam but are settled over a vast area (See Map. No. 3.1). Their villages are situated on the southern bank of the Brahmaputra river from Sadiya in Lakhimpur in the north-east to Gamarighat in Sibsagar in the south-west on the down stream. The distribution of their population in this entire region is not uniform but they are settled in small pockets throughout. One of the largest concentration of the Pagro-Mishing is in Majuli, a river island in the Brahmaputra. The present study was mainly conducted in the Majuli island and in some adjoining areas of Sibsagar district.

In Sibsagar district, the Pagro-Mishing villages are situated mostly on the south bank of the Brahmaputra in the riverine strip of land with a width varying from 3 to 8 miles. The riverine strip is covered with swamps, high reed jungles and stretches of fodder grass. The area is climatically inhospitable and being low lying is subject to periodic floods which render land to very little productive use. The entire riverine strip is inhabited only by the Mishing. North of the Brahmaputra river, and separated from the Sibsagar mainland lying south of river, is Majuli island, where we have one of the largest concentration of Pagro-Mishing population.

Majuli -- the river island

Majuli island forms an administrative part of the district. The island is situated between the Brahmaputra and the Lohit which is a branch of the Brahmaputra itself. Majuli island has been formed chiefly by the silt deposited from the Subansiri river which flows through the district of Lakhimpur and empties itself into the Lohit near Jengraimukh, a Pagro-Mishing village in Majuli. The Lohit leaves the main stream near the point where the Brahmaputra enters the district of Sibsagar. It flows circuitously but generally in a south-westerly direction for about 70 miles till it reenters the mother-stream, nearly opposite the mouth of the Dhansiri river.

Majuli is about 80 miles in length and has an average breadth of five miles between the Brahmaputra and the Lohit rivers which form its southern and northern boundary respectively. A few years ago the island was 380 square miles in area, which made Majuli the largest river island in the world. Although the area of the island has been ever changing due to regular erosion on its sides, in 1976 the erosion took a very serious form when a considerably large portion of the island was eroded resulting in shifting of many villages to safer places.

The soil of Majuli is rich alluvium suitable for cultivation. But the whole of the island is too low for the cultivation of transplanted rice and only staple crops that can grow easily there are summer rice (*ahu*), mustard and pulses.

The only means to reach Majuli from Jorhat, the district town, is to take motor ferry boat which plies between Neemati on the south bank of the Brahmaputra and Kamlabari on the north bank. It takes about two hours to cross the river during winter season and much more during the rainy season when the river Brahmaputra grows very wide and turbulent. The road traffic between the districts of Sibsagar and Lakhimpur also passes via Majuli. The ferry conveys not only the passengers, but also fish, poultry, cattle and other commodities from one side to the other. Lorries and buses, bound for Lakhimpur also cross the river by ferry. At the other end of the island, another ferry crosses the Lohit and empties its cargo in Lakhimpur district, which lies on the northern side of Majuli island.

Majuli is of great relgious significance for the Vaishnavite sect of the Hindus of Assam. More than twenty five *Vaishnavite Satra*[1] are situated here. These *Satra*[1] were established in Majuli during the rule of the Ahom King Rudra Singh (1696-1714 A.D.).

Majuli and its People

The population of Majuli according to 1971 census was 96,015 out of which 33,294 were the Mishing which accounted for 35.56 per cent of the total population. The Mishing population of Majuli accounts for 39.28 per cent of the total Mishing population in Sibsagar district, which is 84,752. The rest of the population of Majuli is composed of several castes among which the principal ones are the Kalita, Keot, Dom, Hari and Brahman. A few villages belonging to other tribal communities like the Deori and Sonowal Kachari are also situated in Majuli. However, the interaction between the Pagro-Mishing and other communities is socially insignificant. A Mishing village, although it may be situated very near a caste Hindu village, has absolutely no institutional communication with it. The Pagro-Mishing are consciously avoided by the caste Hindus who regard the Mishing no better than the untouchables. The Pagro-Mishing too do not feel any necessity---social, economic or ritual---to have interaction with the caste Hindu villages.

The Pagro-Mishing Village

The Pagro-Mishing villages are invariably situated on the banks of the river or a stream. A typical Mishing village usually consists of a population of less than four hundred persons living in about 30 households. The houses in the village always face the running water. They are generally constructed close to one another without much thought for planning of the village. Unlike an Assamese village, the Mishing villages present a bleak landscape because the Mishing houses are seldom surrounded by kitchen gardens or fruit trees, although lately they have started planting some trees near their houses.

A Pagro-Mishing village is distinguished by typical long dwelling houses (*chang-ghar*) of the Mishing which are built on a bamboo platform raised about six feet above the ground on wooden poles. The width of a house is about 20 feet and its length depends on the size of the domestic family that occupies it. Some of the bigger houses are almost 120 feet in length. A Mishing house is not partitioned into small rooms but the entire domestic group lives in one single large barrack like hall. Each house has extended varandah in the front. There are only two doors in the house, one in the front and other in the rear. There are no windows in the house. The architectural pattern of the Mishing house has no variation in any form in the entire country.

A Mishing house built on a platform is highly adapted to the frequent floods that visit most parts of upper Assam and specially the riverine tracts. During normal floods, a Mishing village looks like a vast canvas of water with their houses quite above the water level. Unless the flood water rises as high as seven feet, the Mishing house is quite safe. During the floods, the daily life of the people is modified but is not disrupted. The cattle are, of course, taken to higher grounds, but the poultry and pigs, which every household possesses, are housed on the raised pigsties and platforms. Each household also owns a few large boats and dugout canoes and instead of walking from one house to another, during the flood season they just row their canoes to visit others in the village. Thus the social life of the people is not greatly disrupted. Every Mishing -- man, woman and child -- knows swimming and rowing and they are well adapted to the environmental conditions. The floods usually occur in late May and continue up to mid-July.

If the floods are not serious, they are, in a way, beneficial to the people. First, the villagers would say, it is like an annual cleaning of the underneath of their houses, and secondly, the flood water also deposit rich silt on their fields which enriches its fertility. When floods cause erosion only then villages may be threatened otherwise floods are treated with nonchalance and indifference by them.

The Pagro-Mishing villages are exclusively inhabited by their own people and it is indeed rare to find any village with a mixed population. There may, however, be a few non-Mishing temporary residents in some of the larger villages working as artisans or specialists of some trade like a tailor or a goldsmith. All the households in a Pagro-Mishing village are usually related to one another either consanguineally or affinally. Kinship and affinity form the important cleavages in their village organization. The villages are not necessarily exogamous territorially. Whether a Pagro-Mishing village is exogamous or not depends on the composition of its population. If a village is composed of only one clan, it has got to be exogamous. Presence of two or more affinal clans would imply the possibility of marriage within the village.

The Pagro-Mishing are exclusively settled agriculturists. In their original home in the hills, they practised shifting cultivation and after migrating to the plains, they did not totally abandon this practice. They could practise shifting cultivation initially in the plains because there were vast tracts of grasslands and forests in the alluvial plains of upper Assàm, besides the population pressure was also not much. With the availability of fresh land the Mishing seldom stayed at one place permanently. They moved to a new site after a few years soon after the fertility of the soil was exhausted. For this reason, in the earlier administrative reports, the Mishing have been classified as nomadic agriculturists (Allen:1905).

At present the large scale migration of the Mishing villages has stopped, though there are still rare instances when a few households from a village migrate to a new area and settle there. The paucity of virgin land and increase in the population have, however, rendered the large scale migratory habits of the Mishing impracticable. They may now be classified as settled agriculturists.

Once they became settled agriculturists, it led to change in their concept of the ownership of land as well. Formerly they did not think of owning and cultivating the land permanently and were therefore treated as 'annual tenants' by the Government. The Mishing are now permanent cultivators, but are still classified as 'annual tenants'. However, the Mishing still abandon some of their fields after three or four years of cultivation. These fields are left fallow to be recultivated after a lapse of three or four years. During this period, however, the tenancy rights are not surrendered and the land remains part of the household possession. This practice of leaving some areas fallow is perhaps a vestige of shifting cultivation which was their original form of cultivation. The land tenure system under which the Pagro-Mishing have got land is the annual *Kheraj*[2] system. The annual lease is renewable and hereditary which makes them permanent tenants

The land holdings of the Pagro-Mishing are large as compared to other communities[3]. Their agricultural practices are similar to those of the Assamese peasants. They use simple plough, the draft animals are either the bullocks or male buffaloes. However, they have not yet begun the cultivation of transplanted paddy like the Assamese peasants.

The most important crop raised by the Pagro-Mishing in Majuli is *Ahu* paddy which is sown broadcast in winter and is harvested by about July before the floods come. They also grow another variety of paddy called *"Baodhan"*. This is grown only in Majuli. This paddy crop grows even in water logged fields and therefore can be cultivated in low lying tracts along the banks of the Brahmaputra. This variety is sown broadcast about the end of February and harvested in December. The transplanted winter paddy is not grown by them due to inadequate knowledge of the techniques involved in its cultivation. Moreover, Majuli being a low lying area is not suitable for its cultivation. Other important crops raised by them are mustard, pulses, millet and some cash crops like chillies, potatoes and ginger. The Pagro-Mishing have no slack season in Majuli.

The Pagro-Mishing economy is typically a household economy in which the household is the unit of production and consumption. Though they cultivate mustard, a cash crop, the sale of mustard is just sufficient to enable them to meet the domestic demands of day-to-day necessities which they themselves do not produce and have to depend upon markets. The Pagro-Mishing are occupationally homogeneous.

Besides agriculture, their economy is supplemented by animal husbandry and fishing. Fishing, which is next in importance to agriculture, is a daily activity and is done with the help of various types of nets, traps and harpoons. Fishing, like agriculture, is also meant exclusively for the domestic consumption and is never undertaken for commercial purpose. Though both the men and the women are expert in fishing, it is only the men folk who use nets and harpoons and procure fish for the day-to-day consumption of the domestic family.

Although hunting formed an important activity in the past, it has ceased to be so due to the paucity of the game. However, during the summer months, when the flood water forces the wild animals to seek shelter on higher grounds, wild boars and deer may be hunted. Hunting is done by the men folk only, in groups.

The domestic economy of the Pagro-Mishing is greatly supplemented by animal husbandry. Every household in the village normally owns a number of pigs, poultry and cattle. Of all the domestic animals, pig is the most valuable in their economy. It is essential as a sacrificial animal in almost all their rituals and ceremonies; it also forms an essential part of the marriage prestations. Pork constitutes the most important dish in any communal feast. Besides its value for domestic consumption, there is also a demand for pigs and fowls in the neighbouring towns and cities. Many traders from the towns regularly come to the Pagro-Mishing villages to buy these commodities. Although the Pagro-Mishing households also keep a number of cattle but they are mainly for the supply of draft animals because they neither drink milk nor do they relish any milk products. The only utility of cow for them is for its male progeny. Lately, however, some of the households have started selling milk to milk vendors from towns which may become an extra source of income to the household.

One of the major activities of the Pagro-Mishing women is weaving of silk and cotton cloth. Every household owns a few looms on which its womenfolk weave castor silk cloth or cotton cloth. Silk yarn is prepared by women themselves from the silk-worms which are raised by almost every household. Similarly some cotton is also grown by them for the purpose of making cloth. However, the cloth woven by the women is exclusively for their personal use and never for the market. Lately, the introduction of mill made cloth has become popular which is definitely harming their own traditional crafts.

The traditional dress of the Pagro-Mishing is simple. For women it consists of *geru* ,an unsewn cloth tied round the waist that covers the lower limbs as well. The upper garment known as *gapa* is a rectangular piece of unsewn cloth tied slightly above the breasts and is long enough to cover the hips. But quite often only *geru* may be used to cover both the upper and lower parts of the body. Sometimes a tight fitting petticoat *(egge)* may be worn under the *geru*. The married women sometimes wear a colourful piece of colth, *ribi*, round their breasts which covers the waist as well. Nowadays, however, the younger women wear more or less the same type of dress that are worn by the Assamese women. It consists of *mekhla,* blouse and a piece of cloth that is tied aroud the hips and tucked over the shoulders. The menfolk wear a *dhoti* and shirt. *Dhoti* and vest forms the working dress for men. On ceremonial occasions they wear turban *(dumer)*. During winter a shawl is used to cover the upper part of the body. These shawls are made of *eri* (castor) silk and are woven by the womenfolk of the household.

Traditionally the commonest ornaments were just carved pieces of bamboo worn as ear tops. Bracelets of ordinary metal were also popular. Necklaces of Tibetan beads were also possessed by some women. Now only old women may be seen wearing bamboo ear tops, otherwise common imitation jewellery has become popular among the younger women. The Pagro-Mishing women do not wear any nose ornament, nor do they perforate it.

The Pagro-Mishing food normally consists of rice and curry which is prepared with edible roots and tubers (yams), or when available bamboo and cane shoot may be used along with fish. A few households now grow little vegetables in their kitchen gardens.

The Pagro-Mishing greatly relish fish which is available in plenty throughout the year, except during two months of summer when its availability is meagre. Besides fish , pork and chicken are equally relished. But they do not form part of the daily meal. Pork is generally available when a pig is sacrificed in a ritual, otherwise a pig is seldom slaughtered just for domestic consumption. They, however, do not like mutton. Beef is scrupulously avoided and cow slaughter is deemed to be a sin in the Pagro-Mishing society.

The Pagro-Mishing are extremely fond of *apong* (rice beer) which is brewed in every household. It is in fact part of daily meals. *Apong* is served at any time and to all persons irrespective of age and sex. It also constitutes an important part of the offerings in their rituals. *Apong* is offered as a mark of Mishing hospitality and the guests must be treated with a cup of *apong*.

Culture Contact and Religious Values

The Pagro-Mishing have been influenced greatly by their contact with the Assamese society ever since they settled on the plains of Assam. Though the contact was initially nominal, they had to deal with the Assamese people for various reasons. The constant contact with them have made the Pagro-Mishing bilingual. Most of them now use the Assamese language for communication with the non-Mishing though among themselves they speak in their own mother tongue. Today the Pagro-Mishing society is participating in all the activities of development which have greatly affected the entire milieu of their traditional way of life. It is not only in the domain of their material existence but also in their religious beliefs that one can discern the impact of change. Although the Pagro-Mishing retain their traditional religious values in the original form, they have incorporated religious ideology of the local Hinduism and they now identify themselves as Hindus.

The traditional religion of the Pagro-Mishing is animistic. The entire life of a person, his health and happiness, prosperity and well being, his ills and misfortunes, are attributed to some spirits or *Uii* as they are called. The cosmic phenomena like thunder and lightning, water and fire, earth and air are all abodes of the various spirits which are powerful and benevolent to man and have to be propitiated periodically. *Taleng- Uii* is one such important ritual for every household in which the cosmic forces are propitiated. They also have a very large number of malevolent spirits, and any misfortune is believed to be caused by such spirits. Such misfortune may be in the form of personal illness or in the form of a bad harvest but it is believed to have been afflicted by some *Uii,* which must be identified by the *Miboo,* the 'diviner', who also suggests the remedial sacrifice to ward off the evil spirits.

The cult of *Donyi* (the Sun) and *Polo* (the Moon) is well established. The Sun and the Moon are regarded as the mother and father and hence benevolent. However, there is no specific ritual ceremony to worship them.

The most important religious belief of the Pagro-Mishing is, however, the cult of ancestor worship *(Urom Punam)*. They recognise their agnatic ancestors only, who are worshipped periodically. The Pagro-Mishing strongly believe that the spirits of their ancestors are the guardians of the living descendants whose welfare and prosperity depends on their benevolence which is assured if they are propitiated properly. Their watchful eyes protect the living from most misfortunes. The ancestral spirits also warn their descendants to keep away from any sinful acts. The moral and ethical values of their society and the normative pattern of their kinship values are sustained by the belief in the ancestral spirits which are believed to keep an ever watchful eye on the activities of their descendants. After the Pagro-Mishing had settled on the plains of Assam, they gradually came in contact with the local Hindus. However, a number of *Gossains* (religious preachers), who were the religious heads of various *Satras* (religious institution) in upper Assam took on themselves to proselytise them. The *Gossains* of Sessa, Nomati, Jokai, Budhbari and Khowamara *Satras* were the most prominent ones to influence them towards Hinduism. These *Satras* among themselves divided various territories of upper Assam as their 'parish' and began their work of religious preaching among the emigrants. Slowly they were able to bring some elderly Mishing under their influence who were then initiated into their fold and were taught elements of *Kirtan* and *Bhakti* to God Hari.

Thus, at the operational and ritual level within their society, the Mishing are very much the follower of their traditional beliefs, whereas at the inter-societal level, they believe and recognise themselves as Hindus, like other Hindu communities which surround their society.[4]

Though the Pagro-Mishing may not be fully Hinduised, it is obvious from their relations with the various Hindu castes of the region that they are quite aware of the nuances of the concepts of purity, pollution and untouchability. The local Hindu caste groups have minimal contact with them although the Mishing and Hindu villages are quite nearby. The Mishing are treated almost like the untouchables by the caste Hindus who do not let them enter their houses, nor do they offer water and food to them in their utensils. The Mishing, in retaliation, also do not allow any Assamese, irrespective of his caste to enter their houses. The local untouchable Hindu castes like Dom and Hari are treated as untouchables by the Mishing themselves. However, the Mishing do not equate themselves with any Hindu caste, nor have they accorded any ritual importance whatsoever to the Brahmin. Thus, they believe themselves to be Hindus, but do not seek a position in the caste hierarchy. They are socially autonomous.

The above description of the Pagro-Mishing society does give us an idea that their society has undergone tremendous social change in the course of more than 300 years during which they have been settled in the plains of upper Assam. In the new ecological setting it was inevitable for them to adapt themselves to the existing conditions. Not only the environmental conditions but the political and social conditions in the new habitat were basically different from their original home in the hills. Consequently many of their institutions and their functions lost their significance in the plains. The concept of chieftainship (*Gam*) lost its validity in the new political conditions and completely vanished from their social structure. A more fundamental change has occurred in recent times in the mode of production. They became settled cultivators in the plains and gave up shifting cultivation, and the nomadic way of life. This led to changes in their social values, particularly with regard to the concept of property and the ownership of land, as also they acquired the productive technology of the settled cultivators.The contact with the Assamese for such a long period of time influenced them both linguistically and religiously. They are now, by and large, bilingual and profess to be Hindu while following their own beliefs and rituals as intensely as before.

The close proximity between the Pagro-Mishing and the other Assamese communities was neither intense nor institutionally regular. At best it was confined to matters pertaining to economic transactions which were few and far between. Even the religious preachers, were interested more in collecting offerings rather than in preaching. The cultural isolation of the Mishing have therefore helped them in maintaining their identity due to limited acculturation. They have only adopted from their neighbours their technology and material culture which was essential for their survival and gradually acquired the knowledge of the Assamese language for communication with the members of other communities. In spite of the physical proximity between the Assamese and the Mishing, socially and culturally they kept their distance.

Thus the process of acculturation has been slow and effective marginally for the Pagro-Mishing society. They retain their cultural identity by following their traditions and values, their beliefs and by generally subscribing to the ethos of their culture. Their social organisation has not been affected by their contacts with the non-tribal people. It is their social organisation which provides the continuing and autonomous edifice of their society which in turn is maintained by the social, cultural, and religious values of the Pagro-Mishing society.

4

The Principle of Descent and Structure of Descent Groups.

Having described the ethnographical background of the Pagro-Mishing, I shall now discuss the concept of descent and the structure of descent groups in their society. The frame-work of the Pagro-Mishing society cannot be conceived without a full understanding of their descent groups and the principles on which they are organized. The entire fabric of the Pagro-Mishing society is woven round the descent groups which provide it stability and continuity as well as determine the norms, rules and principles that define the social relationships in their society.

THE PRINCIPLE OF DESCENT

The Pagro -Mishing are a patrilineal people and strictly follow the rule of patrilineal descent. Every individual belongs to one descent group formed on the principle of patrifiliation . It is true that kinship is based on the physical relatedness of the parents and their children, nevertheless, kinship may not always be synonymous with the genetic relationships. Kinship relationships are hence those relationships which are culturally defined on the model of physical relations without always being actually genetic in content. Concept of kinship is biological in conception without being so in content. Kinship may thus be created by incorporation of an individual within the kinship fold although such an individual may not be physically related. Thus the concepts of *pater* (social father) and *genitor* (biological father) signify that by adoption of a child, a man becomes the pater and thereby creates a socially recognized kinship with the adopted child, though he lacks a physical link with him (Radcliffe Brown 1950 : 4).

Physical Paternity and Descent

Descent among the Pagro-Mishing is determined exclusively by the physical ties of fatherhood, though adoption of a child is also allowed, provided the child belongs to the same descent group. The implication of physical fatherhood among the Pagro-Mishing is structurally very important. The membership of a descent group among them is acquired by a person strictly by his physical ties with his genitor who in most of the cases is also the pater. However, in those cases where a child has only the genitor who is not also the pater, he naturally acquires the membership of his genitor's patrilineal descent group. Thus, for example, the child of an unmarried woman becomes the member of his genitor's descent group. Such a child can neither be incorporated into his mother's patrilineal group nor can he acquire the membership of the descent group of the man who may marry his mother subsequently unless he also happens to be the genitor of the child. The position of an adulterine child of a married woman is also similar. The adulterine child becomes member of his genitor's descent group and cannot be incorporated either in his mother's or mother's husband's descent group. The principle of unilineal descent among the Pagro-Mishing is thus strictly adhered to and is exclusively based on physical ties. In other words, the membership of a descent group and the rule of recruitment to the descent group are both determined exclusively by physical paternity. The provision of incorporating an individual into a descent group, with which he has no physical relationship through his genitor does not exist in the Pagro-Mishing society. Such an insistence on biological paternity does not exist in many societies. For example, among the Zulu, an illegitimate child belongs to his mother's agnatic lineage unless redeemed by his genitor or by another man who may have married the woman subsequently (Gluckmen 1950 : 170). Similar rules prevail in some other societies like the Tallensi (Forte's 1970 :55), the Nuer (Evans- Pritchard 1945:64), and the Lakher (Leach 1961 :93). Although these societies are patrilineally organized, yet some of the links in the descent system may actually be through the women which implies that the principle of physically determined patrilineal descent is neither exclusive nor absolute. The Pagro-Mishing do not make any compromise either with regard to the descent rule which is exclusively patrilineal or the membership of descent group which is determined exclusively by actual physical ties. Thus, a child, when he is born, whether legitimately or illegitimately, automatically becomes member of his genitor's descent group with which he remains affiliated for the rest of his life. The physical ties between an individual and his genitor are considered ritually sacrosanct by the Pagro-Mishing whose religious beliefs are based on the cult of agnatic ancestors who are worshipped and propitiated regularly. There are periodic and contingent rituals connected with the worship of one's agnatic ancestors. All the male descendants must worship their ancestors for their (descendants') welfare and prosperity. If such periodic rituals are not performed by the descendants, it is believed that it would result in misfortune, sickness or even death in the family. It is only the actual agnatic ancestors who keep a watch on their descendants, and hence worship of the real i.e. physically determined ancestors is an absolutely essential part of the Pagro-Mishing belief system. Ancestor worship among the Pagro- Mishing is strictly a lineage activity and hence the incorporation of a person into a lineage group is solely determined on the basis of his physical ties through patrifiliation and never through the rule of matrilateral filiation as is the case among the Nuer, Tallensi and Kachin etc. Structural arrangement of Pagro-

Mishing society itself imposes structural constraint on matrilateral filiation as the basis of descent and membership of a descent group. The Pagro-Mishing make a clear distinction between kinship status and affinal status on the basis of exogamous dual division of their society. The kin belong to one's own clan and moiety and the affines to the opposite one. This dichotomisation of kins and affines in two predetermined categories has definite implication on the status assignment of a person in society. Thus, the children of the female agnates (sister,daughter) are treated as affines and not as kin. The birth of a child out of wedlock implies that it is either a consequence of an illicit relation between either a woman and a man belonging to the marriageable category which would categorise the child as an affine of his mother's agnatic group, or such a child is the outcome of an illicit relationship where both the man and the woman belong to the same clan or moiety and hence sexual relationship between them would be regarded as incestuous. Incest is considered a most reprehensible act and invites the wrath of the supernatural powers. The child of such a union is killed and is not allowed to live. The Pagro-Mishing thus make a clear distinction between patrifiliation and matrifiliation; the patrifiliation creates agnatic kins and matrilateral relatives are always categorised as affines. Ritually, and structurally therefore, it is not possible to incorporate an affine into the agnatic category. The Pagro-Mishing allow adoption but they adopt a child who belongs to adoptive father's own lineage and hence does not entail any change in worship of the agnatic ancestors. The Pagro-Mishing woman retains her mundane relationship with her agnatic group even after marriage, but at the ritual level she completely severes her lineage ties and is fully incorporated in her husband's family. The implication of this situation is that though a woman after her marriage maintains affective kinship ties with her agnates, her filial status and ritual bonds are terminated from them. She is fully transferred from her father's jural authority and comes under her husband's jural authority as the politico-jural bonds between a woman and her father and siblings (and agnates) are finally severed at marriage. The principle of full incorporation of the women into their husbands' domestic groups after marriage and the strict adherence to the physically determined patrifiliation as the basis of the membership of descent groups make the Pagro-Mishing a strong patrilineally organized society.

DESCENT GROUPS

The Pagro-Mishing term for the descent groups is '*ope*' which is a generic term for all forms of descent groups that comprise the Pagro-Mishing society. In its most extensive meaning an *ope* refers to the clan which is the largest patrilineal descent group. The subdivisions of a clan are also referred to as *ope*. Similarly, the term for a lineage is also *ope*. Although these descent groups of various orders are not distinguished terminologically, conceptually they are distinctively conceived by the Pagro-Mishing. Its meaning is appropriately conceived according to the operational requirement of the situation.

The Clan

A clan in the Pagro-Mishing society constitutes the largest category of men and women who have descended patrilineally from a common male ancestor. The Pagro-Mishing clans have names which are used as the surnames by the members of the clan. The women, after marriage, use the husbands' clan name and not their natal clan name. The founders of the clans are believed to be real human beings and not mythical characters, although in case of clans, the founder is regarded as a direct descendant of the Creator of the universe itself. Their clan genealogies trace back their origin from the Creator, Sedi. The Pegu clan, for example, is believed to be founded by Pegu, who was a direct descendant of Sedi, the Creator, according to the Pagro-Mishing cosmogony.

The Pagro-Mishing clans are dispersed in a wide area, though many villages belonging to the same clan generally inhabit a contiguous area. Before emigrating to the plains of Assam, the Pagro-Mishing clans were most probably local groups and were also corporate in nature. But after they emigrated to the plains of Assam, these social groups underwent a change in their organisation. As I have described earlier, in most cases, it was likely that the entire clan did not migrate together and moreover it was perhaps not possible for a large emigrating group to settle in one place. Besides, the Mishing, being shifting cultivators in the hills continued to be migratory cultivators in the plains of Assam until very recent time. These were the factors that resulted in the dispersal of the members of a clan over a wide region.

The emigration of the community to the plains of Assam also resulted in changing the political structure of the clans. In the hills each clan had a chief who was known as *Gam*. The *gam* was usually the most powerful and enlightened man of the localised clan and was acknowledged as the leader of the group. He was primarily responsible for maintaining political relationship with the neighbouring communities. In the hills, a clan was usually a local group, but when a clan grew into a large group it dispersed in a number of villages, the headman of each village who in fact might have been only a lineage head, was also called a *gam*. However, the institution of *gam* underwent a radical change after the annexation of Assam and the adjoining hill tracts by the British. The British administration introduced an annual poll-tax on the tribes that came under their jurisdiction. The poll-tax was levied at the rate of Rs.1/- per person annually. The Mishing were also made to pay the poll-tax. The *gams*, who were earlier the political leaders of the clans, were made responsible for the collection of the poll-tax from the members of their clans. The *gam* was given a certain amount as his commission out of the total tax collection. However, the poll-tax on the Mishing was abolished between 1841 and 1844 and in lieu of the poll-tax, the British introduced land revenue on the Mishing as well. They also created the office of Mouzadar (village official) who was responsible for collecting the land rvenue within his circle (Hunter 1879 :239). The position of the *gam* was thus made functionally redundant because he was neither required to maintain peace with other communities, nor did he remain responsible for the collection of tax from the people. Thus as a result of migration and a new administrative, political and environmental set-up, their clan organization underwent a change. Firstly, they ceased to be local groups and had to disperse in a wide area. Secondly, the *gams* lost their legitimacy in terms of their political functions which they performed in the hills, later on even the administrative function, namely the poll-tax collection, ceased to be their responsibility. The Pagro-Mishing clans at present are no more localized corporate groups under a *gam*. Now a clan connotes only a category of agnatic kins who are dispersed in a wide area. The institution of *gam* has been totally lost. However, the unity and identity of a clan based on the idiom of agnatic kinship is immutable in their society as will be discussed presently.

Clan Exogamy and Clanship Norms

The Pagro-Mishing clans are exogamous and clan members identify themselves as *ope birrang-birmang* (*ope* brothers and sisters). Sexual relations within the clan are regarded incestuous *(Yoddak* which literally means 'an act which is morally prohibited'). The clan exogamy and the incest taboo are considered by the Pagro-Mishing as absolute and immutable. The rule of exogamy and incest taboo are valid for the entire clan irrespective of the fact that it may be subdivided into a number of segments. The structurai distance between the members of a clan due to the genealogical proliferation in no way diminishes the observance of these rules in the Pagro-Mishing society. The dispersed nature of the clan neither obliterates its exogamous character nor does it put an end to the observance of incest taboo between the members of various segments of the clan however wide apart they may be settled. The breach of the exogamous rule or the incest taboo is regarded as a very grave sin by the Pagro-Mishing. They believe that the culprits of such sinful acts are punished by the spirits of their ancestors. It is not only the individual culprits who are punished but such sinful acts invoke the wrath of the ancestral spirits for their entire lineage group, which cannot be averted unless the spirits are propitiated in a collective lineage ritual. However, it is the local segment of the clan where the breach was committed which punishes the culprits by either banishing them from the society or by publicly chastising them. In either case, performing the ancestor worship as a purificatory rite is obligatory. The Pagro-Mishing clan is thus a significant agnatic unit of their social structure and due to its rigid and immutable exogamous character provides the foundation of the rules of kinship and affinity in their society.

The clan members regard themselves as agnatic kins and interact within the domain of clanship on the basis of appropriate kinship status which is identified by the kinship terminology. Each member of the clan is ascribed by a kin type by an individual on the basis of generation, age and sex and is referred to by the relevant kinship term. The terminological ascription determines the norms of interpersonal relations among the clan members.

The Pagro-Mishing clan as a category is constituted of persons united by the immutable ties of agnatic kinship and as a conceptional category it is a permanent and continuing unit of the society without ever changing the moral and ethical values of kinship emanating from the belief of a common descent. Though at present a clan has neither economic nor political functions, nor is it a territorially compact group, yet it is structurally and functionally the most important kinship unit in the Pagro-Mishing society.

The Pagro-Mishing clans, however, are not undifferentiated, monolithic structures but are composed of segmented genealogical structures. The genealogical segments of a clan are sub-clans and the lineages.

The Subclan

The subclans, like the clans, are also named groups. The subclans are founded by the descendants of the clan founder, though the members of a subclan cannot recollect their exact genealogical links upto the founding ancestor of the subclan. It is interesting to note that subclan formation among the Pagro-Mishing is not universally present in all the clans. Only some of the large clans have the subclan segments, whereas the small clans are segmented directly into lineages.

Like a clan, the subclans are also of great genealogical span and it is therefore not possible for the living members of a subclan to trace their genealogical links up to the subclan ancestors.

The formation of the subclans, however, does not have important structural significance in the Pagro-Mishing social organization because subclan formation is not based on a uniform generation proliferation. In other words, the subclan formation does not necessarily mean that it was founded by each son of the founder of the clan. A subclan as a distinct unit generally came into existence when the founder of a lineage was singled out for some of his outstanding quality or idiosyncracy and later on was remembered for these. Gradually his descendants were known after these qualities and it became the identifying label of the entire group of his descendants. Such an identifiable category of agntic kins is regarded as a subclan. Thus, for example, a subclan is named as Gunjam Pegu implying that it is a subclan of the Pegu clan. *Gunjam* in the Mishing language means buffalo. It is believed that the founder of this subclan was very fond of buffalo flesh and hence the name Gunjam has been used for his descendants who are at present spread in a number of villages. Since the subclan formation is not structurally determined with regard to the proliferation in every generation or even after some generations, different subclans within a clan need not be of equal generation span. Therefore they cannot be put at the same structural distance from the founding ancestor of the clan. As it has been pointed out that the subclans formation is not a regular structural feature, one is legitimately tempted to find out the functions and significance of the subclans in the Mishing social structure. Although the people themselves do not attach any great importance to the subclans, yet they make it amply clear that the persons belonging to a subclan have closer kinship ties as compared to their kinship relations with other members of the same clan. We can also find that the subclan level seems to be the basis of the formation of village level community. In other words, in a village usually all the households may generally belong to one subclan. However, a few households belonging to other subclans may also be there, but each village has a preponderance of the households belonging to one subclan only.

A number of villages may be occupied by members of one subclan. Most of the villages belonging to one subclan are situated in a contiguous area. However, a few subclan villages may also be situated in distant regions away from the main subclan cluster. Such villages are founded by those households which had migrated from their natal villages in the past in search of virgin land.

Since the subclan membership is structurally more proximate as compared to the relationship between persons of two subclans, the interaction at the intra-subclan level and inter-subclan level is qualitatively different. For example, if a man has to spend a night in some other village he would always prefer to stay in a household belonging to his own subclan. Similarly, a man may participate in a ritual pertaining to ancestor worship with his own subclan members but would not do so when the ritual concerns other subclans. During the marriage ceremony too, we find the importance of subclan affiliation. Among the Mishing (until the culmination of the final ritual ceremony which is held at the husband's place), a bride continues to be part of her own clan. So when the bride is taken to the husband's village for the first time, in such cases where the husband's village may be more than a day's distance away, the bridal party on the way stays for the night in that village where the bride's subclan agnates may also be living. The bride stays in a household belonging to her own subclan. But on her return trip to her natal village from the husband's village, she stays with her husband's subclan agnates and not with her own agnates. The marriage alliances as we shall see are also generally confined to the subclan level of the two exogamous moieties.

Though the Pagro - Mishing do not have a separate term for a subclan which is also referred to as *ope*, there is no confusion in their perception regarding the functions of a clan and a subclan in spite of their being structurally the same. The distinction of clan and subclan levels for a Pagro-Mishing is manifested at the operational level and not at the conceptual level. A subclan like a clan is neither a property owning unit nor are there any specific rituals connected with the subclan. The position of a clan as a discrete bounded segment of the Pagro- Mishing society is of fundamental importance since it regulates the moral and kinship values of its members, who may belong to its segments as well. Generally, therefore, when a Mishing refers to his *ope,* it is invariably the clan, and only on a deeper inquiry he mentions his subclan, although it is also a named agnatic category. The subclan membership, however, becomes manifest at the transactional level in the day-to-day activities of a village where there may be many households belonging not to the same clan, but to different subclans. The interaction between the households belonging to the same subclan are invariably more intimate. Quite often a village may also be named after the subclan to which most of households belong. For example, a Pagro-

Mishing village is named as Gajera and another as **Patir** becuase they are inhabited predominantly by the households of the Gajera and Patir subclan respectively.

From the above discussion it is evident that the clans are the basic structural units of the Pagro-Mishing society. They are basic units because they are the permanent and ongoing bounded segments both in time and space. The strict exogamous rule manifests the moral basis of kinship solidarity within the clan and reinforces the immutable agnatic character of clan. The clans thus provide precisely defined boundary of the agnatic kin category in the society. The ritual basis of norms and values of agnatic kinship ties are great unifying factors within the clan. However, the Pagro-Mishing clans and subclans do not emerge as corporate groups. Now at present, they have no political, economic or ritual functions at the level of the entire clan collectively, which perhaps they had in the former days.

The Lineage

The subclans are further subdivided into genealogical segments of varying orders. These segments are the lineages. The lineage system provides the operational basis of the ritual, economic and domestic life in the Pagro-Mishing society.

The Pagro-Mishing lineage is obviously organized on the principle of patrilineal descent. A lineage comprises persons of both the sexes who are the known descendants of a known and named ancestor in an unbroken male line. A clan is thus constituted of many such lineages. Analytically clan and the lineages within it are two dimensions of the same reality differing only in degree and not in kind.

The genealogical growth of a clan does not change its structure although each succeeding generation entails a change in the structure of lineages. The process of segmentary differentiation is engendered by genealogical growth. Thus while the structure of clan remains the same over the time, the lineages undergo the process of segmentation after every succeeding generation. This means that the genealogical growth of the lineage implies internal segmentation into two or more segments, each one of which is definable by reference to the founding ancestor of the lineage. Segmentation, however, does not alter the existence of a group as such but it creates new groups which have structural relationship within the group. Defining this process, Meggit (1965 : 54) writes that, "segmentation is a process whereby an agnatic group generated subordinate or co-ordinate groups from its own members without necessarily losing its identity...".

Lineage is a relative term since it can be defined with reference to any particular ancestor who is selected as its founder. In other words the generational span of a lineage is not definite. Theoretically, a lineage can be a very large group of persons of any number of generations provided the living persons are aware of the unilineally reckoned genealogical links to the founding ancestor. Similarly, the smallest possible lineage is the sons and daughters of a man. The Pagro-Mishing lineages are, however, characterised by a structured precision according to the number of generations that are incorporated in it whereby lineages of different genealogical depths are functionally differentiated.

The Lineage Structure

The Pagro-Mishing have great interest in recounting their genealogies. By this recollection of the genealogical links to a remote ancestor, usually a large number of living persons can be brought within the frame work of a lineage. Such a lineage may have span of seven or eight generations counting from the oldest living generation. However, this form of lineage group is neither functionally important nor does it emerge as a corporate unit in their society. Moreover, a lineage of this span is not a local group either.

Such a lineage comprises the largest group of agnates who have the knowledge of their agnatic descent from a common ancestor and may be termed as the maximal lineage, following Meyer Fortes (1970 : 37) who defines it as "the lineage of widest span" which "consists of all the descendants in the male line of the remotest common patrilineal ancestor known to the members of the lineage". However, among the Mishing such a 'maximal lineage' is neither a functional and nor a corporate group but it is merely a category of agnates, whereas among the Tallensi the maximal lineage is the basic unit of Tale social organisation that emerges in corporate activities.

Among the Pagro-Mishing the widest lineage which is functionally relevant and which also emerges as a corporate group has a fixed span of generations counted from the oldest living male member. This corporate lineage is further internally segmented and each segment of the lineage is also defined by a fixed number of generations with reference to the founder of the lineage segment.

Lineage Segments and Lineage Terminology

The maximum span of a Mishing lineage that emerges as a corporate group is composed of the agnatic kins descended from an apical ancestor in the fourth ascending generation counted from the oldest living descendant . This widest corporate lineage is further segmented into lineages of lesser span which are composed of agnatic kins descended from an ancestor belonging to third ascending generation from the oldest living generation. These segments are further segmented into lineages of still lesser span which are composed of the agnatic kins descended from an ancestor who belongs to the second ascending generation counted from the oldest living descendant. In the present study, for the largest group of the agnatic kins who comprise an "effective corporate" lineage, I have used the term "effective maximal lineage". This implies that technically a lineage of much wider span may be in existence because of an even more remote ancestor being genealogically known to the descendants, yet such a group of living agnates do not emerge as a corporate group. Thus by the technical definition of a lineage it may be labelled as the maximal lineage if by this we mean "the largest group of agnatic kins who have descended from the remotest-known ancestor". But such a lineage in the Pagro-Mishing society is not operationally a functional unit and whose members merely comprise a category of agnates without constructing a group.

The effective maximal lineage continually expand and proliferates through a process of segmentation after each generation into major segments and the major segments are further segmented similarly into minor segments and finally the minor segments divide into minimal segments. The maximal lineage and its segments of varying orders are functionally differentiated. The segmentation of the 'effective maximal lineage' shows the 'nesting attribute' of segmentary series (Middleton and Tait 1955 : 7). The structure of Pagro-Mishing lineage may be explained with the help of the following diagram (Fig. 4.1).

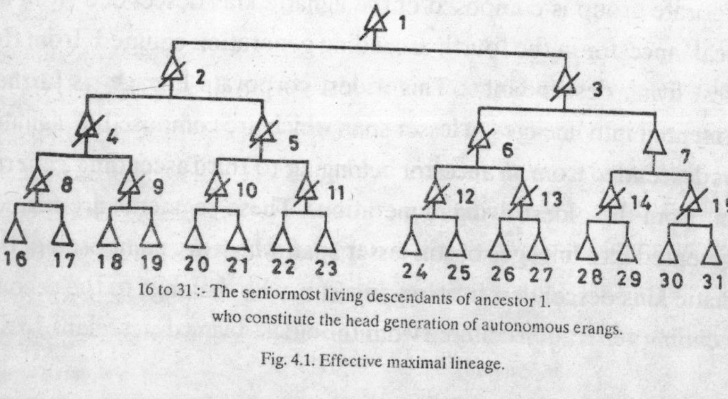

16 to 31 :- The seniormost living descendants of ancestor 1. who constitute the head generation of autonomous erangs.

Fig. 4.1. Effective maximal lineage.

The genealogical diagram (Figure 1) assumes that each male descendant of the male founding ancestor has two sons. Other than this hypothetical assumption, the diagram represents the empirical model found in the Pagro-Mishing lineages. The men in the fifth descending generational level (Nos. 16 to 31) represent the oldest living descendants who are agnatically related to one another and form the seniormost core of an effective maximal lineage by virtue of being the descendants of the same ancestor No.1. It is clear from the diagram (Figure 1) that all the descendants are not uniformly related to one another on the basis of their structural distance from one another. The descendants of No.2 and No.3 thus constitute two 'major lineage segments' consisting of Nos. 16 to 23 and Nos. 24 to 31 respectively. These segments have been termed as 'major lineages'. The major lineages are further segmented by the same principle into what have been termed as 'minor lineage'. The descendants of Nos. 2 and 3 would thus constitute two 'major lineages', and the descendants of Nos. 4,5,6,and 7 would constitute four 'minor lineages'. The segment of a minor lineage has been termed as the 'minimal lineage' hence the descendants of Nos. 8,9,10, 11,12,13 and 14 would constitute the minimal lineages. The Mishing lineage system may thus be seen as a hierarchy of groups in which two or more parallel groups are bound together to form a larger segment which in turn, is grouped with one or more similar segments to form a still more inclusive group.

The structure of the lineage among the Pagro-Mishing is absolutely dependent upon the cult of ancestors. The genealogical proliferation not only segments the lineage into smaller divisions in each generation which emerge as corporate entities in some social context, it also results in splitting the effective maximal lineage. In other words, the Pagro-Mishing effective maximal lineage is not a permanent corporate group but is subject to fission in every generation because the morphological structure of a lineage is defined by the cult of ancestors as will be evident from the following discussion.

Lineage Structure and Ancestor Worship

The different corporate structural forms of lineage and their segmentation among the Pagro-Mishing are based strictly on ancestor worship. Ancestor worship provides the rationale for segmentation of lineage among the Mishing. What Forte's (1970 : 41) writes about the Tallensi aptly describes the Mishing situation because among them too, "ancestor cult is the calculus of the lineage system by means of which the progressive internal differentiation of a lineage is ordered and is fitted into the existing structure".

Ancestor worship is the most dominant feature of the Pagro-Mishing belief system. A man's ancestors are his watchful guardians; the welfare of the living members depend upon the benevolence of their ancestors which is assured by periodic sacrifices to them. The norms and ethics of kinship behaviour are directly linked with the cult of the ancestors who exert a coercive power over their descendants. The breach of a taboo, for instance, is considered a sin for which the punishment to the culprit would be dispensed by the spirits of his ancestors. The norms and the sanctions reinforcing social behaviour in the lineage, clan and the society at large are directly derived from the ancestors who are both feared and venerated by the Pagro- Mishing. The pattern of kinship behaviour in the Pagro-Mishing society is not based merely on jural, economic and other utilitarian consideration; they have a moral binding as well which is reinforced by the fear of the supernatural power of the ancestral spirits which, they believe are omnipresent.

The Pagro-Mishing have very precise and clear notion about the genealogical categories of their agnatic ancestors (Gomin Bulla), who play a decisive role in their day-to-day life. They divide their agnatic ancestors into two categories according to the genealogical distance between the oldest living descendants and the ancestors.

These two categories of ancestors are *Ramnu* and *Ramku.* The *ramnu* and *ramku* mean the near and the distant ancestors respectively. The proximate ancestor *Ramnu,* is a man's deceased father's father, whereas the distant ancestor *Ramku,* is the man's father's father's father, as shown in the following Figure (Fig. 4.2)

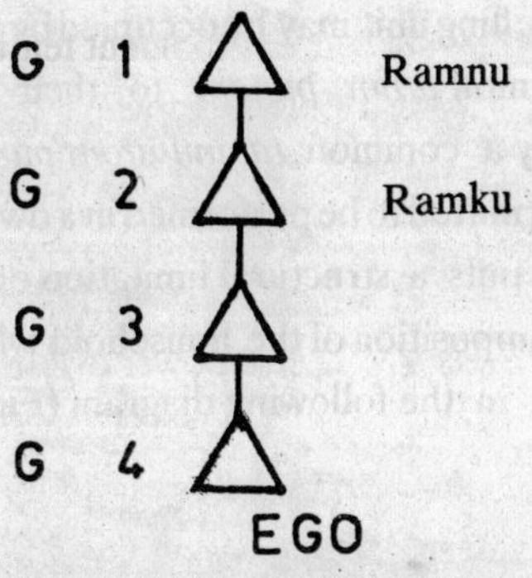

Fig. 4.2. Ramnu and Ramku ancestors.

In Figure 4.2, Ego's (G 4) *Ramnu* ancestor is his father's father (G 2) and *Ramku* ancestor is his father's father's father (G 1). The *ramku* and *ramnu* ancestors are the most important for the members of a lineage from the ritual point. They are regarded as the guardians of the households *(erang)* of their descendants. Any disregard shown by the descendants towards them is immediately manifested by misfortunes. Therefore, these ancestors are invoked at the beginning of every ceremony held by the household besides the obligatory periodic ancestor worship *(Urom Punam)* performed by the concerned descendants. *Urom Punam* is an extremely important and elaborate ceremony involving sacrifice of an especially reared pig and some fowls. This ceremony must be performed by the households periodically.

The Pagro-Mishing believe that the spirits of the *ramnu* ancestors dwell in the rear portion of their dwelling house (*akum*). These ancestors may therefore be called 'house ancestors'. A Mishing house is the dwelling place of a domestic family which is a structurally defined group consisting of the male agnates, their wives and children. But a dwelling unit may be occupied by only those agnates who may offer a common *urom punam* to their *Ramnu* ancestor because as a rule, only a common *ramnu urom punam* ritual for the entire household is permitted to be performed in a dwelling house. This restriction necessarily puts a structural limitation on the composition of a household. The composition of the household which performs the *ramnu urom* is shown in the following diagram (Figure 4.3) :

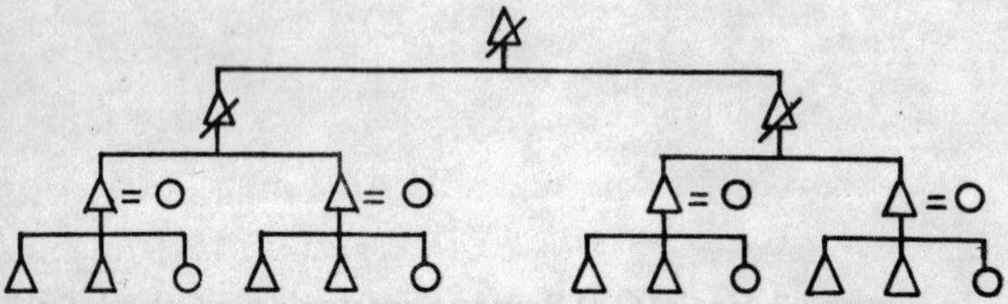

Fig. 4.3. Composition of a household as Ramnu urom performing unit.

Since a dwelling house can be the abode of only one *ramnu* ancestor, it has major implications in the organization of the household and lineage segments. It is evident from the diagram (Fig 4.3) that a house can be occupied, at the most, by a minor lineage which is the basis of a domestic family among the Pagro-Mishing. A domestic unit is therefore composed of those men in the senior generation who have a common father's father and who offer a common *ramnu urom* and occupy one house. It is believed by the Mishing that death of a person in a house where he would not be eligible to offer the *urom* to the house ancestor would pollute the house. Similarly a daughter is not allowed to give birth to a child in her father's house because her child would obviously be member of another agnatic lineage. The ancestors who are believed to reside in the house get offended with the death and birth of those who are not their agnatic descendants. The next higher order of ancestor worship, that is, *ramku urom* is performed by [illegible] major lineage. It includes a group of male agnatic kin who have descended from an ancestor in the third ascending generation counting from the oldest living descendants (Fig. 4.4).

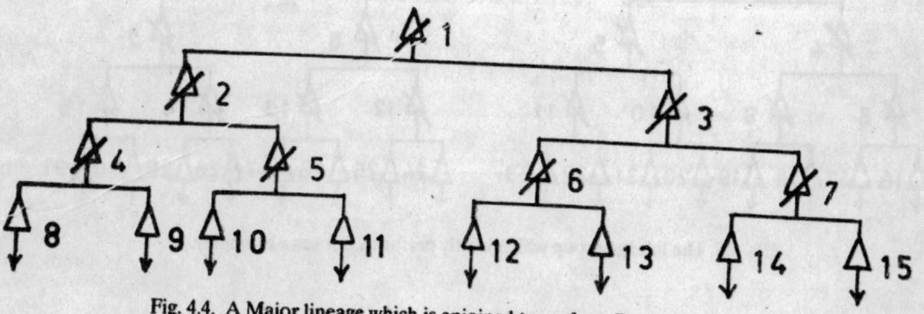

Fig. 4.4. A Major lineage which is enjoined to perform Ramku urom.

In the above diagram (Fig. 4.4), Nos. 8 to 15 are the living descendants of No.1, who is the founder of the major lineage. No. 8 to No. 15 and their descendants constitute a major lineage group and perform jointly the *ramku urom* of their ancestor. Within the major lineage, there may be two or more minor lineages (In Fig. 4.4 only two minor lineages are shown viz. descendants of Nos. 2 and 3) which jointly perform the ceremony. The *ramku urom* ceremony is performed in the house of the seniormost living man belonging to any of the minor lineages that compose the major lineage.

The highest order of ancestor worship among the Pagro-Mishing is an elaborate affair. It is performed jointly by all those household, the heads of which are the male agnatic descendants of a common ancestor in the fourth ascending generation. This worship is called *Bor Seva*.

In other words, the *Bor Seva is* performed by the male agnatic kin descended from an apical ancestor reckoned in the four ascending generations from the oldest living desendant. The *Bor Seva* ceremony is performed by those men who have common father's father's father's father (Fa Fa Fa Fa) (Fig. 4.5).

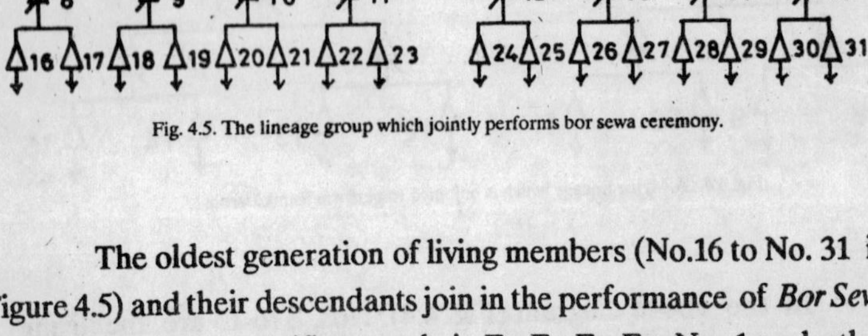

Fig. 4.5. The lineage group which jointly performs bor sewa ceremony.

The oldest generation of living members (No.16 to No. 31 in Figure 4.5) and their descendants join in the performance of *Bor Seva* ceremony to offer sacrifices to their Fa Fa Fa Fa, No. 1 and other remoter ancestors.This agnatic group constitutes the 'effective maximal lineage'. The entire agnatic group that joins for *Bor Seva* ceremony as shown in the diagram (Fig. 4.5) consists of four minor lineages (descendants of Nos. 4,5,6 and 7) or two major lineages (descendants of Nos. 2 and 3). Sometimes a maximal lineage may be of much greater generation span than what is shown in the diagram. But it remains effective only as long as the living descendants remember genealogically the correct agnatic links with the founding ancestor. A maximal lineage may thus continue to grow with every succeeding generation. However, such 'maximal lineage' may undergo the process of fission and split into two or more functional segments due to structural distance between the segments or owing to extraneous factors like emigration. The fission occurs from the generation of the founding ancestor himself. Thus, if No.1 had a brother No. 1a (Fig. 4.5), his (No. 1a) descendants could perform *Bor Seva* separately if it was more convenient due to the physical proximity of the various segments that constitute this lineage. But it is obligatory that all the minor segments of the 'effective maximal lineage' must perform the *Bor Seva* jointly. In such cases, for example, where a minor lineage might have migrated to a new area or to a new village, the head of the minor lineage has to be duly informed regarding the performance of the *Bor Seva* ceremony and his participation in the ritual is obligatory. The day for the ritual ceremony is decided in a joint meeting of the heads of the minor lineages. Each minor lineage contributes equally towards the expenses of the ceremony.

Ancestor worship, thus, provides the blue-print for organizing the lineages of various span among the Pagro-Mishing. An effective maximal lineage is fixed with reference to its founding ancestor and so are the major and minor lineages. From time to time the unity and identity of these segments become manifest in the cult of common ancestors. A major lineage also performs some other rituals jointly. For example, when a dwelling house is struck by lightning, it is regarded with grave concern a manifestation of the supernatural wrath of the ancestors. The event calls for an immediate propitiation of the ancestors to ward off any further calamity. In this ritual the whole major lineage of the affected household must participate. The ritual entails offer of sacrifices to *Taleng Uii* (Spirit of the Thunder and Lightning) and the ancestors. The sacrifice consists of a pig and three chickens and offering of some *apong* to the spirits and the ancestors. The participating lineage members later on partake of the sacrificial meat and *apong* and observe two days' abstinence *(genna)* from all non-domestic chores. This ceremony is performed just outside the affected house. Similarly when the after-death *(Dadgang)* ceremony for an adult member of the lineage is held after ten days of his death, the whole major lineage participates in the ritual. If head of any minor lineage is unable to participate for some unaviodable reasons, he has to perform a ceremony (*Chaki)* at the deceased's house later on. The ancestor worship is performed by that lineage head who is the oldest living male member of the senior generation of the concerned lineage segment. Thus the *ramnu urom* is performed on behalf of the minor lineage by the eldest son of the deceased ancestor; but in case he is dead, genealogically next oldest male agnate performs it. This procedure is followed in all the ancestral rituals. The man who is head of the lineage is called '*ige bone*' ('one who leads'). *Ige bone* is also obliged to symbolically pierce the sacrificial pig for such ceremonies.

Segmentation of Lineage

From the above discussion it is clear that the Pagro-Mishing lineage is not an undifferentiated aggregate of individuals. It is resolved into three segments which are hierarchically arranged and whose structural relationship is marked by points of reference to precisely defined ancestors in the genealogical framework. These three segments of the Mishing lineage have a definite genealogical order because they are absolutely dependent upon the cult of ancestor worship. The largest segment, the effective maximal lineage, is inclusive of the major lineages and the major lineages encompass the minor lineages (Fig. 4.6). Below this level, morphologically there is the minimal lineage which comprises the sons and daughters of a man. But the minimal lineage among the Pagro-Mishing is neither a ritual unit, nor a functional segment, though it is obviously a potential minor lineage.

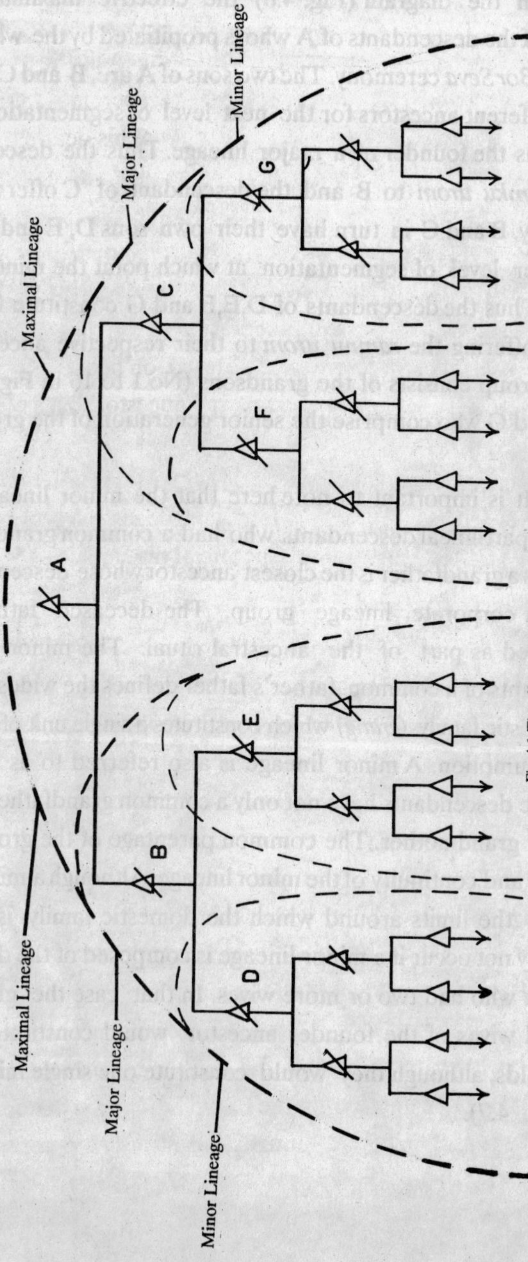

Fig. 4.6. The effective maximal lineage and its segments.

In the diagram (Fig. 4.6) the effective maximal lineage consists of the descendants of A who is propitiated by the whole group jointly in *Bor Seva* ceremony. The two sons of A are, B and C, and they are the referent ancestors for the next level of segmentation because each son is the founder of a major lineage. Thus the descendants of B offer *ramku urom* to B and the descendant of C offer *urom* to B separately. B and C in turn have their own sons D, E and F, G. This is another level of segmentation at which point the minor lineages emerge. Thus the descendants of D,E,F and G constitute four minor lineages offering the *ramnu urom* to their respective ancestors. The lineage group consists of the grandsons (No.1 to 16 in Figure 4.6) of D,E,F and G who comprise the senior generation of the group.

It is important to note here that the minor lineage consists of those partilineal descendants who had a common grandfather (Fa Fa). Thus a grandfather is the closest ancestor whose descendants constitute a corporate lineage group. The deceased father is not propitiated as part of the ancestral ritual. The minor lineage i.e. descendants of a common father's father defines the widest extension of a domestic family *(erang)* which constitutes a single unit of production and consumption. A minor lineage is also referred to as *Ayuke Ope* when the descendants have not only a common grandfather but also a common grandmother. The common parentage of the group ensures the unity and continuity of the minor lineage. Although a minor lineage provides the limits around which the domestic family is organized, yet it may not occur if a minor lineage is composed of the descendants of a man who had two or more wives. In that case the grandsons of different wives of the founder ancestor would constitute separate households, although they would constitute one single minor lineage (See Fig. 4.7).

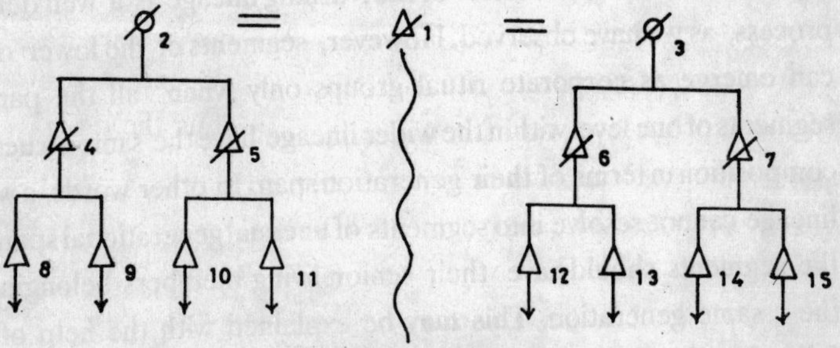

Fig. 4.7. Segmentation of minor lineage on the basis of maternal affiliation.

In the above diagram (Fig.4.7) the grandsons of No. 1 constitute one minor lineage and, therefore, ordinarily should have constituted one domestic family in its maximum extension. But they are descendants of two separate grandmothers (Nos. 2 and 3). So after the death of their respective fathers (Nos. 4,5,6 and 7), the grandsons of No. 2 (Nos. 8,9,10 and 11) and No. 3 (Nos. 12,13,14 and 15) would establish separate households and thus there would be segmentation in the minor lineage on the lines of matrifiliation, though ritually they would constitute one minor lineage.

From the above discussion, it has emerged clearly that the Pagro-Mishing lineage system is structurally related to the ancestor worship. The process of segmentation is, therefore, predictable as it occurs with genealogical proliferation. Thus in the course of development, a minor lineage in the next generation becomes a major lineage and a major lineage becomes an effective maximal lineage. Though two or more maximal lineage segments may contine to join together for *Bor Seva,* they are not obliged to do so. When a lineage grows beyond its ritual limit it ceases to be corporate and the segments beyond the fourth ascending generation are merged in the clan because the ancestors beyond the fourth ascending generation reckoned from the senior living members are not functionally important and they are worshipped only during certain rituals and cease to be the focus of the lineage segments. The segmentation of the Mishing lineage is a well defined process, as we have observed. However, segments of the lower order can emerge as corporate ritual groups only when all the parallel segments of one level within the wider lineage have the same structural composition in terms of their generation span. In other words, a wider lineage cannot resolve into segments of unequal generational span. All the segments should have their senior living members belonging to the same generation. This may be explained with the help of the following diagram (Fig.4.8).

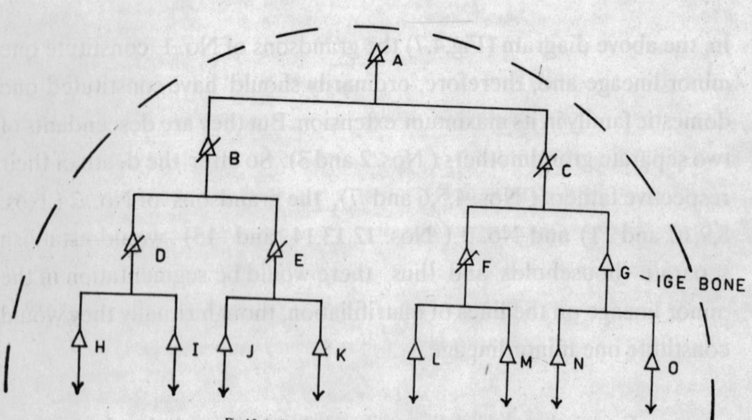

Fig. 4.8. A minor lineage with asymmetrical collateral segments

In the above diagram (Fig. 4.8)(in a hypothetical situation) it has been shown that A, the founder of the lineage, had two sons B and C who also had two sons each namely, D,E and F,G. All these men are dead except G. The deceased D,E,F, and their living brother G also have two sons each viz., H, I; J,K; L,M; and N, O. The descendants of B constitute one ritual unit to offer him the *ramnu urom* (being FF). Logically, since father and grand father of L and M are also dead, they would be expected to offer *ramnu urom* to their grandfather C. Similarly the living descendants of A who are H, I, J, K and L, M should offer *ramku urom* to him (being Fa Fa Fa). Only G along with his sons N and O would not participate in the ritual because G will worship A by offering *ramnu urom* to A who is his (G's) father's father.

However, the formation of ritual units envisaged in the above situation is not possible. The reason is that a lineage of higher generation span can segment into smaller functional units only when every segment is of the same generation span. Thus, in the above example we find that the lineage segmentation is not strictly on the basis of a uniform growth of all the implicit segments of the major lineage. On the basis of this hypothetical case, we find the seniormost living descendant of A is G and therefore he is the lineage head *(Ige Bone)*. The ancestor worship, as already mentioned, is conducted by the seniormost living male descendant of the lineage founder. Therefore, as far as G is concerned the lineage group reckoned from A is still a minor lineage i.e. one which would offer only *ramnu urom* and G, the *ige bone* would propitiate A, his deceased father's father. When he performs the ceremony along with other members of the lineage to propitiate A, other deceased members of the lineage namely B and C are taken care of within the *urom punam*. Therefore, individuals H to M alongwith their households are not obliged to perform the *uroms* of their Fa Fa and the Fa Fa Fa separately. The responsibility for propitiation of the ancestors lies with G who is the seniormost living member of the lineage reckoned from A. After G's death, however, there will be segmentation. The lineage which was one minor lineage until G's life time will divide itself into two minor lineages (reckoned from B and C) and will also grow into one major lineage (reckoned from A) which will then offer *ramku urom* jointly to A, the founder of the lineage.

A Mishing lineage thus segments into minor segments only when all the male descendants of an ancestor, who is the focus of reference for the entire kin group is dead, otherwise even a morphological minor segment may be submerged in a more inclusive lineage due to the presence of a living male in the collateral segment. So even when a sibling group's father and father's father may be dead if their Fa Br is alive he acts as the *ige bone* of the lineage group and the two collateral segments remain one corporate ritual unit.

It is evident from the above discussion that the various levels of segmentation in the Pagro-Mishing lineage are distinguishable by morphological as well as functional criterion. The functional basis of segmentation is provided by the different levels of ancestor worship which in turn defines the morphological structure of each lineage segment. Whenever a lineage emerges as a corporate group in its own right it is identified by reference to its founding ancestor. Although the various orders of lineage are primarily ritual units, yet the functional requirement of different levels of lineage is not the same. Thus the effective maximal lineage is a ritual group that offers *bor seva* sacrifices to the lineage and clan ancestors; the major lineage is ritual unit of a lesser generation span and is responsible for performing the *ramku urom*, the minor lineage is also a ritual unit and offers *ramnu urom*.

The minor lineage more importantly is also the basis of the Pagro-Mishing domestic family which is structured on the basis of the genealogical links between its male members and the founding ancestor. The growth and fission of a domestic unit is therefore directly inter linked with that of the lineage. In this way the minor lineage as a residential unit is the most significant corporate group with jural, economic and ritual functions in the Pagro-Mishing society.

Lineage and the Local Group

An effective maximal lineage is a localized group. It is seldom that two or more effective maximal lineages of the same clan constitute a village although two or more such groups belonging to different clans may form a village community. The composition of a village community among the Pagro-Mishing was related to their migratory nature which until recent times led them to new areas in search of virgin land and consequently establishment of a new village. Although they still migrate, but due to the increase in population and consequently non-availability of fresh land, the habit is dying out.

In the past when a new village was established, it was done only by a few households constituting a 'major lineage' which migrated to a fresh area as a group. A new village was inhabited continuously for many generations. Only when the number of households increased over a period of time, a segment, generally a major lineage or a segment thereof, moved to a fresh area and established a new village. The migrant groups, usually did not go very far away from the natal village and were therefore able to maintain contact with the kin in parent village. Consequently some of the rituals like *Bor Seva* which is jointly celebrated by an effective maximal lineage continued to be celebrated jointly in the village where the seniormost segment of the lineage lived. However, when the men of the senior generation had died and the genealogical distance between the lineage segments had also increased, the migrant lineage segment in their new villages also grew into maximal lineage and attained an autonomous ritual status. The process of migration was therefore the basic cause of the dispersed nature of the clans and also fission in the localized lineage groups. The composition of the village community, and the structure of lineage was directly linked with the economic system followed in the Pagro-Mishing society. The shifting cultivation with primitive means of production forced them to abandon a site after a certain period of time. With the increase in population, it became imperative that the surplus population migrated to fresh area in search of virgin land. Therefore the relationship between subsistence pattern and the population size is an important factor in understanding the Pagro-Mishing lineage structure. It might legitimately be inferred that the limitations of resources of an area put a limit on the optimal size of the village community which generally comprised an effective maximal lineage. As soon as the population increased, some minor segments of the maximum lineage shifted to a new area, which over a priod of two generations grew into effective maximal lineages. Thereafter, the same cycle began once again.

It may be recalled here that the ties of clanship for the Pagro-Mishing are immutable not with standing the genealogical and geographical distance between the segments. The ties of clanship are permanent which bind them to a system of moral values, which is sustained by the ritual values of the society. The continuity and identity of a clan is maintained by a shared body of beliefs and rituals which are reinforced by the supernatural sanctions and the corporate actions of the lineage as well. It is the effective maximal lineage as a localized group and the minor lineage as the residential unit which are the two levels of corporate functions of lineage among the Pagro-Mishing. The corporateness of the local lineage groups manifests at the time of birth, marriage and death besides, of course, for the all important ancestor worship. The minor lineage which forms domestic family is, however, the most important segment of the lineage group as discussed in a subsequent chapter.

So far I have described the internal structure of descent categories and group, the process of their growth and segmentation, and the norms and values that determine the interpersonal relations between the members of a clan. I shall now discuss the framework of the Pagro-Mishing society by examining the system of relationship by which their clans are integrated and provide the structural basis of society.

Dual Organization and Kingroup Relationship

The Pagro-Mishing society is divided into two intermarrying exogamous moieties. Each moiety is composed of a number of clans. Structurally the organization of the society into two intermarrying divisions is the most significant feature of this society which is fully reflected in the rules of marriage, the kinship terminology and the reciprocal kinship behaviour. The basic structural features of an exogamous moiety organization namely, distinction between the parallel and cross-cousins, merging of the patrilateral and matrilateral cross-cousins, and the existence of bilateral cross-cousin marriage are present in the Pagro-Mishing society.

The dichotomous division of the Pagro-Mishing society is a cognitive reality by which the members themselves conceptualize the structure of their society. The Pagro-Mishing conceive of their society as being composed of two parts : one in which a person is born and the other from which he seeks a spouse. The one in which he is born is composed of his agnatic kin and the other division is composed of those who are his affines. These two divisions are complementary. A person refers to his agnatic division by the kin terms as *Biro Birnang* (brother-sister), and the affinal division as *Igo- Magbo* (brother-in-law). Apart from dividing the whole society into two intermarrying moieties, the dual organization of the Pagro-Mishing society has no role in their economic and ritual system. The Pagro-Mishing social organization is characterized by the existence of exogamous moieties, and yet the ethnographical and historical evidence indicate that this was not an original feature of their society but it developed during the period of emigration to the plains of Assam. The dual organization is an outcome of the adaptive process of social change that was engendered by mass exodus of these people.

The ethnohistory of the Pagro-Mishing also describes the formation of the dichotomous division of their society. There are many folktales which narrate the events that resulted in the formation of dual organization. Though, the folktales are not records of history; yet when folktales describe the events that took place only a few generations ago, they cannot be totally ignored for knowing the past of a people about whom there are no other historical records. Moreover, the process of absorption of new clans in the Pagro-Mishing dual organization continued until very recently which gives credence to the events narrated in their folktales regarding the absorption of clans in the past.

The Pagro-Mishing society as already discussed earlier is composed of three phratries and some individual clans. The original nucleus of the society was provided by the Pagro Phratry after which the entire group is known today. The Pagro were composed of two clans (1) Doley and (2) Pegu, and are regarded as the earliest emigrants to the plains of Assam. The two clans were initially loosely related by the ties of affinity which was established firmly between them by exchange of women as a permanent mode of alliance while they were in the process of emigration to the Assam plains. According to the ethno-history, the Doley clan was led by Ranu while they emigrated to the plains. During the period of migration they lived in many places. The Pegu clan, under the leadership of Matsik, was also emigrating and on the way they met the Doley clan at the foothills of the Siyang valley. Ranu and Matsik, the leaders of two clans, met with each other and discovered that they had actually come from the same region and for the same purpose i.e. emigrating to a safe place. Their common concern and a common heritage forged a unity between the two clans who decided to establish permanent relationship between them which was created by the bonds of affinity. Since that time, the Doley and

Pegu clans have become permanent affines of each other. The legend further tells that the Doleys had already settled for a while at the foothills when the Pegus met them. The Doleys were gradually moving in the northerly direction whereas the Pegus were further moving in the southerly direction when they met each other. But once the affinal relationship was established between the two clans, both of them emigrated jointly to the plains of Assam. However, the Doley clan by virtue of its earlier migration towards the plains claimed ownership of land, and the Pegus were given rights to cultivate the land by them.

This original relationship between the Doley and Pegu clans is still reflected, though in the symbolic form, at present. It is customary even now, that any piece of land cultivated by a Doley family and abandoned after some years, as was the practice due to shifting cultivation, would not be cultivated by a Pegu family even after several years without the permission of the Doley family. This prohibition did not affect the Doleys if they wanted to recultivate the land abandoned by the Pegus. Similarly the Pegu households make a token payment to a Doley family to 'buy' earth from which to make the *'maram'* (fire place) inside their house. The Pegus also 'buy' land from the Doleys for burying their dead. All these symbolic acts manifest the claims of the Doley clan as the earlier emigrants and hence the owners of the land.

The Doley and Pegu houses also show a slight variation in the placement of the main support beam of the roof of the house. The Doleys always place the rootside of the wooden pole made out of a tree trunk towards the north and Pegus place the rootside pointing towards the south. The direction of the beam symbolizes the movement of the Doleys and the Pegus at the time when they first met each other.

Over the long period of emigration many other phratries and individual clans from the same region emigrated to the plains and came in contact with the Pagros. These clans were gradually accepted by the

Doleys or Pegus by a fiction of either kinship or affinity. The process of incorporation was to create a fictive kinship with either of the Pagro clans. Once the clan brotherhood was established, the new clan was automatically regarded as affine of the other clan. Thus the Bomi phratry became clan brothers of the Doley and so was the case with the Tayo-Taye phratry as well. The clans belonging to the Bomi and Tayo-Taye phratry, by virtue of their clan brotherhood with the Doley, have automatically become *igo-magbo* (affines) of the Pegu clan. Many other clans like the Kari, Patgui, Lagachu etc. also became clan brothers of the Pegu and thus created 'affinal relationship' with the Doleys. The process of incorporation of a few clans into the dual organization of the Pagro- Mishing has been recorded in the last generation itself.

Initially thus the relationship of affinity existed between the Pegu and Doley clans only. Then with the emigration of various Mishing clans from the hills, the process of incorporation into the dual organization began. Some emigrating clans were already known to either the Pegu or the Doley clan and they re-established their relationship with them. It is said that the Bomi group of clans joined the Doley as their *birnang* (brothers) because they have had this relationship in the hills as well. The Tayo-Taye group of clans also regard the Doley as their kins. On the other hand clans like Lagachu, Patgiri and Kari claimed kinship with the Pegu clan.

The structural basis of the Pagro-Mishing society was, thus, provided by the Doley-Pegu affinal relationship. This dichotomous division provided the model for relationship between the clans. Therefore the clans which were accepted within the folds of the Pagro-Mishing had to follow this structural basis of relationship. Consequently many independent clans or clusters of clan in the past became part of the Pagro-Mishing dual organization without either altering the structural relations or losing their own identity.

Development of the dual organization in the Pagro-Mishing society was an adaptive process and required minimum structural re-adjustment in the relationship of the clans. In other words, the rules of marriage among the Mishing adumbrated the possibility of the emergence of dual organization due to the preferential bilateral cross-cousin marriage that was the basic form of marriage in the Mishing society. So even in the hills, the clans were interlinked by bilateral exchange of women. However, emigration of the Mishing clans did disrupt the relationship between the clans but the creation of exchange relationship with the new clans aptly suited the hitherto existing model of the bilateral cross-cousin marriage. Moreover, the demographic character of the clan size was also a contributing factor in the merger of clans in the Pagro-Mishing group. The clans that joined them were small in size and therefore could not influence the structural relationship between Doley and Pegu clans. Hence the social kinship created with any one of the two original clans in the system put them in an affinal category of the other clan. The dual organization of Pagro-Mishing thus provided the paradigm for clan relationship. It had the flexibility to accommodate any number of clans without altering its basic features. Addition of new clans has merely enlarged the area of exchange of spouses, though preferentially, only those clans and subclans exchange women which have enduring affinal relationship. The process of incorporation of new clans in the Pagro-Mishing dual organization has however augmented its size.

The Moieties and the Clans

The Pagro-Mishing moieties are named as Doley and Pegu after the two original clans. These two clans are also numerically dominant. The Pegu moiety is composed of seven clans : (1) Pegu (2) Kari (3) Patgiri (4) Gettum (5) Patir (6) Pait and (7) Lagachu; and the Doley moiety is composed of eight clans : (1) Doley (2) Yeani (3) Kagyeng (4) Koptag (5) Mili (6) Kuli (7) Kutum and (8) Kumbang (Table 1).

TABLE 4.1

Clans and Subclans of the Doley and Pegu Moieties

Doley Moiety		Pegu Moiety	
Clans (ope)	*Subclans*	*Clans (ope)*	*Subclans*
1. Doley	(1) Letum	1. Pegu	(1) Gudang
	(2) Ledang		(2) Gupit
	(3) Gajera	2. Kari	
2. Yeani		3. Patgiri	
3. Kagyong		4. Gettum	
4. Koptag		5. Patir	
5. Mili		6. Pait	
6. Kuli		7. Lagashu	
7. Kutum			
8. Kumbang			

The Pagro-Mishing do not have any term for the moiety and normally use the term *Khel* to refer to them. However the term *Khel* is also used for the phratry.

Some of the clans that belong to a moiety have more specific ties among themselves. Thus the three clans of Doley moiety namely, Yeani, Kagyong and Koptag are believed to have migrated to the plains together because they were assumed to be the descendants of a common ancestor. These three clans belong to Tayo-Taye *Khel.* Similarly, three other clans namely Kuli, Kutum and Kumbang belong to Bomi *Khel* and are supposed to have a common agnatic descent from a remote ancestor. The Mili clan is a recent incorporation into the Pagro-Mishing society. In the Pegu moiety, the three clans, Patir, Pait and Patgiri are believed to be related as descendants of a common ancestor. They have, however, no collective name. The rest of the clans in the Pegu moiety are independent of each other.

Most of the Pagro-Mishing clans are demographically small and are localized in only a few villages. Many clans are not divided into subclans either.

The two main clans viz. Doley and Pegu are, however, numerically very large and are also dispersed in scores of villages in the entire Pagro-Mishing territory. Both of these clans are further divided into named subclans. The Pegu clan is divided into two subclans which are (1) Gudang and (2) Gupit. The Doley clan is divided into three subclans namely (1) Letum (2) Ledang and (3) Gajera. The subclan names are, however, not used as surnames. Owing to the large size of the Doley and Pegu clans, the subclans formation has been a natural response which facilitates in maintaining closer structural ties among the kinsmen as well as with their affines in the opposite moiety.

Clans and Their Relationship Within the Moiety

Although all the clans that belong to one moiety do not claim to have agnatic ties among themselves, nevertheless they act within the idiom of agnatic kinship. In other words, the members of a moiety regard one another as consanguineal kin regardless of their clan affiliation and identify the members of their moiety as *"Biro-Birmang"* brother-sister) which in turn determines their interactional pattern with the members of the moiety. The moieties are, thus, not only strictly exogamous but sexual relations within the moiety are also regarded like incest. Though any sexual transgression that takes place between members of two different clans within the moiety, would not be strictly regarded incest and does not invite the wrath of the ancestors, the society nevertheless does not tolerate it and would excommunicate the culprits. In fact, such acts are conspicuous by their absence in the Pagro-Mishing society.

In the contemporary Pagro-Mishing society the dual organization provides the structural foundation to the whole society. It binds the segments of society by two strands of relationships, namely consanguinity with in own moiety and reciprocal affinity with the other moiety.

However, the kinship sentiments among the members of various clans of the same moiety are perceptibly and qualitatively different as far as one's own clan and other clans are concerned. For instance one's own clansmen are referred to as *ope birrang* whereas members of other clans are referred to only as '*birrang*'. *Ope Birrang* implies 'clan brothers' and therefore refers to structurally nearer and actual kin, whereas *birrang* connotes a mere social category without any actual basis for it. Nontheless the dual organization is an empirical reality. The basis of the dual organization is provided by the rules of marriage and the idiom of kinship. The system cannot continue if these values are endangered and hence the structural constraints preclude any change in the values that would disrupt the functional interdependence between the segments of the society.

Let me illustrate the point by discussing a case which occurred within last fifty years.

The Doley moiety, consists of a clan which was incorporated into it only about 50 years ago. This is the Mili clan. Mili is a large clan and was keen to align itself with the Pagro-Mishing, but was not able to do so. The male members of this clan sometimes married women belonging to either the Doley or the Pegu clan. Though the number of such indiscriminate marriage was few, it was enough to create structurally anomalous situation contradicting the basic features of the dual organization. In spite of these marriages being regarded irregular ones, they nevertheless contradict the kinship and affinal pattern of the Pagro-Mishing. In other words, the Doley and Pegu being affines of each other, the women belonging to one clan become wives of the men of the opposite clan, and accordingly have a predetermined place in the kinship terminological system. But in a situation, where two women belonging to Doley and Pegu clans were married to the men of Mili clan only, their position became anomalous. The Doley and Pegu women became wives of two brothers and hence became sisters and lost their perpetual affinal relationship to each other. The consequence of such anomalous marriage was that the Doley and Pegu families became common affines of a third clan viz. Mili, and the children born of the Doley and Pegu women thereby became parellel cousins,though under the normal rule of bilateral exchange, the children of a Doley and a Pegu women would always be cross-cousins and hence potential spouses.

The Mili clan, thus created a great confusion by indiscriminate marriage choices. The Pagro-Mishing society took a strong view of these irregular marriages. Finally, a special meeting *(Kebang)* of the various clan elders of the Pagro-Mishing was held and the Mili clan was specifically warned to stop its unorthodox behaviour. The Pagro-Mishing also agreed to incorporate the Mili clan if they exchanged their women with only one moiety. After that the Mili clan identified itself with the Doley moiety because they have a traditional kinship link with the Bomi *Khel* which is part of the Doley moiety. Since then the Mili have become affines of the Pegu moiety. This event occurred according to some elderly informants around 1930.

This case clearly illustrates my contention that the dual organization of the Pagro-Mishing was an adaptive system and incorporation of a new clan was possible only if it did not involve any structural change that led to disequilibrium in the Pagro-Mishing social structure.

The principle of agnatic descent, cult of ancestor worship and the corporate nature of the lineage are fully manifested in the structure and functioning of the domestic groups. Without a proper understanding of these principles and values, the domain of domestic relations in the Pagro-Mishing society would have remained merely at the level of form without uncovering the model on which they are structured.

5

The Family System : Structure and Organization

The domestic family is one of the most important functional units of the Pagro-Mishing social structure. The descent groups viz., the clan and lineage provide the framework of the Pagro- Mishing social structure, but it is the domestic family as an autonomous unit of the society which provides the basis for the crystallization of kinship interaction which is both intense and regular for its members. It is within the domestic family that the children are born and come to maturity and learn cultural conceptions, values, norms and the rules of kinship and it is within this unit that each individual finds food and shelter. The domestic family is a resource holding as well as a production and consumption group. To be born and to grow up in a particular domestic family gives an individual the jural and social status, determined by his physical relationship which forms the basis of his domestic and extra domestic rights, duties and obligations. Among the Pagro-Mishing, without being member of a domestic family an individual has no social existence because he attains his rightful place in the society through his domestic family alone. If an individual commits a wrongful act, it is not treated merely an individual's private act but the blame and its correction are both allocated to his domestic family. It is therefore the obligation of the domestic family to redress, what they consider, wrongs to the members of the society, and to safeguard their interests.

Thus among the Pagro-Mishing, the concept of the responsibility and accountability is familial, not individual. Consequently those persons who do not belong to a domestic family have no jural status in the society. For this reason, a Pagro-Mishing individual has always to be member of a domestic family.

I will discuss and analyse the different dimensions of the Pagro-Mishing domestic group in the present chapter as well as in the three following chapters.

In this chapter, I will discuss the concept of the family and the domestic group in the Pagro-Mishing society and then proceed to analyse the structural basis of the composition of the domestic groups including the rules of recruitment and the typological variations in the domestic group. I will then examine the relationship between the ethnographical data and the rules governing the composition of the domestic groups. A description of the Pagro-Mishing dwelling house and its relationship with the structure of the domestic group will form the concluding part.

Concept of the Family and Domestic Group (*Erang*)

The Pagro-Mishing term for the family is *erang* which connotes a family unit having an autonomous economic, social, political and ritual status with a common residence. To a Pagro-Mishing, then *erang* means a domestic group, the membership of which is determined exclusively on the basis of kinship and affinity. Any other type of residential unit which may not be based on the familial relationships, either conjugal or filial, is not called an *erang*. For example, the Pagro-Mishing have no term to identify a household having only one person, because it lacks the minimum requirements of being a familial group and hence to be called an *erang*.

A Pagro-Mishing conceives of his *erang* to be his family and his home. The *erang* is, therefore, not merely an abstraction of a kinship group but it is also an empirical reality. The term *erang* nicely conceptualizes in the Mishing language both the home and the family. An *erang* is not only an autonomous family group but it is also the most significant group in the society because an individual has to be a part of an *erang* in order to exist in the society.

Sometimes, the term *erang* may also be used to refer to a larger social group incorporating a number of domestic groups. They may be jointly referred to as one *erang.* But the term *erang* is used in this sense only for those independent domestic groups which are headed by full brothers. This extended meaning of the *erang* implicitly emphasizes the prepartition position of those *erang* which are autonomous now but which were part of one single erang when the father or father's brother of the present heads of the independent *erang* was alive and all of them constituted only one domestic group under either the father or the father's brother. Such independent domestic groups constitute one unit for the purpose of *ramnu urom* worship. The term *erang* in this sense refers to all those domestic groups of the minor lineage who jointly offer ancestor worship to the common father's father and who once constituted a single domestic group.

Nuclear Family and Domestic Group

The Mishing make an analytical distinction between a domestic group i.e. *erang* and the nuclear family. A man's family of procreation consisting of ego, his wife and his unmarried children is identified as his *ope*. A nuclear family is always identified with the husband/father as the point of reference. So a woman is part of her father's *ope* before her marriage and of her husband's *ope* after marriage. She is not made a point of reference in an ope, only her husband is. In fact, even if a man's wife is dead, leaving behind the children, this unit is still called *ope*. The term *ope* it may be recalled, is also used by the Pagro-Mishing to refer to a clan and a lineage. The extension of the term *ope* to a man's family of procreation emphasizes the continuity of the lineage through the nuclear family because in this context, it basically refers to the minimal lineage, that is, a man and his children. Since the mother is not a point of reference, the emphasis is clearly on the patrifiliation only.

A nuclear family for the Pagro-Mishing is primarily a conceptual unit and they differentiate it from the domestic group. So when a nuclear family is also an independent domestic group, such a household is referred to as an *erang* and not an *ope*. An *ope* is therefore a conceptually defined unit by conjugal and filial relationships and not by the household functions. An *erang*, on the other hand is a domestic group irrespective of its typological form but conforming to its structural boundaries. A joint-family *erang* is thus composed of as many *ope* as there are married men within it along with their wives and children.

Agnatic Kinship as the Basis of Composition of Domestic Group

The fundamental rule on which the Pagro-Mishing household is organized is based strictly on the principle of agnatic descent. The Pagro-Mishing follow the rule of virilocal-patrilocal residence and hence the sons continue to live with their father after their marriage whereas the daughters have to leave their father's household on marriage and become members of their conjugal households. The core of the Pagro-Mishing household is thus constituted by male agnatic kin, their wives and children. But the genealogical ties among the agnates who constitute the domestic group are further defined by the cult of ancestor worship. Owing to this ritual injunction, as it has been discussed earlier, a Pagro-Mishing household can be composed of only those men constituting the seniormost generation along with their wives and children who have descended from a common Fa Fa Fa, because only they can worship jointly the ancestral spirit of their Fa Fa Fa. Thus in its widest extension, a household may comprise those men in the seniormost generation and their wives and children who are agnatically linked to a common Fa Fa Fa. This is the genealogical limit of the growth of a domestic group, but on the empirical level, the domestic group is generally composed of only those men constituting the seniormost generation who have a common grandfather (Fa Fa). Since only one agnatic ancestor worship can be performed in the house occupied by a domestic group, it is obvious that a household would be constituted by genealogically related men and their wives and children. A Pagro-Mishing domestic group is thus invariably a familial group based on descent and conjugality. Any other person, for instance, a wife's brother, or a son-in-law, or a sister's son, cannot be members of this domestic group because they are affines and not agnates of the male members of the household. It is, therefore, obvious that the Pagro-Mishing society does not have any households which are based on the uxorilocal or the avunculocal rule of residence. The Pagro-Mishing domestic group is strictly based on the patrilineal descent and patrilocal-virilocal rule of residence.

The genealogical basis defined by the cult of ancestor worship clearly specifies the rules of recruitment to the Pagro-Mishing household. An individual is incorporated in a Pagro-Mishing household by the virtue of birth, marriage and adoption alone.

Every individual in the Pagro-Mishing society is born in a particular *erang* and owing to the prevalence of the rule of virilocal residence, it is always in the *erang* of the child's father. The ties of patrifiliation form the basic principle of recruitment. The ritual constraint manifested in the cult of ancestor worship has important bearing on the kinship composition of the domestic group among them. The ritual dimension, as mentioned above, not only defines the agnatic core of the household but it also precludes incorporation of any other male person in the household who is either an affine or a non-relative of the agnatic core of the household. Thus among them a household cannot be formed with an uxorilocal son-in-law, because he is not an agnate, and more importantly he cannot be permitted to perform any ancestral or other rituals in his father-in-law's house because the Pagro-Mishing firmly believe that the agnatic ancestors of the male agnates who form a domestic family do not allow any other man to be part of their descendant's domestic family. Any breach of this rule, it is believed, would be inviting calamity for the members of the household. Since only the agnatic ancestors are propitiated by them, the uterine ancestors are not considered important. For this reason the household cannot incorporate the descendants of the daughters as its members. Consequently the avunculocal residence as a basis of domestic grouping is totally absent in the Pagro-Mishing society.

The absolute emphasis laid on the agnatic principle organizes the Pagro-Mishing domestic group strictly as a patrilocal-virilocal residential group without any exception. The only non-agnates who become members of the household are the women who marry men of the *erang.* The birth of a child which takes place in the residential house, is also a ritual event. It pollutes the members of the household for three days during which they observe *'genna'* i.e., they do not participate in any ceremony in the village nor do they engage themselves in any agricultural activity. On the third day, the child is duly blessed by the elders of his major lineage by invoking the lineage ancestors. The ritual basis of the household organization does have an important bearing on the events like birth. It is ritually prescribed that only those women can be allowed to deliver a child in the residential house, who are legally married to the male agnates of the household. In case of any other woman, if such an emergency arises, the delivery of the child takes place outside the house. For example, if an unmarried girl becomes pregnant, she is not allowed to deliver the child in the house but she is confined in a hut constructed outside the house. Even a married daughter would not be allowed to deliver her child in her father's house. The reason for such prohibition is the belief that the residential house is also the abode of spirits of the ancestors of the agnatically related members of the household. The birth of a child who is not an agnatic descendant is thus offending to the ancestors. The custom among the Pagro-Mishing is therefore that the birth of a child should take place only at the genitor's house and nowhere else, because the membership of the household and the descent group is acquired strictly from one's genitor. Just as the Pagro-Mishing concept of descent is based strictly on physical paternity the membership of the *erang* is also similarly determined. Under no circumstances an adulterine child or an illegitimate child can become a permanent member of his pater's household or his mother's household. In some rare cases, an adulterine son may remain a member of his mother's household until the time he is married. But as soon as he is married, he has to separate from his mother's household and establish his own household. A man remains member of the *erang* or a segment of it throughout his life in which he was born unless he is adopted by some other man. For a daughter, however, the membership of her natal *erang* remains only up to the time of her marriage, after which she is incorporated into her husband's *erang*. A married woman can never come back to her natal *erang* to become its permanent member, even if she is widowed.

For the Pagro-Mishing woman, marriage signifies a sharp break in her ritual, social and jural status. The rule of residence is strictly virilocal, therefore marriage introduces a change in the residence of a woman. After her marriage and subsequently after birth of a child, a woman comes completely under the ritual guardianship of her husband's ancestors. Her own agnatic ancestors cease to be important to her. A married woman is not allowed to participate in ancestral rituals performed by her agnates. After her marriage a woman comes fully under the jural control of her husband's *erang*, and her own father's *erang* has no right to interfere on her behalf in any of her domestic matters. In this sense, marriage signifies the liquidation of her membership in her natal *erang* and her incorporation as a member in the husband's *erang*.

Adoption as a Basis of Recruitment

Adoption (*utak*) is a common practice among the Pagro-Mishing and is another means of recruitment to the *erang*. It also helps in augmenting the size of an *erang* to some extent. *Utak* literally means 'to purchase', which implies that an adopted child is 'purchased' by the adoptive parents. The 'purchasing' of a child is a symbolic act which signifies the ritual and jural transfer of a child from one *erang* to another *erang*. A man usually resorts to adoption when after a few years of marriage, his wife fails to beget a son, though she may have given birth to daughters. The position of a son is of ritual significance among the Pagro-Mishing. A son is also regarded as an economic assurance by the parents specially for the old age. The ritual consideration, however, outweighs any other reason. The Pagro-Mishing believe in the existence of the soul after death which does not get peace until it is periodically propitiated by one's direct male descendants. The welfare of the descendants of the deceased also depend upon the benevolence of the spirits of their ancestors. Though the Pagro-Mishing emphasize biological kinship which obliges even an adulterine child to propitiate his genitor's ancestors, they (the Mishing) give an adopted son the same status as they do to one's own son. An adopted son is fully incorporated---ritually, jurally and socially -- in his adoptive parent's *erang* and severs his relations from his own natal *erang*.

The importance of a son in the Pagro-Mishing society can be well understood by their beliefs in the cult of ancestors and the wish to perpetuate one's own lineage i.e. *ope*. In an agnatic society a son assures the continuation of the lineage. Every man in the Pagro-Mishing society is ultimately also a founder of an *ope* i.e. a lineage. As far as the daughters are concerned, their contribution in perpetuating their father's *ope* is nil. A daughter cannot be part of her father's *ope* for ever and her children automatically become member of her husband's *ope*. Therefore, every Pagro-Mishing has a cherished desire to have a son.

The choice for adoption of a son is not made haphazardly, theoretically though any boy from one's own clan may be adopted. Thus a Doley may adopt any Doley boy. But in practice, the choice for adoption is limited by many factors. Firstly, the boy to be adopted should be a nephew (Br So) in relationship to the adoptive father. Such a boy may be a son of a real brother or a classificatory brother. A man may thus adopt either his own brother's son or his father's brother's son's son. A man, however, preferably adopts a boy who is his father's brother's son's son as shown in the following diagram (Fig.. 5.1).

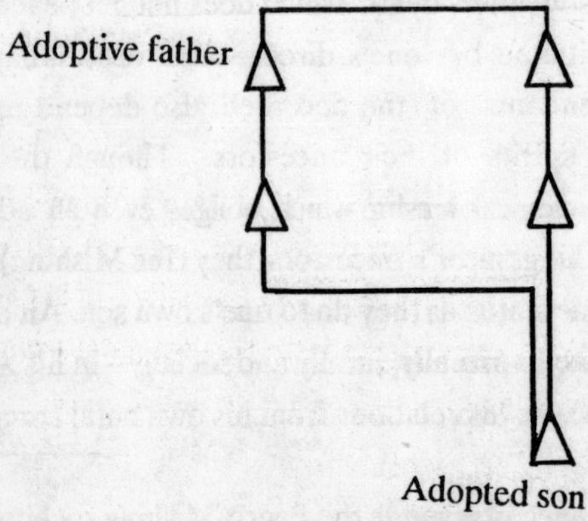

Fig. 5.1. Preference in adoption.

Though a man is allowed to adopt his own brother's son, but in practice it is not done. The reason for avoiding the brother's son is that since the brothers usually live together as members of the same household, an adopted son from the same household would not be fully weaned away from his own parents. Similarly when an *erang* is composed of a group of full male siblings and their father's brother's sons, the choice of an adopted son would be made from outside the domestic group. The choice of an adopted son is thus made from outside one's own domestic group but is generally confined to the minor lineage.

An adopted son is also the eldest son of the adoptive couple (in case if they have their own sons after the adoption of a son). This is not altogether uncommon because usually a couple adopts a son not in the middle or old age but only after four or five years of marriage when the age of the man may not be more than thirty to thirty five years or so. Thus adoption takes place when the couple is still in the reproductive age group. However, the subsequent birth of a son in no way alters the position of the adopted son either jurally, ritually or economically. In fact, the presence of an adopted son has no effect on the structure of Pagro-Mishing household and it goes through the same course of development cycle. Let me describe a few cases of adoption from Kumarbari village to illustrate the above mentioned points.

Marka Doley did not have a son of his own and therefore requested Mantum, his father's brother's son, who had four sons, to allow him to adopt one of them. But Mantum agreed to part with his next son, that is the fifth son, when he would be born for adoption to Marka. When Mantum's wife gave birth to her fifth son, he was adopted by Marka. The genealogical relationship between Marka and his adopted son is shown in the following diagram (Fig. 5.2).

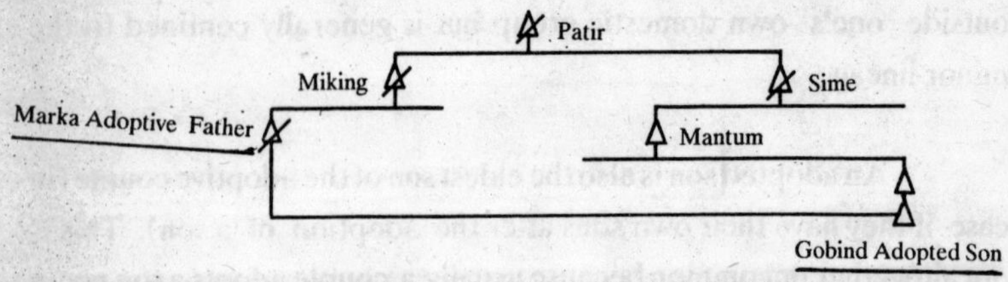

Fig. 5.2. Genealogical relationship between Marka (adoptive father) and Gobind (adopted son).

Marka thus, adopted his own father's brother's son's son, Gobind. At present there are two *erangs* of the descendants of Patir (Marka's grandfather) : one *erang* is composed of Miking's sons and the other is composed of Sime's sons. Gobind is the head of one *erang* and offers *Urom* (ancestral sacrifice) to his adoptive father's father i.e. to Miking - and not to Sime, who was his genitor's father. After the death of Gobind, his sons shall worship and offer sacrifices to Marka and not to Mantum, who was the biological father of their own father, Gobind.

There is another case in which the present head of the *erang* is the son of an adopted son and hence he offers ancestral sacrifice to his father's adoptive father and not to his own father's genitor (Fig. 5.3).

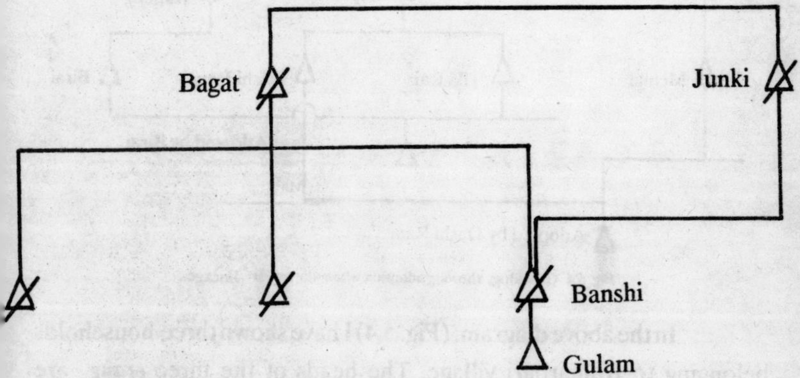

Fig. 5.3. Gulam offers Ramnu urom to junki, his adoptive father's father.

Gulam, who is the head of *erang,* is the son of Banshi. Banshi was the son of Bagat, but he was adopted by Junki, the younger brother of Bagat, because he had no son of his own. After the death of his grandfather and father, Gulam performs *Ramnu Urom* for Junki, the adoptive father of Banshi and does not offer *urom* to Bagat, the actual father of Banshi. Although in this case Junki has adopted his own elder brother's son yet the adoption of a brother's son is not usually preferred. The adoption of a son is generally confined to one's minor lineage only. The rationale for confining the choice of an adopted son to the minor lineage, according to some informants, is that the *erang* which have become structurally distant in two generations are again brought closer by adoption of boys belonging to these households. This will be evident from another illustration. (See Fig. 5.4).

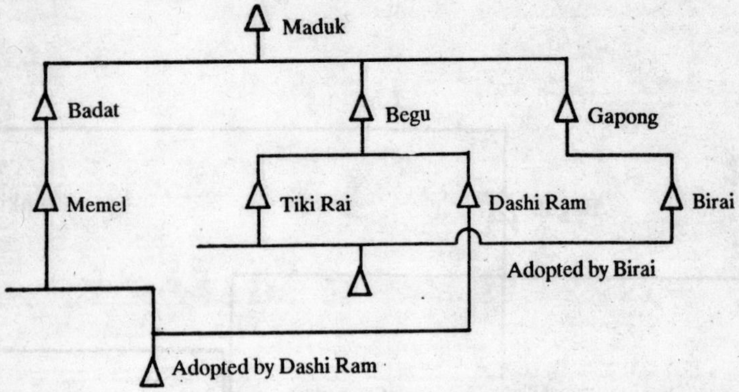

Fig. 5.4. Genealogy showing adoption within the minor lineage

In the above diagram, (Fig. 5.4) I have shown three households belonging to Kumarbari village. The heads of the three *erang* are Memel, Tiki Rai and Birai who are the grandsons of Maduk. They constitute one minor segment of the major lineage and hence perform *ramku urom* to the same ancestor, Maduk. The agnatic ties between these three independent households are further reinforced due to adoption of the sons. Memel's son has been adopted by Tiki Rai's younger brother Dashi Ram, and Tiki Rai's son has been adopted by Birai. The choice of an adopted son being confined to the minor lineage manifests greater emotional and effective ties between the sons of the siblings, who also constitute one ritual unit.

The adoption of a son is thus an institutionalized practice in the Pagro-Mishing society, and like birth and marriage, forms one of the modes of recruitment of a member in the *erang*. The adopted child is given the status of an actual filial kin, though, as a matter of fact, he is already a kin of the man who adopts him. The status of an adopted son is socially, ritually and jurally undifferentiated from that of a real son in the Pagro- Mishing society.

Thus far I have mainly discussed the concept of the Pagro-Mishing domestic groups and the structural principles that govern its composition as well as the modes of recruitment to the domestic group. I will now examine how far the empirical ethnographical situation corresponds with these principles that define the normative pattern of the domestic group.

STRUCTURE AND COMPOSITION OF THE DOMESTIC GROUP

The Normative Pattern

The Pagro-Mishing household ideally consists of a patrilineal joint family of three generations. Such a joint family/ comprises a man, his wife, their married sons and their wives, and the unmarried children, including the grandchildren. A married daughter leaves her natal household and becomes a member of her husband's household. The marriage of a son, on the other hand, implies not only an addition of a new member to the household but also an expected change in the structure of the household by extending it lineally. Besides the partilineal joint family based on the filial ties of father and son, there is another type of joint family among the Pagro-Mishing. In this type of domestic group, the component nuclear families of the men in the senior generation are joined by the ties of siblingship. Such a joint family comprises the nuclear families of two or more brothers, their wives, their married sons and unmarried children. The two types of joint families are structurally different as one is initially based on the filial ties and the other is initially based on the sibling ties. The first type of the joint family may be analytically called 'lineal joint family' and the second type may be called 'fraternal joint family'. Some Pagro-Mishing households however, comprise a man, his wife, his unmarried children and married sons and their unmarried children. This kind of household has lineal as well as collateral extension. But the primary structural link in this household is also that of father-son relationship, hence we may identify it as a lineal joint family. Similarly a fraternal joint family would also be extended lineally when the sons of the brothers, whose families constitute the joint family, are married and have their own children. The defining structural basis of role allocation in such a household is the brother-brother relationship and hence we may call this a fraternal joint family. In both the lineal and fraternal joint families, at times, there may be supplementary relatives like widowed mother and/or unmarried siblings of the head of the household. In some rare cases a distant agnatic kin may also be a member of the household. We have already noted that a Pagro-Mishing household does not have a place for any other male except those who have specific agnatic ties with the head of the household and the women who are married to them. One may also come across few nuclear family households (*erang*) among the Pagro- Mishing. A nuclear family household may also contain some other relatives like the widowed mother or unmarried siblings of the head of the household.

With due regard to disturbances in both the life cycle of the individual and the developmental cycle of the domestic group, both of which affect its empirical expression, the actual distribution of the household types among the Pagro-Mishing exemplifies the joint family ideal. An independent nuclear family household is merely a phase in the developmental cycle of a domestic group and comes into existence because of the demographic structure of the original household. Furthermore, the developmental phase through which the Pagro-Mishing household passes, renders even these above mentioned typologies meaningless except in terms of the structural principles by which it is crystallised at a given moment in time. Therefore, to distinguish and classify the domestic groups as nuclear family, lineal joint family and fraternal joint family is only an analytical device to understand the process of cyclical change rather than categorizing the households into a larger number of types as an end in itself. The addition of supplementary members in the nuclear or joint families, therefore, does not really matter, as far as the organization of the household is concerned. Keeping this point in view for analysing the empirical ethnographic situation, I have classified the households in three basic structural types viz. 'nuclear family households', 'lineal joint family households' and 'fraternal joint family households'. The following analysis is based on the study of 121 households distributed in five Pagro-Mishing villages of Majuli.

Distribution of Domestic Groups

The five villages which are exclusively inhabited by the Pagro-Mishing are not uniform in their population but are fairly representative of the typical Pagro-Mishing villages. The population and the number of households in each village is given in Table 5.1.

TABLE 5.1
Distribution of Households and Population in five villages

Village	Number of households	Population Male	Population Female	Total Population	Average size of the household
Kumarbari	42	430	352	755	17.93
Amguri	17	137	129	266	15.70
Jengraimukh	14	71	69	140	10.00
Majsherpai	31	259	248	507	16.3
Sherpai	17	120	113	233	13.7
Total	121	1017	911	1901	15.71

The Pagro-Mishing households, as is clear from the above table (Table 5.1), are numerically large in size. The average size of a household is 15.71 persons.

The frequency distribution of the households on the basis of their size is given below (Table 5.2).

TABLE 5.2
Size of the Household (N = 121)

Number of persons per household	Frequency	Number of persons per household	Frequency	Number of persons per household	Frequency
3	1	14	6	27	4
4	3	15	4	28	2
5	4	16	4	30	2
6	9	17	4	31	2
7	3	18	5	34	1
8	9	19	2	38	2
9	7	20	5	40	1
10	10	21	4	44	1
11	8	23	2	51	2
12	6	26	2	63	1
13	5				

It will be observed that the Pagro-Mishing households show a very wide range of variation in their size. The smallest household consists of only 3 persons whereas the largest household has as many as 63 members. Households having 10 or less persons account for 37.3 per cent of the total and the households having more than 30 persons account for 7.3 per cent. The majority of the households, as is evident from the table, consists of more than 10 persons but less than 31 persons. Such households account for 55.4 per cent of the total households. There is one household in Kumarbari village which has 63 members. Now let us see the distribution of the households into various structural types.

Types of Domestic Groups

The distribution of various types of domestic groups in the five villages is given in the following table (Table 5.3).

TABLE 5.3
Distribution of Domestic Groups on the basis of Typological Variation (N=121)

Village	Number of Nuclear Family Households	Number of Joint Family Households	Percentage of Nuclear Family Households	Percentage of Joint Family Households
Kumarbari	4	38	9.53	90.47
Amguri	5	12	29.4	70.6
Majsherpai	6	11	35.3	64.7
Sherpai	8	23	25.8	74.2
Jengraimukh	4	10	28.5	71.5
Total	27	94	22.4	77.6

It is clear from Table 5.3 that the distribution of the joint family and the nuclear family households is more or less uniform in all the villages. A very high frequency is indeed observable in the incidence of the joint families. Out of 121 households, 94 households, representing 77.6 per cent of the total households, are composed of joint-families. The number of nuclear households is 27 which represents 22.4 per cent of the total households. This is quite a significant number. However the above figures showing the variations in the household types merely describe the empirical situation at a given period of time and reflect the phases in the developmental cycle of the Pagro-Mishing domestic groups. The existence of the autonomous nuclear family households in the Pagro-Mishing society is an exception rather than rule. The presence of nuclear family households does not indicate the Pagro-Mishing ideology in favour of the nuclear families because they are neither the ideal household type nor do they form a regular cyclical phase in the developmental cycle of the domestic group. An independent nuclear family comes into existence only due to some situational constraints, for example, when death of the parents reduces a joint family consisting of a father-son household to only a nuclear family household. In a rare case, a son may separate from his father after a few years of marriage to establish his own household. But this tendency among the Pagro- Mishing is absolutely against the normative pattern of patrilocal-virilocal residence. A son does never have any idea of separating from his father'a household after his marriage. It is noteworthy that during the course of my field study, not a single case was found where a son had established his household independently after marriage. The residence after the marriage, is strictly patrilocal-virilocal which has consequently resulted in a preponderance of the joint families among the Pagro-Mishing. A concomitant effect of the rule of patrilocal residence for the sons is that the heads of the Pagro-Mishing households are generally the older men and seldom the younger men. This kind of composition of the household is appropriately in tune with the importance given to the age and generation in the Pagro-Mishing society.

Another significant point that emerges from the typological classification of the joint families is that there is a higher percentage of the collateral joint families as compared to the lineal joint families (Table 5.4). The presence of the higher percentage of the collateral joint families is related to the cyclical growth of the Pagro-Mishing domestic group. A lineal joint family has only one married couple in the senior generation and the husband-father is the head of the household. In a collateral joint family, on the other hand, there may be as many couples as the number of married brothers in the senior generation. The head of the household belongs to the same generation to which other members of the senior generation belong. The relationship of the head of the household to other men in the senior generation is that of an elder brother. Some collateral joint-family may be lineally extended too, but owing to its operational organization it has been labelled as collateral joint family.

TABLE 5.4
Frequency of the lineal and collateral joint families

Village	Total Number of Joint Families	Frequency of Lineal Joint Families	Percentage	Frequency of Collateral Joint Families	Percentage
Kumarbari	38	16	42.1	22	57.9
Amguri	12	3	25.0	9	75.0
Majsherpai	11	3	27.2	8	72.8
Sherpai	23	7	30.6	16	69.4
Jengraimukh	10	3	30.0	7	70.0
Total	94	32	34.0	62	66.0

It is clear from the distribution pattern (Table 5.4) that out of 94 joint families, as many as 62 joint families representing 66 per cent are collateral type and the rest, that is, 32 which constitute 34 per cent, are lineal joint families.

The discussion has clearly shown that the domestic family among the Pagro-Mishing emerges as the pricipal unit of their social structure. They conceive of tne family as a residential group subsumed in the concept of *erang* and the jural and social status of an individual is defined through his domestic family only. The acts of an individual are also adjudged as acts of the domestic family being regarded as a corporate unit. So in the Pagro-Mishing society, it is the domestic family that links an individual to the society at large. Further, the organizing principle of the domestic family among them is strictly related to the cult of ancestors which defines its structure and composition. In other words, a domestic family, being a ritual unit for the worship of the ancestors, can comprise of only those men in the senior generation who had a common father's father and who is treated as the focal ancestor of the domestic family. This is the maximum structural distance between the male agnates who may constitute a joint family, and this also defines the optimum structural boundary of the Pagro-Mishing domestic family. These structural constraints preclude the inclusion of any other person in the domestic family who would not be included in the ritual group. The married daughters are not part of their natal family and they are incorporated jurally and ritually in the husband's *erang*. Any affine, other than women married to the men of the household, is also excluded from being a member of the household. The rule of residence is strictly patrilocal-virilocal, which consequently results in the formation of patrilineal and collateral joint family households. We have seen that these structural constraints in the composition of the Pagro-Mishing domestic group are manifested fully at the empirical level as well. The variations that are observable are only in terms of their composition, i.e. in their size and the generational depth and not due to deviations in the principle that underlies the organization of the domestic group.

Having analysed the structure of the Pagro-Mishing domestic family and its variation, I will now examine another important feature of the Pagro-Mishing household. This pertains to the structure of the dwelling house it occupies. Among the Pagro-Mishing the allocation of the space in the residential house is intimately related with the structure of the domestic group, and allocation of space reflects the normative behaviour pattern of its members.

Domestic Group and the Structure of the House

The Pagro-Mishing live in platform houses (*Ekum*). A Pagro-Mishing house is a long, rectangular, unpartitioned hall, constructed on wooden piles. In other words, there are no apartments or cubicles inside the house. When a large joint family, consisting of a number of married couples, resides in it, an unpartitioned barrack like structure may seem awkward to those who are used to living in separate rooms because in the absence of physical partition, one may not be able to maintain any privacy in the strict sense of the term. It may therefore create an impression in their mind that the Pagro-Mishing do not have any sense of privacy because they live in an open hall where one can watch all the other occupants without much difficulty. On the contrary, the members of the Pagro-Mishing household interact with one another within the house with utmost care and restraint and their inter-personal relationships are determined by the norms of kinship behaviour.

A joint household may consist of many conjugal couples and their children. Inside the big rectangular house, each married couple along with their children sleep at one place. The place (floor area) for each couple is earmarked. Unmarried young girls sleep slightly at a distance from their parents, whereas little children sleep quite close to them. The young unmarried men of the house, however, do not sleep inside the house, rather they have no place earmarked for them. They usually sleep in the open platform in front of the house. When a boy is about 15 or 16 years of age he does not sleep in the house and roams in the company of his peers for a good part of the night. This practice appears to be the remnants of the traditional institution of *Murang*, a youth organization of the former times, which has disappeared from their society after they settled on the plains.

The floor area of the house is longitudinally divided into two parts. The right hand side from the entrance is used for keeping household goods, the left hand side is the sleeping area. In the centre, the fire place is built. The Mishing do not use any bedsteads but sleep on the mattresses which are spread over the bamboo floor.

The sleeping area of the *ekum* is divided among all the married couples which constitute a domestic family. The area which is occupied by each married couple and their children is known as *ope soar*. Each married couple keeps its personal belongings on both sides of the space allotted to it. By keeping their belongings in this fashion, they make a demarcation between the sleeping area of two nuclear families. The clothes of each *ope* are hung on a clothes line tied parallel to the side wall. The space used by each married couple is between 15' to 20'. This area i.e. *ope soar* is exclusively used by an *ope* and there is no trespassing into this space by any other member.

Though there is a set pattern in the allocation of the space among the various nuclear families of the *erang*, the allocation varies with the stage in the developmental cycle of the domestic family and also depends on whether the *erang* is composed of a patrilineal joint family or a fraternal joint family. However, the difference is reflected only in the space or "*ope soar*" of the oldest male member of the *erang*. His *ope soar* may be either located in the front or at the back side of the house. The middle portion of the house is allotted in a set pattern in all cases

In a patrilineal joint family the head of the *erang* and his wife occupy the rear part of the house. The reason for this is that the rear portion of the house is also supposed to be the place of the spirits of the ancestors and therefore it is treated as the sacred area in the house for the performance of rituals. The cooking is also done there. The head of the house and his wife are more involved with rituals and religious activities and therefore they can perform these rituals without disturbing the whole household. Besides, the main entrance of the house is in the front side, therefore, the front side which is nearer the entrance is occupied by a relatively younger man who may receive the guests and also keep a watch on those who might enter the house. The back door of the Pagro-Mishing house is never used by the guests as entrance and the people who visit the house enter from the front door and sit in the front portion. In fact, the front portion of the house is occupied by the man who also acts as the chief spokesman of the *erang*. In a patrilineal joint family, if the father who is head of the *erang* is old, then the next man in the domestic group would occupy the front portion. This would be the eldest son of the head. The rest of the floor area is allocated on the basis of seniority of age of the married sons.

When an *erang* is composed of a fraternal joint family, the rear portion of the house is occupied by the eldest brother and other brothers take their place according to seniority; the second elder brother occupies the front portion and the others next to him.

The domestic group grows with the marriage of its male members and the floor area has to be allotted to each member after his marriage. As I have mentioned, each man with his wife and children has a fixed place, therefore, when a man's son marries and brings his wife, the son is accommodated next to his father's *ope soar* and not at a place of his choice. Before a man's marriage, his father's brother's *ope* might have occupied the place next to his father, but after his marriage he would occupy the space between the father and father's brother. Thus the young men who are married sleep next to their parents. It is significant to note that a man and his sons, with their own nuclear families, occupy contiguous space in the house. Thus as the domestic group grows, the number of the married couples also increases and ultimately a bigger house may have to be constructed to accommodate a large joint family.

The space in a house is thus earmarked for a man and his sons who upon marriage bring their wives and take the space next to their father. When the father dies, his portion remains with his sons. For example, when an old man who occupied the rear portion of the house dies, his portion remains with his wife and children.

The structure of the house, and the system of utilization and allocation of the house floor among the Pagro-Mishing is of basic importance in understanding the behaviour pattern of the members of the household. In the open and unpartitioned big hall all the members are in full view of each other. This, however, does not mean that the members of the family pry on each other's personal affairs. The members of the household are always conscious of the presence of other members in the house which restrains their behaviour with others and inhibits them in expressing open fondness for even the spouse. One has to be discreet even in his most personal and intimate relationship and consequently the interpersonal relationships are quite restrained which are fully determined by the norms defined by the kinship position that is occupied by each member of the household.

The Pagro-Mishing themselves believe that due to the openness of the house there is greater cohesion among the members of the family, and there is lesser chance of familial disorganization. They believe that if they began living in separate and closed apartments, the behaviour pattern of the members of the family would undergo a change, and they would tend to become individualistic. Furthermore the traditional style of sharing the open living space also curbs the natural curiosity to know about the affairs of other families because one cannot do any such thing as might go against the interest of the whole household. 'In the large Pagro-Mishing joint families, comprised of several nuclear families, sharing one single unpartitioned large hall, the feeling of secrecy and separation does not arise among the constituent nuclear families; but such feelings would certainly crop if there had been a separate room for each nuclear family.' This is quite a plausible explanation put forward by the people themselves for existence of cohesive and harmonious domestic groups regardless of their large size. The allotment of the floor space to the different units of the Pagro-Mishing household is, one may infer, functionally related to the intra-familial kinship relations.

It may be briefly mentioned here that the Pagro-Mishing observe scrupulously the normative pattern of behaviour between various relatives on the basis of their respective kinship positions. The norm of behaviour between a woman and her husband's elder brother is that of avoidance. They scrupulously avoid to have direct encounter and do not address each other directly. Similarly a daughter-in-law has restrained behaviour with her father-in-law and his brothers. Owing to this restriction in the behaviour pattern, an elder brother does not go to the *ope soar* of his younger brother and similarly a woman does not go to the *ope soar* of her husband's elder brother or that of her father-in-law. She does not go to their *ope soar* even during the day time when the entire household is busy outside the house.

The allocation of the floor space seems to be quite congruent with their patterned behaviour. The seniormost man occupies the rear side of the house and also uses the rear door. He confines his activities to his own *ope soar*. The front side of the house is occupied by the next senior man and the rest of the floor space is allocated according to their seniority in terms of age. Thus an elder man does not unnecessarily go beyond the portion occupied by him. During the day time the movement is not so restricted but at night, a person confines himself to his own ope soar. Since the men generally do not go beyond their own *ope soar*, the women who are their *ighe* (Yo Br Wi) feel quite at ease in their respective *ope soar* which are situated according to the relative age of their husbands. It is imperative that the behaviour pattern of the members of the *erang* living in one single large hall must be highly formalized and institutionalized to ensure its smooth functioning. The pattern of interpersonal relationship in a Pagro-Mishing household, fully reflects the norms of kinship behaviour.

6

Developmental Sequence of the Domestic Group

So far, I have analysed the structure of the Pagro-Mishing domestic group, and have also presented an analysis of the empirical data concerning their composition, which was essentially synchronic in nature. On analysing the empirical data, it was seen that basically two major types of domestic groups have emerged : one, those comprising the joint-families and two, those comprising the nuclear families. The percentage of the joint-family households is, however, 77.6 as compared to the percentage of the nuclear family households which is 22.4 per cent of the total. On further typological classification, the collateral joint families account for 66 per cent and the lineal joint families account for 24 per cent of the total joint families. Thus, postulating the typical household in terms of its incidence, one may generalize that the collateral joint-family household is the typical household among the Pagro-Mishing. Such an analysis is, however, fraught with dangers of misinterpretation, if this is considered to be the final aim of a study, because it is meant to classify the domestic groups on the basis of their genealogical composition referring to the point in time. This static model cannot be understood by itself. The passage of time was of no significance in this approach and the typologies were constructed on the basis of genealogical relationship. The dynamics of domestic relationships is, however, governed by several factors, both internal and external to the domestic group, which manifest over a period of time, are not taken into consideration in this approach. The factors that effect the structure of the domestic group are the demographic factors of birth, age and death, and the social factors of adoption, partition and marriage. Besides, the moral values, kinship norms, ritual constraints and economic factors also affect the composition of the household. The effect of these factors is manifested in the variation of numerical and genealogical composition of the household in different points in time of its existence, because the domestic groups are neither fixed nor static, but are intrinsically dynamic. Meyer Fortes (1958) realized the futility of static approach in the study of the family system and proposed the concept of "developmental cycle in domestic groups" to analyse the structural process of the family systems. Here I am concerned with presenting the dynamic analysis of the Pagro-Mishing family system/by using the concept of developmental cycle in domestic groups.

The concept propounded by Fortes involves the idea of a domestic group (as distinguished from the nuclear family) which grows through a cycle of development (i.e the members and activities which unite them go through a regular sequence of changes) while the group as a unit retains the same form. Thus the original unit dissolves giving place to one or more units of the same kind. Fortes makes an analytical distinction between a nuclear family and domestic group. A nuclear family i.e. the nucleus around which domestic relations are organized, is constituted solely by the bonds of marriage, filiation and siblingship whereas the domestic group is constituted by kinship, descent and other jural and affectional bonds. "The domestic group is essentially a householding and housekeeping unit organized to provide the material and cultural resources needed to maintain and bring up its members... the domestic domain is the system of social relations through which the reproductive nucleus is integrated with the environment and with the structure of the total society" (Fortes,1958 : 8). The significant feature of the developmental cycle of the domestic group is that it is at one and the same time a process within the internal field and a movement governed by its relations to the external field. The status of every member in the domestic domain receives definition and sanction from the politico-jural domain. Residence patterns of the domestic groups are nothing but'crystallizations' at a given time of the developmental process (Fortes 1958 : 3).

Developmental Cycle : First Phase

A Pagro-Mishing household comes into being after partition takes place in the parental household when it has reached the final phase in the developmental sequence. The segments that replace it are generally three generational joint-families. Therefore, the developmental process in the Pagro-Mishing domestic group may be analysed by taking an agnatic joint-family as the normal starting point of the developmental cycle.

The domestic group composed of an agnatic joint family consists of a man, his wife, their sons, sons' wives, other unmarried sons and daughters and the sons' children. The man is the head of the domestic group in his role of father of the sons whose individual nuclear families (*ope*) are subordinate segments of the household. He controls the resources of the *erang*, which provide the economic base for the group. Not only the sons of the head of the *erang*, but all the members who compose the household, including his wife, are jurally under his authority. As the head of the household he represents and acts on behalf of the members of his erang in relation with other households and their heads. As the seniormost man in the domestic group, the head is responsible for the periodic offerings to the agnatic ancestors. He also represents the *erang* at the time of periodic ancestral ritual when his entire lineage group performs it. He is the one who sacrifices the animals on behalf of the *erang* to different spirits. The domestic group is, thus, an organized jural, ritual and economic unit under the authority of the head. The component nuclear families are its segments, but they are devoid of any economic, jural and ritual autonomy. The nuclear family (*ope*) initially is merely a reproductive unit of the *erang*. For all other purposes - economic, jural and ritual- a component nuclear family is fully dependent upon the domestic group.

The children during their infancy are solely dependent on their mother, who gives them constant company, even when she might be busy in outdoor chores. The infant is kept tied to her back most of the time. The father of the child is seldom concerned about looking after it. During the early childhood period it may be looked after by his (infant's) elder siblings, real or classificatory. Most of the children of the household constitute play groups on the basis of age grades. With the passage of time, such a domestic group acquires more members by marriage and birth. This happens as the children and the grandchildren of the head progress into adulthood and attain marriageable age. The man when he attains the age of 22 years or around it and a woman, when she is about 18 years, are thought to be marriageable. However, when a boy has attained the age of 14 years or so, he no longer sleeps in the dwelling house of his *erang*. There is, in fact, no place for the unmarried boys to sleep in the '*ekum*'. They move with the boys of their age group in the village and sleep on the open platform of any house in the village. The girls, however, continue to sleep in the house. In former days, the Pagro-Mishing also had bachelor's dormitories (*Morung*), and this practice of sleeping outside the house is a remnant of the olden days.

During the later period of bachelorhood a boy may be married to a girl, chosen by his parents or he may elope with a girl of his choice and marry her. A young man is, however, still under the jural authority of the head of the domestic group. Even if he wants to elope with a girl, he must seek the permission of the head because the final negotiations after the elopement, including the payment of '*aalig*' (bridemoney) has to be paid by the boy's *erang* to the *erang* of the girl.

After the marriage, a son is provided sleeping space in the house. This space, called *ope soar*, is allotted to the man next to his own father's *ope soar.* This is the space in the house where the young man establishes his own nuclear family (*ope*) over the course of time. In due course of time, other sons and grandsons of the head of the household also get married and establish their own nuclear families. The girls of the household leave it after marriage and join their husband's erang. Thus the composition of the domestic group changes with marriage and birth. The change in the domestic group is not merely in terms of additions and replacements of the personnel but is also brought in by the additions of new nuclear family units (*ope*) in the *erang.* Thus seen over a long period of time, the domestic group goes through a change in its composition and the interpersonal relation among its members. The younger male members grow up, marry and have children of their own. These younger males may be sons or the grandsons of the head of the household.

So long the head of the *erang* is alive, the sons are jurally subordinate to him. A son may establish his independent household after marriage, but the Pagro-Mishing ideal is that the sons should continue to live with the father. This ideal is strictly followed. The ideal and the actual norm in fact have no discrepancy at all. The moral, kinship, ritual and economic constraints are so strong that a son would never think of establishing his household during the lifetime of his father. Owing to these constraints, the Pagro-Mishing domestic group continues to grow with the additions of the new members and component nuclear family units.

Although the jural, economic and ritual status of the sons formally remains the same vis-a-vis the father, there is a definite change in the day-to-day functioning of the *erang* at the operational level. The elderely sons, whose own nuclear families have grown due to the marriage of their sons, begin to take more and more decisions in day- to- day activities. With the growing age of the father and head of the *erang*, his sons assume greater responsibility in the management of the house. The most important change is in the management of the productive resources of the household. Besides this, the grown up sons begin to take decisions with regard to their own sons' and daughters' marriage. The *erang*, however, remains one single consumption, production and resource owning group. For ritual purposes, the father, as the eldest male member, remains the representative in ceremonies pertaining to ancestor worship at the lineage level. But over this period of time the *erang* is affected by the changes in the cyclical growth of the constituent nuclear families inside the *erang* as well. Several phases in the developmental cycles, therefore, manifest simultaneously inside the erang. In other words, the nuclear families of the sons of head of the erang are in the different stages of development as compared to the nuclear families of the grandsons of the head of the erang. Thus, if the erang, when it came into being, was composed of a lineal joint family constituted by opes (of father and sons) in two generations only, it grows into a lineal joint family with the addition of the *ope* of grandsons in the third generation as well. But generally, the death of the father as head of the *erang* may occur before the *erang* acquires any ope in the fourth generation. The *erang* is thus restricted to three generations. It begins with three generations and remains a three generational *erang* even after the death of the head.

Second Phase

With the death of the father, as head of the *erang*, a new phase in its developmental cycle sets in. The sons of the deceased head have two courses open before them. One of them is that they continue to live in the same *erang* and the second is that they may split and establish independent erangs. All the sons of the deceased are now jurally equal and are entitled to take independent decisions regarding their future. However, the ideal in the Pagro-Mishing society is that the brother should continue to live in one single *erang* under the headship of the eldest brother. The Pagro-Mishing norm is also that the brothers must live together till such time that all their unmarried brothers and sisters are properly married. It is the jural responsibility of the *erang* to marry its members. Even in the event of all the brothers being married, they live together at least until each one of the brother has his own sons and daughters got married. In other words, they continue to live together until the *ope* of each brother is lineally extended by additions of the ope of their sons as well.

In this phase, the *erang* is composed of the full male siblings, their wives and children. The widowed mother is the other member. The most important change that occurs is in the change in the headship of the *erang*. Now, in place of the father, it is the eldest son in his position of being the eldest brother in the sibling group who succeeds as the head of the *erang*. He acts jurally, socially and ritually on behalf of the entire *erang*. As a production, consumption and resource owning group, it continues to be one single group. The solidarity among the brothers in the Pagro-Mishing society is very strong. The proper code of behaviour between the younger and the elder brother is respect, authority and obedience. However, with the growth of *erang* by additions of the *ope* of the brothers and their sons, there is a shift in the interest of the brothers. They begin to take more interest in their own growing family. Although the domestic group remains one resource owning group and a common production and consumption unit, each married man and woman may also earn some extra money by some additional cultivation or by rearing of chickens and pigs in their spare time. The money thus earned is spent by a man on his own nuclear family. However, this extra activity is never done at the expense of the domestic group. The kinship, moral and ritual factors are in favour of the fraternal joint family. The Pagro-Mishing also believe that the ancestors of the siblings are never happy to see the full brothers living separately. After all, the ancestral ritual has to be performed by the eldest brother and therefore even if the brothers live in separate households,they will have to join together to perform the rituals. More importantly, independent *erang* of each brother would be a small household with few adult men and women to do all the productive activities and, thus, its economic condition would be more precarious. Therefore, the Pagro- Mishing households seldom split, after the death of the father, among his sons. Thus a fraternal joint family continues to exist as one *erang* as long as the constituent segments regard it to be a well balanced production-consumption unit.

Third Phase

The economic viability of the *erang* is determined by its size. When the brothers realize that it is not possible for the entire household to continue as one economic unit due to dwindling resources, and there are strains on its economic viability, they may decide to partition the *erang*. When partition occurs in a fraternal joint family, each brother along with his wife, his sons and their wives and unmarried children separates as one segment and establishes a separate *erang* under his headship. Separation in the Pagro-Mishing *erang* never occurs on the basis of the nuclear family of each man, but on the basis of the constituent segments of the *erang* which are the lineal joint families of each brother. Thus the new domestic groups are also structurally patrilineal joint families and not the nuclear families.

The newly established household may continue to live in the same *ekum'* for some time and only gradually construct new houses for themselves. Once the separation takes place, the *erangs* become separate resource owning groups as well as independent production-consumption unit. They also become jurally and socially distinct unit in the village. However, the separation is not complete in all respects. This group of *erang* continues to be single ritual unit under the leadership of the eldest brother who is responsible for the propitiation of the common ancestors. The younger brothers have to cooperate with him in the periodic rituals. In this context, this group of *erangs* may be referred to as only one *erang*. This is the extended meaning of *erang*.

Partition of fraternal joint family is not inevitable in all the cases. The course of the developmetal cycle in such domestic group depends largely on the demographic factors and also on the resources at the command of the household. Thus, if the economic constraints are not there and the size of the *erang* is also not too large, the brothers may not split at all and continue to live in one single domestic group. For example, when there are only two brothers whose families constitute the *erang*, they may not separate. Thus partition of the fraternal joint family is not a normative phase in the developmental cycle.

The Final Phase

In the fraternal joint family, after the death of the head, the next brother takes over as head of the *erang*. With the death of all the brothers, the domestic group undergoes an important structural change, which is now composed of full brothers, their male parallel cousins (father's brother's sons), their wives and children. This domestic group now comes under the headship of the eldest male sibling. There is now a possibility of its splitting into at least two erangs, each one consisting of full brothers and their families. But if this domestic group continues, which it may if the number of its members is not large, then this domestic group will be in its final phase of the developmental cycle. In other words, the final phase is attained when the domestic group is constituted of full brothers, their parallel male cousins (father's brother's sons) and their wives and children. With the death of the male members in the senior generation, the domestic group dissolves and new group comes into being. This split is inevitable even if the size of the *erang* is not too large and the economic viability is not at stake. It is because of the ritual of ancestor worship that such a domestic group cannot exist as one unit in the Pagro-Mishing society.

The Pagro-Mishing *erang*, as I have already discussed, is an ancestor-focussed domestic group. As we have seen, an erang is strictly defined in genealogical terms through its male members and may consist of only those male agnates (and their families) who have had a common father's father. Such a domestic group is also the optimal ritual group, because only they can offer ancestral sacrifice to the common ancestor (Fa Fa) in the same house. The optimal phase in the developmental cycle in the Pagro-Mishing domestic group is therefore fixed and predictable. When partition takes place in such a household after the death of all the senior male members, the domestic groups that emerge are constituted of only those male agnates who have a common father's father. Such a domestic group may therefore consist of only full brothers and their families; and their father's brother's sons and their families. I have emphasized that this is the final phase of partition of the domestic group because the new domestic groups have not only jural, social and economic autonomy but they also attain ritual autonomy. In the entire developmental sequence of the Pagro-Mishing *erang*, the ritual authority lies only with the eldest living brother (own or parellel cousin) and therefore, the *erangs* of the full brothers may be independent, yet ritually they will not be autonomous. With the completion of the final phase of the developmental cycle in the Pagro-Mishing domestic group, the new erang that emerge are fully autonomous with the head of the each *erang* attaining the ritual authority as well.

In the discussion so far, the ideal pattern of the developmental cycle in the Pagro-Mishing domestic group has been presented. The Pagro-Mishing domestic group is organized on the basis of certain basic principles which clearly specify the norms of the membership of the domestic group.The principles are fixed and inviolable. Thus the Pagro-Mishing domestic group, the *erang*, has to be composed of only those male agnates and their spouses who constitute a single ritual group which is defined by the genealogical ties linking them to a common father's father. In other words, the Pagro-Mishing *erang* is not only a familial group but it is also a ritual group. Further, the rule of patrilocal-virilocal residence is strictly followed.This is the ideal in the Pagro-Mishing society. This ideal is sustained in the society by kinship, moral and ritual constraints. In fact, this is not merely an ideal but the normative pattern in the society. The strict adherence to this rule obviously implies that the marriage of a son would not lead to the establishment of an independent household composed of a married couple, or subsequently of a neolocal nuclear family, of which a son is the founder.

The most significant point that emerges from the above discussion is that a nuclear family is not a regular phase in the entire developmental cycle in the Pagro-Mishing domestic group.The existence of the nuclear family households which are, of course, present is due mainly to the demographic reasons or because of some serious shortcoming of a son, for which he was forced by his father to establish his own independent household. The inference is that the nuclear family, as the basis of an *erang*, comes into being by the cirucmstances beyond the control of the individual and are not governed by the voluntary choice of a man. Similarly, there is no choice in the Pagro-Mishing society for keeping an uxorilocal son-in-law for patrilocally residing daughter whereas an adopted son is indistinguishable jurally, ritually and socially from a natural son of a man.

Phases of Developmental Cycle in Domestic Groups in Kumarbari

Now let us see how far these norms and principles are followed in the real situation. This I shall do, in the description that follows, on the basis of the numerical data from the village Kumarbari.

Kumarbari village was composed of 42 domestic groups which were in different phases in the developmental cycle. Typologically the domestic groups were classified in the following categories (Table 6.1).

TABLE 6.1
Classification of the Domestic Groups in Kumarbari Village

Basis of Kinship in the composition of Domestic Groups	Type of the Domestic Group	Frequency	Number of generations
1. Husband, wife and unmarried children	Nuclear Family	3	2
2. Husband, wife and one married son, other unmarried sons and daughters; and grandchildren	Lineal Joint Family	1	3
3. Husband, wife, and two or more married sons, grandchildren and unmarried sons and daughters	Lineal-cum-lateral Joint Family	15	3

4. Two or more full brothers, their wives, married sons and their wives and grandchildren	Lateral-cum lineal Joint Family	13	3
5. Two or more full brothers, their parallel cousin, (father's brothers son) their sons, sons' wives and unmarried sons and grandchildren,	Lateral-cum-lineal joint family	10	3
Total		42	

It may be observed from the above table (Table 6.1) that the range of the households in terms of their composition is not very wide. There are only three domestic groups which are composed of nuclear families. Two of the independent nuclear families were originally constituents of the same *erang* i.e., one nuclear family household is composed of a man, his wife and unmarried children and the second one is composed of his son, his wife and a child. The son lived patrilocally for about 12 years. But the son and his wife did not pull on well with their father i.e. head of the *erang*. The behaviour of the daughter-in-law was impolite and therefore the father asked his son to leave the *erang* and establish his own household. In fact, the son did not want to separate from his father but he was not acceptable to his father. Thus the existence of these two nuclear family domestic groups is due to deviant behaviour of the son. The household of the son, is however, ritually part of the father's *erang*, but economically it is an independent unit. The third nuclear family household came into being when the father of the head of the existing *erang* died leaving behind his only son, son's wife and two unmarried daughters. His mother had died earlier. Over a period of time, however, these nuclear family households would again grow into joint-family households.

The remaining 39 domestic groups are distinctly in four different phases of developmental cycle.

In the first phase there is only one domestic group which is composed by a man, his wife, one married son, son's wife and his own and son's unmarried children. This is the phase when growth of the *erang* is assured by additions of new members by birth and also by creating new nuclear family units within the *erang* with the marriage of other sons and subsequent birth of grandchildren. Next there are 15 domestic groups which are already in the second phase. The composition of the domestic groups in the second phase is constituted by a man and his wife, their two or more married sons, their wives and unmarried children and grandchildren. These households are structurally different as they are extended lineally as well as laterally because they contain *ope* of the father and two or more sons.

Another group which consists of 13 households which have developed into the third phase. This phase is characterized by the fact that the head of the domestic group is not in the kinship status of father of the men constituting the senior generation, but he is the eldest brother of the group of the male agnates who constitute the senior generation of the erang. In other words, when the father is dead and has left behind his sons whose opes constitute the erang, then the third phase begins. This type of domestic group is basically a fraternal joint-family with the lineal extension of each brother's *ope*.

The remaining 10 domestic groups are in the fourth and final phase of their developmental cycle. These households are composed of full male siblings, their wives and married sons and unmarried children, and also the male parallel cousins i.e. father's brother's sons, their wives and children. These households are composed of those male agnates in the seniormost generation who had a common father's father but different fathers. In other words, they are composed of the *opes* of male siblings and their male parallel cousins. This type of household has reached the optimum point in its growth because it constitutes one single domestic family which may live in one *akum* and offer common ancestral sacrifice to the founding ancestor i.e. Fa Fa in the same house. After the death of all the male members in the senior generation, the domestic group will split into independent segments that will be composed of only full siblings or sons of the full male siblings and their opes. The partition of the *erang* at the death of the senior generation is inevitable.

Analysing the above sample, classified on the basis of the household composition existing at a given time in Kumarbari, we notice the phase by phase developmental sequence of the Pagro-Mishing *erang*. It may be noted however, the penultimate phase, that is, the third phase, need not always develop into the last i.e. fourth phase. This means that an *erang* composed of full brothers and their families, may not in all the cases, remains one single domestic group even during the life time of the brothers. Owing to economic exigencies, they may partition the household during their own lifetime and thus each brother may become head of an independent *erang*, though for ritual performances they will have to continue to act under the leadership of the eldest brother. Yet, the existence of 10 households in my study in the optimal phase of their development makes it amply clear that the cycle of the Pagro-Mishing erang takes a full turn only when the development in the third generation from the founding ancestor, after which the *erang* divides itself into a number of *erangs* which are composed of full siblings and their *ope*.

In the light of the above discussion, it is now possible to generalize the normative form of the developmental process within the *erang* on the basis of its existing composition. The normative form may be generalized and described as follows :

(1) If there is a nuclear family *erang* and the man is survived by an only son and daughters, the daughters will be married virilocally and the son will bring his wife and continue to live with his father and the developmental cycle in the domestic group will be in the son's own family of procreation.

(2) When the *erang* consists of more than two sons, at the time of father's death, the developmental process will be quite different. After the death of the father, both the brothers will continue to live together under the headship of the elder brother. The brothers' joint family will continue to grow until all the sons and daughters of both the brothers are married. Their own sons will continue to live in the same *erang*, whereas the daughters would leave it to become members of their husbands' *erang*. When their (brothers) own families of procreation have grown to become lineal joint families, the brothers may separate and form two lineal joint family households.

(3) There is, however, alternative in the above case in which the brothers may continue to live together in the same *erang* even after each brother has a lineally extended *ope*. In case the elder brother dies, his younger brother will become the head of the *erang*, but functionally there will be no change in the *erang*. After the death of the other brother, their sons, who are already married may continue to live together and the eldest male in the sons generation will become the head. In this case also there are alternatives, either the sons of each brother may

establish a separate *erang* or the full brothers and their male siblings may continue to live together in one *erang*.

(4) When an *erang* consists of full brothers and their male parallel cousins, it can last only during their life time. After the death of all the male members in the senior generation their sons will have to establish separate *erangs*, structured around a core of full male siblings because this is the optimum point of structural viability of a Pagro-Mishing *erang* due to the cult of ancestor worship at the level of Fa Fa which defines the organization of the household.

(5) When a man has two wives and both of them have sons, or when he has an illegitimate son, the *erang* after the death of the father will continue in the existing form until all the sons including the illegitimate son have full lineal joint families of their own within the *erang*. At this stage, the fission in the *erang* is oriented on the basis of matrifiliation. In otherwords, sons of one wife of the dead man establish one household and the sons of another wife establish a separate household. The illegitimate son also comes under this structural rule. Though he is alone, he has also to establish a separate household along with his own sons and grandchildren.

The main courses of the developmental cycle of the Mishing *erang* shows no deviation in the developmental process, for instance, there is no possibility of a married daughter continuing to live with her father. An adopted son is not at all distinguishable from other sons of a man and, hence unlike an illegitimate son, he is not singled out at the time of fission. The most significant point is that a nuclear family does not emerge as the basis of a Pagro-Mishing domestic family in the course of its normal development.

7

Kinship Norms and Interpersonal relations

From the discussion so far it clearly emerges that the structure of the Pagro-Mishing domestic group is characterised by two principles : (1) the composition of the domestic group is based strictly around a core of male agnatic kins who are genealogically related to each other with reference to a common ancestor who provides the boundary of its internal structure, and (2) the patrilocal-virilocal rule of residence which entails that the male members of the domestic group continue to live with their family of orientation after marriage along with their wives , whereas the female members of the domestic group leave it upon marriage. Thus, the composition of the domestic group is structurally invariant, although typologically its organization may vary at different stages of the developmental cycle.

The prescriptive rule of patrilocal-virilocal residence results in the emergence of joint family as the basic form of the Pagro-Mishing domestic group, and the strict adherence to the rule of genealogically defined agnatic kinship among its male members determines its kinship composition. The existence of these principles, however, does not mean that there are no domestic groups composed of elementary families.

Normatively household among the Pagro-Mishing is composed of patrilocal - virilocal joint family and a person normally remains a member of a joint family household throughout his life. The composition of a joint household inevitably creates a wide range of interacting statuses. A man in the Pagro-Mishing household is brought up amidst a large number of his male agnatic kins and their wives. They are his father, mother, brothers and unmarried sisters; father's brothers and their wives; father's brothers sons and unmarried daughters; father's father and mother. When he grows up, he interacts with a few more relatives. They are his own wife, younger brothers' wives, sons and daughters and brothers' sons and daughters, finally daughters-in-law and the grandchildren.

For the continuity of a large joint family household for over three generations, much depends on the recognition and institutionalization of the member's playing appropriate roles based on a set of norms which define the reciprocal relationships. The normatively prescribed reciprocal relationship precludes the individual members from acting independently in pursuit of their personal goals. The members of the domestic group thus share a core of values that results in mutual or complementary expectations of behaviour. The patterns of behaviour within the domestic group are also related to the norms of interpersonal relations at the extra domestic level.

In this chapter I will now describe the role differentiation within the Pagro-Mishing domestic group and analyse the structure of interpersonal relationship in different kinship dyads by delineating the patterns of behaviour between various kinship categories which embody and signify defining properties, directions for behaviour and sanctioned norms of right and duty.

The structure of interpersonal relationship in the Pagro-Mishing household is hierarchical, based on the criteria of generation, age and sex. Thus the people of elder generation are superior to those in the younger, within each generation the elder have preference over the younger, and the men are superior to the women. This hierarchical pattern of relationship is the model for interpersonal relationship in the wider context of the Pagro-Mishing society itself.

I shall first discuss the structure of dyadic relationships within the domestic group and afterwards discuss them in the extra domestic context.

Father and Son

In a society which is organized rigorously on patrilineal descent system, with physiological paternity as the basis of legitimate kinship status in the society, and where kinship provides the principal framework of the social structure, the bond between father and son assumes socially the most significant relationship. The bonds between father and son have many facets which impinge upon the entire life cycle of a son and influence his field of action. The prominent dimensions within which the father-son relationship may be analysed are ritual, jural and economic.

As we have seen, the Pagro-Mishing strictly follow the principle of physiological paternity as the basis of jural fatherhood as well as for ascription of the membership of the descent group. So even an adulterine son becomes, *ipso facto*, a member of his genitor's clan, and cannot be affiliated to any other clan. A father in the Pagro-Mishing society is, thus always related physiologically to his son, who acquires his ritual, social and legal status from him.

The position of a son among the Pagro-Mishing is very significant due to his reilgious obligations to his father ,especially after death. In their religious system, the concept of soul *(Yalo)* exists. They believe that after the death of a person, his soul is released from the body and it goes to its abode *(sine-mobo)* from where it can visit the living descendants. However, a person's soul must be propitiated periodically by his legitimate son in order to keep the soul in peace. If the soul of a man is not propitiated, it remains restless and turns into an evil spirit (*uii*) which can also inflict misfortune on its living kins. So if a man dies without leaving behind a son, his soul will never rest in perpetual peace. It will turn into a ghost or an evil spirit. The belief in the existence of soul forms the basis of the cult of ancestor, which is the most important aspect of their religious system. The ancestral spirits are believed to be endowed with supernatural powers which they may use to help or harm the descendants. However, the benevolence of the ancestors is assured only by their periodic worship (*urom-posum)*, in the absence of which the descendants are likely to be afflicted with misfortunes. The ancestral spirits are the guardians of the living and watch over one's whole life, right from the moment of birth. The cult of ancestor worship and the belief in the existence of soul has made it a ritual necessity for every Pagro-Mishing man to marry and have a son because it is only a legitimate son who may propitiate the ancestral spirits as well as the soul of his deceased father. A son performs the rites and secures for his deceased father and grandfather an eternal place in the abode of the dead and in turn assures their benevolence for himself and his descendants. For this reason, every man in their society wishes to have a legitimate son. If a married man fails to beget a son after a few years of his marriage, he adopts one. An adopted son has the same status as one's own son.

Notwithstanding the ritual significance of a son, the relationship between a father and son is formal, aloof and restrained. The formal relationship between them is manifestly an outcome of authority of father and subordination of son. Birth of a son is, no doubt, a significant event, but it is not considered a big social event. However the ancestral spirits are propitiated and their blessings are sought for the safety of the infant on the third day of his birth.A man is generally not concerned with looking after his child and child's mother, which is the job of other women of the *erang* e.g. his own mother or sisters-in-law. During infancy, it is the mother who looks after the child who is constantly tied to her back even while she performs her household chores. The attitude of a father towards his son, during the latter's infancy and childhood, is of indifference. There is no manifestation of love and affection either by fondling the infant or by carrying him around. A child is looked after exclusively by his mother or his little siblings. A father seldom shows any indulgence for his little son, though a son may sometime share food with his father from the same plate. An open expression of a greater affection and fondness for one's infant son is contrary to the expected behaviour of a Pagro-Mishing father. Such behaviour on the contrary may bring ridicule to him. For example, Kandura was very fond of his infant son and he used to take him around in the village. But very soon he attracted the attention of other villagers for his unusual role of looking after the child. He was ridiculed not only by the men but also by the women of the village. They promptly gave him the sobriquet *'gero'*, which actually refers to a woman's lower garment and is considered unclean. Thus, Kandura was ridiculed and insulted by equating him to the unclean part of a woman's garment and hence contemptible. When a son has attained the age of eight or nine years, he starts participating in the tasks meant for men only, viz. helping in the agricultural fields or in fishing etc. At this stage he seeks company of other boys and remains mostly with them. In a joint family, his own brothers and parallel cousins of the same age group comprise the play group. The relationship between him and his father remains cool and aloof. But a father may sometimes scold his son if he is careless in the domestic chores. This pattern of aloofness of relationship is the characteristic feature of father-son relationship throughout their life. During adulthood close and intimate encounters between a father and son are not frequent. They converse only when they must, and it is confined to specific problems concerning household work etc. A son does not address his father ever in a raised voice even when he is being scolded by his father. One can notice that a young man seldom looks straight into his father's eyes while talking to him. The adult status of a son does, however, endow him with a certain jural status. Now as an adult he may work on an extra piece of land and earn some money out of it. The income he earns in this manner is his own.

But such income is rather insignificant. At this time of his life, a young man generally becomes more interested in girls in his age group and also establishes friendship with them. As a young man he may also like to marry a girl of his choice; or his father in consultation with other members of the erang may arrange his marriage. However, if a young man wants to marry his beloved, he may not do so unless he has his father's consent. A father is jurally responsible for the acts of his son. If a son, for example, impregnates a girl it is not only he but his father and his entire erang which have to face the consequences of his misadventure because it is the boy's father and the erang who pays the fine to the girl's father and *erang*. In an arranged marriage, as well as in the elopement marriage bride price *(aalig)* is paid. The responsibility for the payment of *aalig* money rests with the father and his *erang*. A son, howsoever, old he may be, cannot take an independent decision about his marriage and act upon it. Since such an act will be flagrant breach of jural authority of the father as well as of the entire *erang*. It will also evoke moral indignation of the entire local community. Thus, if a man marries against the wishes of his father and other kinsmen, he may be thrown out of the *erang*. Since, during the life time of the father, a son has no jural right in the household property, it may be impossible for a man to start his life from scratch. Besides facing economic hardships, he may also be cursed by his ancestral spirits who are believed to uphold the parental authority. The moral values of the society would also not allow such a man to be welcome anywhere amongst the Pagro-Mishing. In short, the moral, jural, economic and ritual constraints help the perpetuation of asymmetrical interpersonal relation between a man and his son. The rule of patrilocal-virilocal residence implies the continuity of a son's association with his natal domestic group. Marriage, no doubt, confers certain rights on the son. His marriage establishes his relationship with his wife's domestic group. He also participates in some ceremonies at his wife's place. He may also earn some money independently which he may spend on self or his own nuclear family over which he has authority. Though he acquires certain elements of jural independence in his actions, within the context of the domestic group however, his position in relation to his own father remains the same. A married son does not become economically independent, nor does he acquire more authority in relation to his father. Since the domestic group among the Pagro-Mishing has a norm of temporal continuity based on jural and economic position of the father, marriage of son does not set in even an incipient fission in the domestic group. Thus as long as the father is alive, a son remains jurally, economically and ritually subordinate to him.

The relationship between a man and his father's brother is also marked by formality and respectful distance. A man does not indulge in loose talks with his father's brother, nor does he joke with him. A man obeys him as he would his own father and conversely, a father's brother is equally responsible for his deceased brother's children. In case of unmarried children the responsibility to marry them devolves on the deceased man's brother, who initiates the negotiations for their marriage and makes the *aalig* payments. For all intents and purposes, there is thus no difference in behaviour towards one's father and father's brothers when they are members of the same domestic group. The kinship term for father is *babu* which is extended to father's brothers as well, though a terminological distinction is made on the basis of their relative age. If the father's brother is older than the father, he is addressed as *babatta* and if he is younger, the kinship term is *baboi.* These kinship terms are also extended to father's male patrilateral parallel cousins. However, a man has more intimate and affectionate relation with members of his own nuclear family and the affective ties are definitely more intimate with one's own sons than with the brother's sons.

Relationship Between Brothers

In the patrilineal ideology of the Pagro-Mishing with joint family as the basis of the domestic grouping based on patrilocal-virilocal rule of residence, the relationship between the brothers tends to be of great structural importance. This is next in importance to the father- son relationship since even after the death of a man, his sons continue to live together in the same domestic unit which manifests economic, jural and ritual solidarity among the brothers.

The relationship between the brothers is comparable in content to the relationship between father and son. The relationship between the brothers is also hierarchic. In the father and son relationship the criterion of hierarchy is generation, whereas in the brother-brother relationship, the criterion is of relative age. The brothers are collectively referred to by the kinship term *birrang,* but the terms of address for the younger and elder brothers are different.

During childhood the brothers form a playgroup along with their cousins and other children of their age group. There is no marked difference in their behaviour towards one another. But gradually the children learn to accept the authority of their elder brothers, which is accelerated by differentiation of peer groups according to various age categories, and the role differentiation that is associated with this. The older brothers become responsible for many household chores and are assigned specific tasks like fishing, ploughing and harvesting . The younger brothers still look after infant siblings or carry out the orders of the elders. The elder brother can force the younger brothers into obedience by using physical force as well. Thus during his childhood, a boy may receive beating at the hands of the elder brother. But this phase of relationship is of short duration and later on, when the brothers have grown up to adulthood the younger brothers obey their elder brothers, which is the normative behaviour.

In adulthood and in the later part of life there is no informality between the brothers. Their relationship is neither intimate nor relaxed. This formal relationship is more pronounced if the age difference between them is greater. The younger brother shows great deference for his elder brothers and does not talk loosely if the elder brother is within hearing distance. The brothers are seldom seen talking platitudes, and they never talk about sex. Their conversations are mostly confined to the topics of mutual concern, especially in relation to the household activities. The younger brother, while coversing with his elder brother, does not look straight into his eyes, as is done by a son while talking with his father. This is not merely an ideal pattern of behaviour but it is the normal practice. No one really tells them to do so, but this manifestation of formality is really an expression of respect for one's elders. Quarrels, both verbal and physical, among the grown up brothers are extremely rare, almost non-existent. In fact, violence between the brothers, as well as between a father and son, or between the kinsmen or between the affines is supposed to be *'genna'* which implies a 'ritually forbidden act'. The punishment for the infringement of this code of conduct is meted by the ancestral spirits. During the course of this study, I never came across a single case of violence between the brothers or for that matter, in any other collectivity. The disputes, it is believed must be settled by arbitration and this applies equally to the brothers also.

The eldest brother becomes the head of the *erang* after the death of the father. He represents the household unit in ritual, social economic and political spheres. All other brothers abide by the decisions of the eldest brother. It is the duty of the brothers to look after their younger brothers specially with regard to their marriage after the death of the father. In spite of seemingly cool and formal relationship between the brothers, their relationship is based on amity, cordiality and affection. A group of full brothers have intimate interest in each other's children.

It may be recalled that the brothers continue to live in the same domestic group till the time each of the brother has got his sons married

At this stage the domestic group may go through the process of fission and each brother may establish his own independent *erang*. The brothers separate mainly for economic reasons when the domestic group becomes unmanageable, and seldom because of personal conflicts. Even after separation, the brothers continue to be part of the same ritual unit and perform the worship of their ancestors jointly under the charge of the eldest brother. The brothers remain a ritual unit during their life time and their sons continue to be part of one ritual unit for the performance of *ramku urom* which is jointly performed by them to propitiate their grandfather.

The relationship between the patrilateral parallel cousins is, more or less, the same as between the brothers. The behaviour between them is also patterned according to their relative age. The kinship terms for them are the same as for one's own brother. However, the genealogical distance between the parallel cousins leads to their separation into different ritual units. But, as we have noted earlier, the Pagro-Mishing domestic groups may be composed of full brothers and their parallel cousins -- who had a common grandfather. Thus, the relationship between the brothers and their parallel cousins is ritually, economically and jurally quite enduring.

Mother and Son

The relationship between a mother and son is very different in content and actions from that of father and son relationship. The son has more intimate and loving relationship with her. She is more affectionate and indulgent towards him. A son may quarrel with her over small things; he may pick up an argument with her and sometimes he may also disobey her. A son does not hold his mother in awe as he holds his father, he has love and affection for her.

From the time of his birth a son is looked after by his mother. He is totally dependent on her until he is weaned at the age of about three years. As an infant, his mother carries him all over the place tied to her back with a sling. A child is never left alone but is always carried on the back of his mother. One can see many women with their infant children tied on their back, working in the fields, or pounding rice, or spinning thread or carrying water from the water sources. When a child is able to walk, he is looked after by his elder siblings. The entire burden of feeding the child, cleaning him and looking after his general health is on the mother. A father is absolutely unconcerned about his son's up-bringing.

A women is seriously concerned regarding the marriage of her son and advises her husband on this matter. A son may also confide in her, if he has himself chosen a girl. Similarly, when a boy wants to marry a girl of his choice by elopement, he takes his mother into confidence who may convince the boy's father for the subsequent settlement with the girl's parents.

A son is morally responsible to look after his mother when she is widowed. However, the uterine ancestors have no important place in the Pagro-Mishing belief system and therefore a mother is not a link with the ancestors. After the death of the mother, a son offers sacrifices to her soul but it is not worshipped periodically.

The format of relationship of a man with his father's brother's wife is similar to that of one's own mother. However, there is a qualitative difference in his attitude towards her as compared to his own mother; they are not so intimate and indulgent.

Father and Daughter

The position of a daughter in the Pagro-Mishing household is marginal. After her marriage she severes her relationship with the natal *erang*. Perhaps for this reason a father's attitude towards a daughter is more affectionate and his behaviour is also more indulgent. A daughter usually looks after her father by serving him meals or *apong*' and also washes his clothes. A man is responsible for the marriage of his daughter. The *aalig* money is settled by him as her jural guardian. If a daughter elopes with a man, the man's father through his *erang* has to negotiate, symbolically with the girl's father to legitimize their unions. Symbolically, because it is the decision of the *erang* and not merely of the father.

Mother and Daughter

The mother and daughter are more intimate in their relationships. The behaviour of a daughter towards her mother is affectionate. A daughter is physically more closely associated with her mother owing to similar domestic chores which both of them perform. However, a mother is more concerned about the morals of her grown up daughter and may also reprimand her if she misbehaves. In case, a daughter is suspected to be intimate with some boy, it is her mother who takes a very serious view of this and may even give her a severe physical punishment. However, a father would never beat his daughter. A women, in the absence of her husband, cannot settle the *aalig*. This is done by the head of the *erang*. A mother has no right over the *aalig* money.

Brother and Sister

The relationship between brother and sister is almost opposite of the brother and brother relationship. A sister is very informal with her brothers -- both elder and younger, though the elder brother is respected and obeyed and the younger brother is loved. However, the younger brother does not care too much for his elder sister's command and may not always obey her. A brother has a very important place in the life of a sister. The Pagro-Mishing attach a great significance to the presence of brothers in the family of a girl while they negotiate for her marriage with their son. A girl who has no brother has difficulty in getting a spouse. A brother-in-law (wife's brother) is a dependable relative. Moreover, the absence of a brother implies that the marriage alliance between the two families cannot be perpetuated in the succeeding generations, which is the common practice in their society. The brother and sister are thus also potential parent-in-law of their children.

The relationship between the sisters is very affectionate and intimate. They work together and may also confide in each other. The sisters may even know each other's personal affairs. But the brothers scrupulously aviod all such talks in the presence of their sisters.

Husband and Wife

Within the domestic group, the relationship of maximum intimacy is firstly between the husband and wife and then between parents and their children who constitute the nuclear family unit. Although a nuclear family may not be an autonomous unit, its distinctive character is manifested in the emotional and affective nature of the relationship of the husband and wife. The intimacy of the husband-wife relationship is however, never exhibited publicly. Owing to the structure of the Pagro- Mishing dwelling unit which is an unpartitioned room and is shared by several nuclear family units of the domestic group, the husband and wife can never openly express their affection for each other. The relationship between the two is subdued and they interact with one another without open expression of emotions. This fact is all the more striking because many a husband-and-wife couple, prior to their marriage, have been intimate lovers and have married only because of their love for each other. However, once the lovers are married their status becomes that of a husband and wife, consequently the behaviour pattern between the two converges on the formal, expected norm.

The husband and wife relationship is asymmetrical and she is regarded subordinate in all domestic and extra domestic spheres.A wife is fully incorporated in her husband's group. She is jurally and ritually transferred from her own natal domestic group to that of her husband. Sometimes the relationship between them get severely strained and a husband may even beat his wife. Similarly in some, cases a man may have extramarital relations with unmarried women but the wife is unable to check him, though she definitely resents this. On the other hand, a wife is ideally expected to be fidel, and she usually is. A husband may marry a second woman without any consideration for his existing wife, but a wife on the other hand, cannot even think of divorcing her husband, though divorce is permitted. In fact, the incorporation of a wife into her husband's domestic group and lineage implies that her own agnatic kins cannot interfere in her affairs. Moreover, since a woman can remarry only those men who belong to certain predetermined categories, who all happen to be her husband's kin and who would not accept any such woman as a wife. The greatest constraint on divorce, however, is of kinship values. A woman who has quarrelled with her husband and his domestic group may not be acceptable to any other domestic group as a wife. A divorced woman cannot even go back to her own natal family. However, the relationship between the husband and wife is normally harmonious and affectionate in spite of a husband being excessively dominant in his attitudes and behaviour towards his wife.

Grandparents and Grandchildren

The structure of relationship between these alternate generations is quite opposite of what we observed for the father and son relationship.

The relationship between grandparents (Fa Fa) and grandchildren is of familiarity and equality despite the age difference.

Though the kinship term of reference for grandchildren are *uo-ume,* a grandfather addresses a grandson as *tata* and the grand-daughter as'*mimbur*' (woman) or '*yayo*'. These are the kinship terms for father's father and father's mother respectively. Thus the relatives in the alternate generations use the same terms - *tata* and *yayo* while addressing each other. Similarly two men, who are in the classificatory relationship of grandfather and grandson, may also sometime address each other as '*Salpati*', a term used to denote wife's sisters, husband implying that they could be co-brothers although the wives of these two men may not be sisters. This only reflects the equivalence between the two persons in alternate generations. The jokes between Fa Fa and So So are however only verbal though their content may be vulgar. A grandfather may joke libidly or may even indulge in vulgar talks with his grand son's wife, who in turn, may also reciprocate in the same vein. Similarly a grandson may joke uninhibited with his grandmother, (real or classificatory) and this form of behaviour is extended by him to all men and women who may be only in the classificatory relationship of *tata* and *yayo*. The paternal grandparents are usually the constant company of their grandchildren. When grandparents are quite aged and have ceased to be active members of the household, they become all the more fond of little grandchildren. A grandfather may even carry his grandchild on his back which, perhaps, he never did in the case of his own son or daughter during their infancy.

AFFINAL RELATIVES

Brothers-in-Law

As has been discussed earlier, the kinship terms *igo-magbo* are used for the entire category of affinal relatives besides referring to particular kin types. As the affinal category, members of the opposite moiety are collectively referred to as "igo-magbo". The particular relatives covered by these terms are *WiBr* and *HuBr*. The one who is older than Ego (both male female speaking) is called *magbo* and the one younger than Ego is called *igo.* These two terms are also used for bilateral cross-cousins i.e FaSiSo and MoBrSo, who are also part of the affinal category.

The relationship between a man and his wife's younger brother or a man and his wife's elder brother or with the elder sister's husband is of joking and familiarity. *igo-magbo* may discuss freely all things including sex and personal affairs of one another. They may even abuse each other, but none takes any serious note of it. The relationship is in contradistinction of Br-Br relationships which is based on restrain.. The relationship between the brothers-in-law is more or less uniform for all the men who stand in *igo-magbo* relationship and is not confined to the actual *igo-magbo*. Thus the male bilateral cousin (FaSiSon-MoBrSo) also have joking relationship though none of the two may be married to either's sister.

Though the relationship between them is of familiarity yet with one's real *Magbo/Igo* (SiHu,WiBr), one shows extreme courtesy also. The jokes between them are seldom rough and are confined to only verbal exchanges. They do not indulge in horseplay. The *igo-magbo* relationship is thus characterized by respect and familiarity and not by respect and restraint. There is also a formal character of *igo-magbo* relationship. The Pagro-Mishing concept of affinity is based on the ethics that the affines should never quarrel over anything or not even use angry abusive language for each other. The relationship between the affines is a continuation of the affinal ties which were created in the past and are likely to continue in future generations also. Cooperation between the real brothers-in-law is an expected norm. They also participate in the family rituals at each other's place.

Sisters-in-law

Women affines in one's own generation address each other as *mamo* and *igne.* The relationship between an unmarried *mamo* (HuElSi) and *igne* are friendly and cordial and they share many secrets of each other. The actual *mamo* (El Br Wi) and *igne* (HuYoSi) also interact on friendly terms, though in some cases there seems to be a little tension between them especially when the Hu Yo Si is still unmarried. An unmarried daughter is less busy in the domestic chores in her father's home and consequently she gets more time to do her own work like weaving cloth for hereself whereas, a daughter-in-law remains busy for long in the household chores. As a bachelor, a man also gives more attention and shows affection to his sisters and also brings small presents for them. But after his marriage his attention is shifted to his own wife. This diversion of sibling affection sometimes causes tension between *mamo* and *igne* interaction and which may sometimes manifest in the shape of a verbal clash. Within the course of daily routine a woman and her husband's unmarried sisters have less chances of meeting and gossiping because of different roles performed by them. They (*mamo-igne*) also do not go out together in the village. Only the unmarried girls do. A married woman and an unmarried woman have very different activities in the household due to different roles they have to perform. Therefore the *mamo-igne* relationship does not develop into intimate relationship, though an *igne* is also a prospective sister-in-law of the *mamo* due to cross cousin marriage.

Hu El Br-Yo Br Wi

Though a woman refers to her HuElBr as *magbo* and he refers to her as *igne,* the relationship between the two is of avoidance. They do not talk to each other or address each other directly. Though a woman does not veil her face in the presence of her *magbo,* she certainly does not come in his presence without wearing a serious countenance. Though all the brothers for a considerable length of time inhabit the same house, the interaction between *magbo* and *igne* is minimum. A younger brother's wife may serve food to her HuElBr but she neither looks directly at him nor does she talk to him unless it is necessary to do so.

The partition of the sleeping places in the unpartitioned house, as discussed earlier, is such that an elder brother has no business to go beyond his own sleeping place; the younger brother's sleeping place is always after that of the elder brother. If there are house guests, they sit at the elder brother's place or with head of the *erang.* Similarly a daughter-in-law of the house would also not stop over the sleeping places of her HuEIBr. Thus in spite of the open structure of the Pagro- Mishing house, the relationship between a *magbo* and *igne* are kept at respectful distance.

The relationship of avoidance between a classificatory *magbo* and *igne* is not very much rigid and they may even converse but it is always restrained. Joking between them is, of course, forbidden.

The relationship between a man and and his wife's younger sister, who are also *magbo* and *igne,* is of familiarity or of joking. However, a man does not take much liberties with his real wife's younger sister, he is restrained in his behaviour with the *igne*. A man may, however, marry his WiYoSi after the death of his wife but not during the lifetime of his first wife.

The reason for a married man's restrained behaviour towards his *igne* is that a WiYoSi is ultimately destined to be his yo BrWi (real or classificatory) with whom his interaction is not very free, hence a married man generally behaves in a restrained manner towards his real WiYoSi. But the relationship between a man and his classificatory *igne* is quite cordial and have the content of familiarity as well.

A man, though unmarried, has the same term of kinship for his FaSiDa and MoBrDa if they are younger to him. In such cases, the relationship is not at all restrained. On the contrary, it is of friendliness and may develop into an intimate relationship culminating ultimately in marriage.

ElBrWi -Hu Yo Br

The relationship between a man and his ElBrWi is just the contrast of the *magbo-igne* relationship. A man has joking relationship with his ElBrWi whom he addresses as *Mamo.* The jokes between them are rough and sometimes lewd too. In former days, according to some informants, a man could even indulge in sexual relations with his ElBrWi if the ElBr was away for a considerable period of time, though it was denied by others. Of course, I did not come across any evidence of the practice. The important fact that emerges from this information is however, the attitude of the people who think that sex relations between a man and his elder brother's wife are not absolutely prohibited. Sex relations between ElBr and YoBrWi are, condemned and are thought to be extreme case of moral perversion. They, however, do not consider such acts as sinful and incestuous.

The custom of 'widow inheritance' is institutionalized among the Pagro-Mishing. It is confined to the elder brother's widow who may be remarried by husband's younger brother. An elder brother is not allowed to keep his younger's brother's widow. After the death of her husband, the widow, if young, is remarried by her HuYoBr. It is however, not necessary that the next immediate brother should remarry the widow. Any of the younger brother can remarry her, though mostly it is the next brother. Sometimes, a man may be already married and yet remarry the widow.

In some cases, a widow may merely cohabit with the HuYoBr. The children born to her by this union are regarded as that of the cohabiting brother and not of the deceased brother. This practice is neither levirate, nor widow inheritance. This happens in those cases when the widow is not young enough to be taken as wife by a younger man, and besides, she may also have a number of children. Under these conditions she has no chance of getting an acceptable husband and so she may simply have sex relations with her unmarried *igo*. Such relationships are known to the people but they are hardly talked about. The Pagro-Mishing have no term for this relationship.

The above mentioned pattern of behaviour between the *mamo* and *igo* is not confined to the actual relatives but is similarly extended to all women (married or unmarried) who are addressed as *mamo* by a man.

MoBr-Si So

The position of MoBr in the Pagro-Mishing society is understandable only within the framework of the total system. A mother's brother belongs to the opposite moiety and hence belongs to the part of the affinal category. The bilateral cross-cousin marriage by which the Pagro-Mishing create alliance relationship with the affinal moiety places the mother's brother in the position of the FaSiHu and also as the father of the spouse (Hu Fa, Wi Fa). The kinship term for MoBr, FaSiHu, and HuFa, WiFa is the same, namly, *Kaki*.

There is no ambiguity in the Pagro-Mishing conceptualization of the position of mother's brother. They regard him as an affine and not as a kin. Although the Pagro-Mishing have strong agnatic kinship and the ties of patrifiliation are utilized in the formation of lineages, the ties between a brother and a sister are not enduring. A woman after marriage and eventually after the birth of a child loses her jural and ritual status in her natal family. She is fully incorporated in the domestic group and the lineage of her husband's ancestors. Her own agnatic ancestors do not remain important for her after her marriage. In fact, she does not participate in any rituals concerning her own agnatic ancestors, except in her father's and mother's funeral ceremonies (*dadgang*). The position of a woman in the Pagro-Mishing society is similar to the one that existed in rural China (Yang 1945 : 240). Thus, a woman in the Pagro-Mishing society has no status by complementary filiation. The implication of this situation is that among the Pagro-Mishing, as I have pointed out earlier, an individual is affiliated with the descent group of his genitor and he has neither a choice to choose any other group nor does he become member of his mother's agnatic group. The function of complementary filiation in some societies is to provide for individual choice in some areas of social alignments in systems with unilineal corporate descent but it has no relevance in the Pagro-Mishing society where the factor of choice for affiliation to a descent group does not exist . The Pagro-Mishing thus fall in that category of the societies in which, according to Leach (1961 : 123) "unilineal descent is linked with strongly defined rule of 'preferred marriage' where 'complementary filiation' may come to form part of the permanent ongoing structure..."

The ties between a man and his sister are not defined in jural and ritual sense but on affective norms. The relationship between a man and his sister's son are similarly based on affective factors. Thus among the Pagro-Mishing, a MoBr has no jural authority over the SiSo, and a SiSo has no right in his MoBr property. In fact, the concept of avunculocal residence does not exist among the Pagro-Mishing because a man and his SiSo belong to separate descent groups and therefore they propitiate separate ancestral spirits who must not be worshipped in the same dwelling unit.

Although a man has no jural, ritual and economic relationship with his sister after her marriage and the same is extended to the SiSo, yet a man does have positive affective attitude towards his sister and her children. A MoBr is concerned about the welfare of his sister's children. The existence of bilateral cross-cousin marriage obviously makes a MoBr as a prospective WiFa as well. However, a man need not marry the actual MoBrDa, it is not really prescribed. But it is not prohibited, either. At the same time the Pagro-Mishing conceptualize their own system in the model of dichotomous divisions as consisting of kinsmen and affines. Thus a MoBr is regarded as belonging to the affinal category and not to the category of consanguineal kinsman.

The Mosi also belongs to the affinal category. Although a man uses the same kinship term *'Yaue'* for Mo and MoSi (real and classificatory), yet MoSi (classificatory) may sometime be taken as a wife. This is not considered to be a proscribed relationship though it is not regarded a desirable alliance, either. So the point that needs to be stressed is that all the women in the opposite moiety including MoSi, are the possible spouses and the men including MoBr are regarded as affines.

The relationship between a man and his MoBr is generally of familiarty and cordiality but is devoid of obscenity. This type of behaviour is extended to the classificatory MoBr as well. However, a man behaves very differently towards his WiFa who is terminologically the same as MoBr, namely Kaki. The relationship between a man and his WiFa is based on respect and restrain as discussed below.

Parents-in-Law and Son-in-Law/Daughter-in-Law

A son-in-law shows very high respect to his father-in-law, in fact, sometimes it may look as though he is avoiding his father-in-law. Both of them generally talk very little between them, and avoid each other's gaze. A man feels 'shy' *(aaning)* in the presence of his father-in-law. Whenever a son-in-law pays a visit to his father-in-law, he takes the gift of *apong* and '*tamul*' (betel leaf and areca nuts) for him. A son-in-law's behaviour towards the brothers of his father-in-law is if they constitute a single household. In case other brothers of the father-in-law are also present when he visits them, he offers '*pan-tamul*' first to WiFaBr and only then to the father-in-law (WiFa). This act signifies the same respect for him (WiFaBr) which he accords to his own father-in-law. A father-in-law and his brothers are referred to as *Attode* and they address and refer to the son-in-law as *Magbode.* However, the kinship terms for the same persons prior to marriage are *Kaki* and *Uo* respectively. Only after marriage *Kaki* becomes *Attode* (WiFa, HuFa) and *Uo* becomes *Magbode*. However, the term of address remains *Kaki*.

Likewise with a mother-in-law, the relationship is formal. A son-in-law shows respect by keeping a low profile and sitting at a distance from his mother-in-law and generally would not talk to her unless talked to. On the other hand, the relationship between a daughter-In-law and father-in-law/mother-in-law is not very formal or restrained. A daughter-in-law serves food to her father-in-law and does not feel shy (*aaning*) in his presence. The social intercourse between the two of them is, however, restricted to minimum because she remains busy doing household chores whereas a man generally remains involved in out-door work. A wife's and husband's mother are both referred to as '*Ayode*' but the term of address remains the same viz. *Nyanni*.

The daughter-in-law and mother-in-law relationship is more intimate and cordial. Both work in the same sphere. The daughter-in-law obeys her mother-in-law, chats with her and shares the same work. There is seldom any occasion when a daughter-in-law has to be rebuked by her mother-in-law. The relationship between the parents-in-law and the daughter-in-law is devoid of conflict because of the relationship that existed between them even before marriage. A duaghter-in-law belongs to the kin type of a brother's daughter (for the mother-in-law) and sister's daughter for the father-in-law. This relationship may be, of course, classificatory, yet a newly married girl does not feel a stranger in her husband's place. She already has a model of social interaction with the members of her husband's family based on norms of behaviour between the affines. When she actually becomes a wife and attains the status of an affine, there is little modification in her interactional pattern with the husband's kin. Besides, all the daughters-in-law in a joint family *erang* belong to the same kin type viz. classificatory sisters, a fact which also mitigates the fear of being lonely. A woman addresses her HuFa as *Kaki* and HuMo as *Nyanni*.

From the above analysis of the pattern of kinship behaviour between different dyads in the Pagro-Mishing kinship universe, certain norms can be highlighted. The dichotomization of the entire kinship universe into two categories namely, kins and affines, is fully reflected in their social behaviour. The members of one's own consanguineal kin group are generally shown respect, mutual reserve, obedience and authority, on the basis of generation and age difference, though in case of alternate generation, there is greater laxity and cordiality between them. The cross-sex relationship shows more or less a uniform pattern of normative behaviour irrespective of the fact whether it takes place between actual kins or classificatory kins. Thus, for example, relationship between a man and his sister is devoid of any sexual undertone and the same pattern is observable between a man and any of his classificatory sister. However, the Pagro-Mishing seem to make a distinction between a 'lineage and clan kin' i.e. a kin within the *ope* and a kin within the widest category of the moiety.

The *ope* kin are collectively called 'ope birrang' whereas the member of one's moiety are referred to simply as 'birrang'. The pattern of behaviour between these two categories shows certain variation although the general form is the same. Thus sexual relationship between a man and a woman belonging to the same *ope* is treated as incest and entails elaborate purificatory ritual ceremonies besides awarding physical punishments to the culprits; whereas a similar act between a man and woman belonging to different *ope* within the moiety is not treated as an incestuous act and the culprits are punished only by the community and the act does not entail any ritual ceremony. Similarly, respect behaviour and mutual reserve tends to become diluted in actual behaviour between classificatory kin types.

The relationship between the members of the opposite moieties are of familiarity and laxity. The relationship between the men of the opposite moieties are cordial, jovial and are based on joking; the cross-sex relationships are also based on familiarity and joking which have sexual undertones as well. Thus mutual reserve, restrain, and authoritarian attitude of intra-clan behaviour is completely absent from the interpersonal behaviour of the members belonging to the affinal clans.

8

The Economic Dimensions of the Domestic Group

In the preceeding chapter our attention was focused mainly on analysing the structure of interpersonal relationship by discussing the role of the members of the domestic group within the context of kinship. The structure of interpersonal role relationship, as we have seen, is basically hierarchical, being determined by the criteria of generation, age and sex, and are further defined by a set of norms of interpersonal behaviour as well as a description of rights and duties which are jurally defined. In this chapter I will now discuss the role of the members of Pagro-Mishing domestic group in their economy.

The Pagro-Mishing Economy

The Pagro-Mishing are an exclusively agricultural community with plough cultivation. Besides agriculture, their economy is supplemented by animal husbandry, fishing and by raising of certain cash crops. The Pagro-Mishing economy is a household economy in which the household is a unit of production and consumption. The members of the domestic group provide work team and labour power for agricultural and other economic activities which are geared mainly towards production of food and other basic consumption needs of the domestic group.

STRUCTURE OF PRODUCTION

Resources : Land and Livestock.

Land is the basic asset in the productive resources of the Pagro-Mishing society. Before discussing the rules governing the possession of land, however, I would like to recall the historical background of the Pagro-Mishing society because the contemporary pattern is directly related to it.

It may be recalled that the Pagro-Mishing were formerly practising shifting cultivation and were not sedentary cultivators. The Pagro-Mishing had settled, when they migrated to the plains of Assam, on the low lying banks of the rivers. These tracts were almost uninhabitable and therefore the Mishing had a vast stretch of land to choose from. Due to the practice of shifting cultivation, they did not settle at one place and moved to a fresh area as soon as the cultivated land lost its fertility. Thus the practice of shifting to new areas and easy availability of land made them rather indifferent towards owning land permanently. Land was therefore, not considered a part of the household property. Since it was available in abundance, land was not considered a part of heritable asset either.

The consequence of such ecological conditions and cultural norms is reflected in the total absence of disputes pertaining to land in their society. However, with the passage of time, the conditions also changed. With the increase of their population as well as of other communities, land ceased to be abundantly available in the hitherto uninhabited areas. Moreover, the Pagro-Mishing were also forced to change their mode of cultivation for the same reason. Thus they became settled agriculturists from shifting cultivators. However, even now, land is not considered a marketable commodity in their society.

Possession of Land and the Domestic Group

The Pagro-Mishing are settled on the land owned by the government. They cultivate land that has been leased to them on periodic tenancy which is renewed without exception. Thus for all intents and purposes, the land possessed by a household is like permanent property, provided the tenant pays the land revenue regularly.

The initial practice in the society was that each household would clear as much virgin land as was essential to meet its domestic needs. The Pagro-Mishing economy being basically a household economy, no household deemed it fit to possess more land than was necessary in spite of its availability. Another significant consequence of the regional geographical factor is that among the Pagro-Mishing there are no landless household, nor is there a class of people who can be hired as labourers. A household itself acts as a unit of labour.

The possession of the land is in the name of the head of the domestic group who holds the lease of land on behalf of the household. Anything that is cultivated on the land, belongs to the household and is utilized for the household consumption. Since the Pagro-Mishing relationships with any cultivable land were tenuous and the possession of land was on the basis of periodic tenancy, we do not find formal rules of inheritance of land among them. Only until the previous generation, land was not even regarded as an important asset of the household because each and every unit of the domestic group could clear a fresh patch of land when it established itself as an independent *erang.* So the disputes over land among the surviving sons of a man were never a cause of the fission of a domestic group. Correspondingly, the fear of being dispossessed of a share in the family and is also not an integrating factor of the father and son ties. Nowadays, however, each son of the original lease holder is given a share in the land when they separate from one another. The share of each segment of the domestic group is determined on the basis of its size. Thus the segment with a larger number of persons would take more land than the segment with few persons. Moreover, each segment can also augment its possession of land by clearing a virgin piece of land, if available. The other productive resources of the domestic family consist of livestock---cattle, pigs, poultry---boats and canoes, fishing and agricultural implements, and in some cases, an elephant.

A Pagro-Mishing household generally owns a large herd of cattle but they have no economic use of the milch cattle because they neither drink milk nor use it in any other form. They are not beef-eaters, either. The cows are valuable only for their male progeny, namely, oxen which are used as draft animal.

The possession of pigs and fowls is, however, economically very gainful for the household. Pigs and fowls also provide an important source of protein of their diet. In any ceremony ---- ancestor worship, marriage, funeral ceremony, or the worship of the cosmic power *(Taleng Uii)* or any other spirit --- the sacrifice of pigs and fowls is an essential part. The pigs and fowls also constitute part of the marriage gift. Therefore there is a great demand of pigs and fowls in the domestic group for various ceremonies which makes it imperative that each domestic groups possess them in large numbers. In addition to the domestic consumption and ceremonial needs, pigs and fowls have a ready market in the nearby towns. The villagers sell them to the traders who visit the villages regularly from these towns. Owning of an elephant is, of course, a great economic asset to the family economy. It is used to harness the elephant --cart which hauls paddy from the fields to the granary. During non-harvest season, the elephant may be hired to the forest contractors for hauling timber. An elephant may earn roughly about Rs. 5000/- or more in a season, lasting about six months. Every household also owns a number of boats and dug-out canoes which are essential part of the household assets. They are used for fishing in the deep waters; for bringing paddy from the fields which may lie across the rivers. During the flood season, boats and canoes are the only means of transportation in most of the Pagro-Mishing villages

PRODUCTIVE ACTIVITIES

Agriculture is the most important productive activity of the Pagro-Mishing. The agricultural products are mainly raised for the domestic consumption except a small amount of cash crops for the market. The most important crop is rice. Other crops consist of pulses, cotton, mustard, black gram, tobacco and potato. The Pagro-Mishing engage in great deal of fishing in the rivers and ponds which abound in their area. Fishing is the second most important economic activity after agriculture and is meant for only domestic consumption. For this purpose, every household owns a number of fishing nets and traps.

Other productive activities of the Pagro-Mishing are weaving of both cotton and silk cloth. They raise a small quantity of cotton, though now-a-days, cotton weaving is done with the mill made yarn bought from the market. Silk is processed by rearing silk worms and the entire process upto weaving the finished product is totally confined to the domestic family. The finished product is also meant only for the use within the family and never sold in the market.

Household Property and Individual Property

The Pagro-Mishing have two categories of property on the basis of its ownership; one the property owned by an individual member of the household and the other, the property owned by the domestic family. The individually owned property is known as *riksing attar* and the one owned by the domestic group is called *akum erang attar.*

Formerly the Pagro-Mishing had only movable property but consequent to becoming settled agriculturists, land is now being regarded as property. The property of the household consists of agricultural land, the house, the granaries, boats and canoes, fishing and agricultural implements, livestock including the elephant , and other household effects like utensils . The agricultural products like paddy, pulses, mustard, tobacco and potato . belong to the entire household. Any income earned by selling the cash crops or by hiring the elephant forms part of the *akum erang attar.* The household property and wealth is managed by the head of the household.

The individually earned wealth, *riksing attar,* is solely owned by the person concerned. The household has no right over this wealth. An individual may earn a little money by cultivating a small patch of land to grow cash crops like mustard or potato. This may be done by both the men and women. The women may also earn money by selling fowls and pigs which they raise individually. The men, however ,do not raise pigs and poultry. The money thus earned by a woman is exclusively hers and even her husband has no right over it. The unmarried daughters may weave cloth for their own use. An individual may, however, earn money only after having completed his assigned domestic chore. An individual would therefore work on a patch of land or look after the pigs and poultry only during his spare time. However, the domestic chores leave very little spare time with the members. Moreover, the norm of the domestic life obliges its members to devote maximum time to the household chores and therefore an individual's interest is always treated subordinate to that of the household. When a member is suspected to be neglecting his domestic duties in preference to his personal interests, he may be warned and reprimanded. If a daughter-in-law is found guilty of such neglect, she may not only be scolded but beaten by her husband. Thus, although, the Pagro-Mishing recognize the individual's right to own some wealth, it is hardly possible for any individual to earn substantially. The marriage gifts consisting of utensils are also treated as the man's property to whom they were gifted though they are pooled together with rest of the household utensils for daily use.

The role of the individual wealth *(riksing attar)* cannot be totally ignored in the organization and the fission of the domestic group. When a married man or woman earns some money, she/he generally spends it only on her/his spouse and children. Of late, the parents have become more concerned about the higher education of their children. But higher education costs money and in a large household it is not possible to send all the children to the higher educational institutions. Therefore, there is a tendency nowadays to earn privately more money so that a man may send his sons for higher education by supporting them individually. This may result in some disparity in the educational attainments of the boys belonging to the same *erang* but to different constituent nuclear family units within it. This disparity in education among the sons of the brothers constituting a single household may cause conflict among the brothers and may also accelerate the process of partition in the fraternal joint-family. Those brothers, whose sons are not studying may, rightly feel that their own sons are working in the fields for the household whereas the sons of other brothers are improving their career without contributing to the household economy. Thus, if the economic roles of the members of the *erang* conflict with the common goals of the household as a single consumption-production unit, a joint family household is likley to partition into smaller segments. However, this type of conflict among the brothers is an exception rather than a rule. The brothers, as we have seen, have moral and affective bonds which are strong enough to keep them as a cohesive group.

Partition of the Domestic Group and Distribution of Property

When a household undergoes the process of partition, the household property (*ekum erang attar*) is divided, mostly equally, among the sons including the adopted son, if any, of the deceased man. The cultivable land, cash money and heads of cattle are equally shared among them. However, the eldest brother may sometime get a bigger share because he is said to have brought up the younger brothers like a father. Sometimes the shares may be proportionate to the size of the ensuing household of each brother. If the household owns an elephant, which is the case for the more prosperous households among the Pagro-Mishing, one of the brothers may keep it and compensate the other brothers according to the value of the animal. The household utensils are divided equally among the brothers, but the utensils which were received as marriage gifts by each brother and his sons are treated as exclusive property of the respective brothers. The pesonal effects are, however, not subject to any division. In case of the deceased son, his share goes to his sons. The house and the granary are shared according to the size of the respective households, although after sometime each *erang* constructs a new house for its own use. The debts incurred by the household are also shared equally. The women have no right in the household property. Neither the daughter nor the wife has any right to inherit her father's or husband's property. A wife has, however, the right to maintenance and she lives with her sons when they establish their own households. A woman does not have any right in her husband's property even when she is divorced. A woman has no right in the *aalig* (bride wealth) money which may be negotiated at the time of her daughter's marriage. It is the right of her husband, or in his absence, of her husband's brothers to keep the *aalig* money. So the rights in the economic resources of the household are exclusively vested in the male members of the household, and among the male members also, they are vested only in those who belong to the senior generation. So long the father is alive, as we have already noted, a son has no right to demand any share in the household property.

ORGANIZATION OF DOMESTIC WORK

Though the Pagro-Mishing domestic group is composed of a plurality of interrelated conjugal dyads which are the nuclei of familial life yet it operates as a highly cohesive unit of social organisation with precise division of labour among its members. There is a near integration of the family life and its economic enterprises.

The allocation of the economic roles in the Pagro-Mishing family is precisely defined in terms of age, sex and generation by which various members of the domestic group are placed in specific kinship positions. The goods and services are produced and consumed directly for and by the domestic groups. Basically nothing is produced for exchange outside the domestic group, nor the services for the production brought from outside the domestic group. Thus in the economy of the Pagro-Mishing, based on agriculture, major efforts of the domestic group are concerned towards the maintenance of the domestic group. The members of the domestic group work for it and not for any other individual or unit outside it. In other words, the domestic group provides the work team and is the source of labour.

The functioning of the domestic family may be analysed from two dimensions. One pertains to the activities of running the household in its day-to-day existence and the other relates to those activities which are carried out outside the confines of the household. These two dimensions may be termed as internal dimension and the external dimension of domestic activities. The internal dimension of the domestic activities are not directly related to the procurement of the needs of the family but are concerned with the processes and preparation of the goods that have been procured by external activities. Both these activities are interlinked, though distinct in their aims. So the external activities relates to production and the internal activities relate to utilization of the goods.

The activities and the role allocation of the members of the domestic family are clearly earmarked in both these dimensions of activities as discussed below.

DIVISION OF LABOUR

External Dimension of Domestic Activities

Agriculture, fishing and looking after the livestock constitute the main activities in the external dimension of the domestic activities. Of all activities it is agriculture in which the maximum amount of time and labour of the members of the household is invested.

Agriculture requires the labour of the entire domestic group except the infants, the infirm and the aged members. The productive activities are well defined in terms of gender differentiation.

The ploughing, levelling of land and breaking the clods are done by men. Sometimes boys of 15 or 16 years of age may also plough the fields. The sowing of seeds is done mainly by men, though when there is need of extra hands, women may also do it. Weeding is done exclusively by women, including the young girls of the household. Harvesting of the crops is shared equally by men and women. The harvested crop is tied in bundles and then carried to the granaries by the male members only. This is a very strenuous job and it takes several days for the menfolk of the household to convey it to the granaries. Once the crop is stored in the granaries, the male members do not have any further chores to do with it.

Fishing forms another important productive activity. For day-to-day consumption, fishing is done by men only, who fish with the help of cast nets, dragnets or traps. In the summer time, fishing is done with the help of spares. When fish is required in larger quantity, many men may cooperate in the activity, otherwise only one man is allocated this job. Women also do fishing but only occasionally and also only using various types of basket traps.

Although the Pagro-Mishing households own a number of cattle, but they do not have any use for milk. The value of cows is lower and only the bullocks are cared for properly. A household does not have a cattle pen and they are generally tethered under the platform of the dwelling house. The cattle are looked after by the boys of the household. Other domestic animals like pigs and fowls are looked after by the women.

Thus, the agricultural work is done by members of both the sexes, and there is a precise allocation of their roles. Both men and women contribute their labour in this productive activity although the men have heavier load of work to perform,

Now, it is true that the Pagro-Mishing have well defined sex roles pertaining to agriculture and other external productive activities. However, in the large domestic groups which may be composed of a number of nuclear families, the distribution of, or the allocation of specific chores amongst the various members of the household is essential. In the absence of allocation of specific tasks to different members of the household, it would be difficult to manage the household activities efficiently. Therefore, in a large household the head of the *erang* generally divides different tasks among the members who then confine their activities to the assigned chores only. Thus in a joint family household, men in the senior generation, if they are not very old, may be made to look after either agriculture or fishing or repair of house and granary or the household tools and implements. In this way, one of the elder male is made responsible for procuring fish for daily consumption, while another man will be made responsible for the organization of the entire agriculture operation. He decides for each crop: which fields will be cultivated and which will be left fallow. He also assigns tasks like ploughing to other male members in the household. He is the man in the household who knows how much paddy and other cereals are produced and what exactly is the situation of paddy in the store. Similarly another man may be assigned the exclusive task of looking after the elephant, belonging to the household, he feeds the elephant, drives the elephant cart and also takes the elephant, whenever it is hired by any contractor.

The distribution of important task to various male members of the household is done not by a formal procedure but develops gradually over a period of time and is accepted tacitly by all concerned. Since the boys of the family help in most of the agricultural tasks, some of them are gradually given more and more responsibilities by their seniors i.e. men in the father's generation, and when they are grown up married men, they fully take over the work from the men in the parental generation. Usually the eldest man in the son's generation is the one who looks after the agricultural activities of the entire family. In a large joint family, the productive activities are mostly done by men of the middle generation (sons) and the junior generation (grandsons), whereas the senior generation (parental) men gradually become free to indulge in social activites. Thus, as I indicated above, the factors of generation and age are important in the allocation of roles in the domestic group. The males of the parental generation have power and authority, and the males in the son's generation contribute greater amount of labour in performance of the economic chores for the household.

Internal Dimension of Domestic Activities

Food processing and preparation, looking after the infants and children, washing utensils and clothes, looking after pigs and fowls and spinning and weaving are the most important activities that pertain to internal dimension of the household activities. The internal dimension of the household chores is managed exclusively by the women of the domestic group. The organization of work among the women is based on age and generation by which they are positioned in the kinship structure.

The staple food of the Pagro-Mishing is rice. But no household stores any measure of rice, instead it is paddy that is stored in the granaries. Threshing of paddy is done by women in the front porch of the granary with the help of cattle or sometimes by beating with wooden staff. Threshing is done once in a few days, but husking of paddy is almost a daily affair. Each day, early in the morning a certain quantity of paddy is husked. The quantity is equivalent to the daily need of the household. Husking is done by the young married women, though occasionally unmarried girls may also do it. When a woman has married sons or married nephews (HuBrSo) she does not do this work. It is specifically allocated to the women who are in the position of younger daughter-in-law in the domestic group. Cooking, which is done for the whole household in one place, is done exclusively by the women who belong to the daughter-in-law category. Sometimes the older women (mothers-in-law) may also do it, but only when the younger women are busy in the agricultural fields. Washing the cooking utensils, fetching water from the water source and collecting and bringing fire- wood is also done by the younger women. The dishes used by men are washed by the women, but the women wash their dishes personally. The elder women (mothers-in-law) prepare *apong* (rice beer) which requires a high degree of experience and competence. The younger women also lend a hand in preparing its ingredients. However, the older women keep busy with the care of infants and children. When the women are free from the domestic chores and are also not busy in agricultural activities, they tend the silk worms, or keep busy in spinning yarn or weaving of cloth on the looms which are fixed under the platform floor of the house. The older women also weave thick cotton blankets which is usually given as a gift to the daughter at the time of her marriage. The unmarried girls of the household always keep busy with the loom and generally weave silken cloth. The aim of every unmarried girl is to prepare as much dress material as possible before her marriage because once she becomes a daughter-in-law of a family, her entire time is spent in the household chores. Besides these domestic chores, child care is exclusively done by the women. A woman looks after her child until the age of two or until the time of weaning. Until this age, an infant is almost inseparable from the mother who tucks it on her back and carries it whenever she goes. After this age, an infant is looked after by the infant's female siblings who may be just seven or eight years old. The older women (child's grandmother) may also look after them at this stage. The men have absolutely no interest in looking after their children.

Among the Pagro-Mishing, there is no concept of wage labour. The domestic group is the unit of production, consumption and labour force. However, in times of dire need, a household may requisition the help from other households of the village. A need is felt when a household is unable to finish its important agricultural work through its own work force. Such occasions occur when the crop is not harvested and there is danger of impending floods. Under this genuine need, a household requests all other households in the village to cooperate in its work. Each household then sends a young man or woman on an appointed day and the entire work is finished in one day. This reciprocal cooperation in economic activity is called *rikbo*. The cooperation in *rikbo* is obligatory for every *erang* in the village, even during the peak agricultural season. There is no payment for this work and at the end of the day, all those who join in the work force are entertained with *apong* by the host *erang*.

From the above discussion it is clear that the members of the domestic group have well defined allocation of economic roles.

However, in terms of labour contribution, the share of the men is less as compared to the women of the household. The women share almost equally the agricultural chores. They do weeding, harvesting, threshing and pounding. In the internal dimension, the women do entire processing and cooking, besides they also look after the infants and children, fetch water and fuelwood, prepare *apong*, wash utensils and, over and above this, they also tend silk worms, and pigs and poultry. On the other hand the male members have no internal domestic chores to perform. They remain busy during the agricultural season and rest of the time they have few gainful activities to perform. The women, on the contrary, have no leisure time or slack season. However, among the men, it is the son's generation and among the women, those married women who are in the category of daughter-in-law who have the largest work share in the household economy. The men and women in the senior generation have greater access to power and control of resources and relatively lesser contribution of labour in the economic activities of the household.

Pattern of Consumption

The domestic group is the unit of consumption. The head of the household controls the resources and also manages the income that accrues to it by selling of cash crops, and hiring of elephants, if the household owns one. Of course, the head has no control over the individual wealth.

The entire agricultural products are kept in the granaries and are utilized for the entire household. The meals of the household are cooked at one place irrespective of its size. There is no independent allocation of foodgrain to anyone of the nuclear family units of the household. The major portion of rice crop is used as food, but a huge quantity of rice is consumed in preparing *apong* which is drunk in great quantity by the men, women and children along with meals and also when they return from the day's work in the evening.

The food, no doubt, constitutes the major part of the expenditure from the resources of the domestic family. There are some other expenses that have to be met with from the common funds. One of the major items of expenditure is the performance of various rituals which are solemnized periodically. The *urom apin* (ancestor-worship) involves huge expenditure in terms of paddy. The ceremony involves feeding a large number of agnates and at least one man from each household in the village. Other ceremony like *taleng uii* is also performed in the same manner. The household incurs expenditure in the marriage of the men and women of the household. The marriage feasts are usually large scale affairs and hence involve heavy consumption of rice for feeding the guests, as well as for preparing *apong* which is also consumed in large quantity.

Some basic necessities of the members are also met with from the common pool of the household. These include expenditure on clothes which are bought annually at the time of *Bihu* (spring festival). The women members usually do not get any clothes from the household funds because they make cloth for their use on the looms. The individual members of the domestic group use their personal income for buying those things for which the household funds cannot be utilized. Thus, cigarettes, tobacco and shoes etc. may be bought by a person from his own income. But a married person generally uses his self- earned money on his spouse and children and not only on himself.

The Pagro-Mishing domestic group is a production and consumption unit. The domestic economy is geared to satisfy the basic necessities of the members of the group. Their maximum efforts are to produce only that much which they can consume themselves. The total economic activity of the Pagro-Mishing is centred around the domestic family in which there is hardly any place for individual entrepreneurship.

9

The Marriage System : Rules of Exchange

The Pagro-Mishing are divided into two exogamous moieties, each one of which is composed of a number of clans. By extending the concept of consanguinity, the Pagro-Mishing regard all the clans of one's moiety as nonmarriageable categories making it the widest boundary of exogamy. Hence it is marriage alliance which provides the articulating link between the clans belonging to the opposite moieties thereby creating an organic solidarity between the discrete segments of the Pagro-Mishing society. I will now concern myself with an analysis of the rules of marriage and their relationship with the structural framework of society. This will be done by analysing the empirical situation, in order to find the relationship between it and the normative model of marriage system by which the Pagro-Mishing conceptualize it.

Dual Organization and Exogamy

The Pagro-Mishing dichotomize their society into two clear categories of kins and affines. The members of one's own moiety are kins and the members of the opposite moiety are affines. The two moieties, *Pegu* and *Doley*, are therefore interrelated to, and interdependent upon one another as affines. And hence through the principles of consanguinity and affinity, the entire Pagro-Mishing society is organically structured. The idioms of kinship and affinity also provide the conceptual basis of an individual's interactional activities in the society. In the real life situations, these ties provide the basis of his day-to-day interpersonal relationships with other members of the society. It is of interest to recall that in spite of the existence of patrilineal descent groups, the Pagro-Mishing do not recognize any consanguineal kin outside it even through matrifiliation. Relatives through the non-lineage parent viz. the mother, belong to the affinal group of relatives. The Pagro-Mishing, consequently recognize no right and jural status of an individual in his mother's clan or lineage. Among the Pagro-Mishing thus this right which has been termed as 'residual claim' of a 'non lineage kin' (Goody 1973 : 42) or the rule of 'complementary filiation' (Fortes 1953 : 33) is not present because they have clear structural divisions between the kin and affines on the basis of their moiety affiliations.

The classification of the entire society into two kin of relatives -- *birrang* and *igo-magbo* ---thus, provides the blueprint for the interactional pattern between the members of the society, and the concepts of kinship and affinity encompasses the entire society. In other words, conceptually all Pagro-Mishing stand in relation to one another either as kinsmen or as affines and no member of the society is regarded as a non-relative. It is, therefore, a usual practice among the Pagro-Mishing to ascertain the type of relationship that may exist with another person. Thus, for instance, when they encounter a stranger the first question that is put to him is somewhat like this, '*Tani ae Mipag ?*' (man or stranger ?) [The Mishing identify themselves as *Tani* (man) and rest of the humankind is called *Mipag]*. If the other person identifies himself as *Tani*, then the next question is '*Igo-Magbo ae Birro ?*' (affine or a kin ?). This they find out by referring to their respective clans. Once the correct identity is established between them, they interact and address each other accordingly. If the two belong to affinal clans, they immediately address each other as *Igo* or *Magbo;* the younger one addressing the older one as *Magbo* who reciprocally addresses the younger one as *Igo.* Similarly, when boys and girls of distant villages meet, especially during a marriage ceremony, the first thing the boys would like to find out is the correct relational positions of the girls. This is very important because boys and girls of the affinal clans have joking relationship whereas making any lewd remark for a girl of one's own moiety is considered reprehensible. The pattern of public behaviour is thus based on the recognition of the two kinds of relatives in the society. Hence the conceptualization of the entire society into kin and affinal categories not only determines the rules of marriage but also provides the model of social interaction to the Pagro-Mishing at the societal level.

The rule of exogamy entails exchange of women between the two moieties which stand in affinal relationship. Exogamy is therefore essentially a rule of reciprocity between the two divisions of the Pagro-Mishing society which are complementary halves, and the manifestation of reciprocity between them is the existence of symmetrical exchange of women. The perpetual affinal relationship between the *Doley* and *Pegu* moieties are reflected in their dichotomous terminological classification of the entire society as well. The affines, as we have noted, are collectively called *igo-magbo*, the implication of which is that conceptually one marries only an individual who is already an affine i.e. one who belongs to the *igo-magbo* category of relatives.

The direct or symmetrical exchange between the moieties makes them 'wife givers' and 'wife takers' simultaneously. Since the ramification of the classificatory kinship and affinal ties encompasses the whole society, there is always a pre-existing affine tie between the prospective spouses. Although the existence of the exogamous moieties defines the outer limit of the choice of a spouse, the Pagro-Mishing have certain prescribed rules of marriage which enjoin them to marry only certain relatives who belong to a definite kin type. In other words, the Pagro-Mishing have positive rules of marriage, and their kinship system has the characteristics of 'elementary structure' (Levi-Strauss, 1969 : XXIII) [1]. This system of positive rules of marriage has been called 'marriage alliance' or simply ' alliance' by Dumont (1957 : 3).

The Rules of Marriage

The positive rule of marriage in the Pagro-Mishing society is that a man and a woman should marry the daughter or the son, as the case may be, of his or her *Kaki* and *Nyanni.* In other words it means that a woman may marry a man who is related to her as *Magbo/Igo* and a man may marry a woman who is related to him as *Igne/Mamo.* The kinship term Kaki, as we have seen, refers to mother's brother, father's sister's husband and the spouse's father. Similarly the term *Nyanni* refers to father's sister, mother's brother's wife and the spouse's mother. The mother's brother's son and the father's sister's son are both called reciprocally *igo* and *magbo* and the daughters are called *igne* and *mamo.* Thus mother's brother's son and daughter, and father's sister's son and daughter i.e. the bilateral cross-cousins are *Igo-Magbo* (male cross- cousin) and *Igne-Mamo* (female cross-cousin) of each other. This clearly shows that the marriage is preferred between the bilateral cross-cousin as shown in the following diagram (Fig. 9.1).

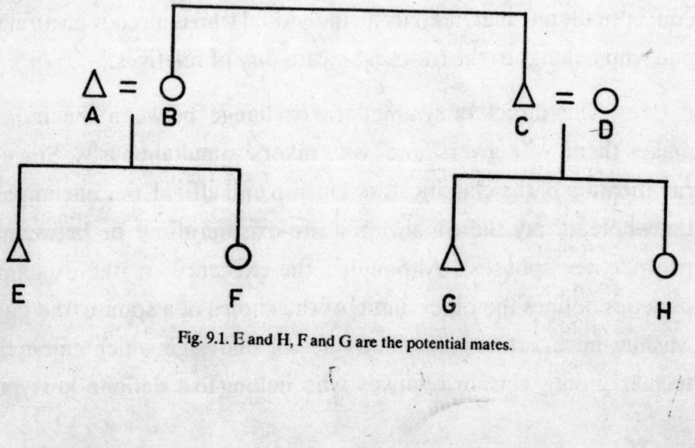

Fig. 9.1. E and H, F and G are the potential mates.

E and F address C, their mother's brother, as *Kaki,* and D, the mother's brother's wife, as *Nyanni.* Similarly G and H address B, their father's sister as *Nyanni* and A, the father's sister's husband, as *Kaki. Kaki* is thus father's sister's husband as well as mother's brother and *Nyanni* is not only father's sister but also mother's brother's wife. The cross-cousins address each other by reciprocal terms. Both the pair of brother and sister, E and F, and G, H, address the son of their father's sister, and mother's brother as *Magbo* if older than self and *Igo* if younger. The daughter of MoBr and FaSi is addressed as *Mamo* if older and igne if younger than self. Thus these kinship terms have reference to the following relatives :

Kaki = Mother's Brother; Father's Sister's Husband; Husband's Father; Wife's Father.

Nyanni = Father's Sister; Mother's Brother's Wife; Husband's Mother; Wife's Mother.

When the Ego is older than the referred person	*Igo*	=	Mother's Brother's Son; Father's Sister's Son; Wife's/Husband's Younger Brother
	Igne	=	Mother's Brother's Daughter Father's Sister's Daughter; Wife's/Husband's Younger Sister.
When the Ego is younger than the referred person	*Magbo*	=	Mother's Brother's Son; Father's Sister's Son; Wife's/ husband's elder Brother
	Mamo	=	Mother's Brother's Daughter; Father's Sister's Daughter; Wife's/Husband's elder sister.

What emerges from this rule is that a man/woman may marry his/her *Kaki's* and *Nyanni's* daughter/son; provided that they are related to each other as *magbo* and *igne* and not as *igo* and *mamo*. This clearly shows that the age of the husband should be more than that of his wife. Thus, not only the bilateral cross-cousin marriage is the ideal among the Pagro-Mishing but the relative age of prospective spouses is also important.

The ideal rule, however, is not so strictly followed as to limit the choice of the spouse to the real FaSiDa or MoBrDa. However, the Pagro-Mishing extend the kinship terms *igo/magbo* and *mamo/igne* to include the children of their classificatory *Kaki* and Nyanni. The exact genealogical reckoning of the relationship between the spouses is not so much emphasized as the categorization of the potential spouses in preferential kin types within the affinal group. The Pagro-Mishing kinship terminology categorises all individuals of same sex and generation in the wife exchanging group by a single term. It is, therefore, not the genealogically determined kin but anyone within the same kin type that qualifies to be an ideal spouse.

Although the preferred spouse should be from the *Magbo/Igne* category, this ideal pattern may not be adhered to in all the cases. Marriage with affines of the adjacent generations is also possible and it does take place. In such cases a man may marry his SiDa, (generally classificatory) or FaBrWiSi or even a classificatory MoSi. The main emphasis that is laid in the Pagro-Mishing affinal relationship is on the perpetuation and continuation of exchange of women between two lineages. This implies, that if a man takes a wife from a lineage, sooner or later his lineage would want to give back a woman to that lineage. This mode of exchange of women, which does not necessarily take place immediately, is to perpetuate the *igo-magbo* (affinal) relationship over generations between two lineages.

During the course of my fieldwork, a few cases were also recorded in which marriage was contracted between the affines of adjacent generations. However, such marriages are not regarded as serious breach of norms. Let me cite some cases of such marriages to elucidate the point.

In one village three related men Pakali, Kula and Gela have married three women who are parallel cousins and belong to same *erang*. (Fig. 9.2)

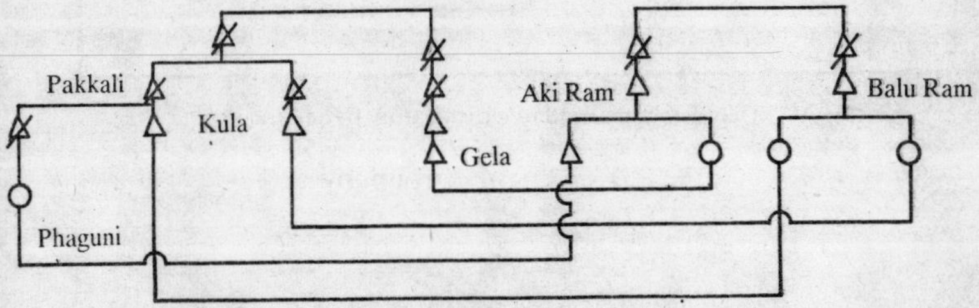

Fig.9.2. Asymmetrical marriage alliances in kumarbari.

Two of the men, Pakali and Kula shown in the diagram (Fig. 9.2) are second cousins and Gela is their FaFaBrSo SoSo. All three have married the daughters of Baburam and Aki Ram who are first cousins. Pakali's elder brother's daughter Phaguni, is also married to Akiram's son. Thus the spouses of Gela and Phaguni belong to their first ascending generation and interestingly, belong to same *erang* from which their own FaBrWi (own for Phaguni and classificatory for Gela) has come. Before this marriage, the relationship between Phaguni and her husband was that of classificatory *Kaki (*MoBr) and *Eime* (SiDa), and between *Eime* Gela and his wife was that of classification *Yaue*

(MoSi) and *Awo* (So). In another case two sisters have married two men who are related to each other as classificatory FaBr and BrSo (Figure 9.3)

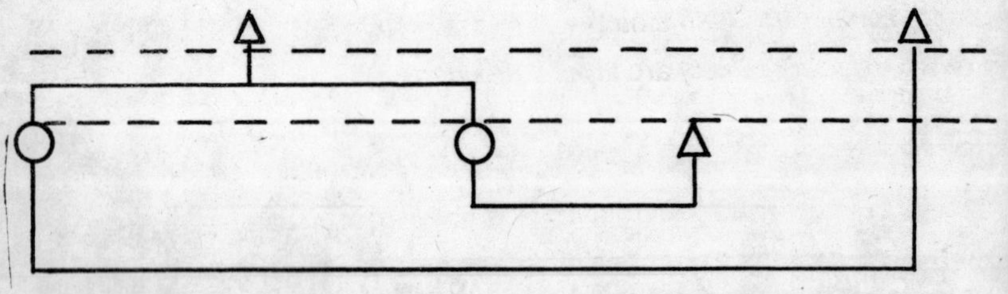

Fig. 9.3. Two sisters married to classificatory father and son.

Such marriages are however, not viewed as the breach of rule by the Pagro-Mishing, they are regarded only anomalous. The frequency of such non-preferential marriage is, however, not high. Moreover, an arranged marriage seldom involves persons of adjacent generations. Such irregular marriages are confined to those cases where a boy and girl decide on their own to marry after a period of courtship. Such marriages fall within the self-arranged category of marriage.

Ideally then the preferred spouses among the Pagro-Mishing are bilateral cross-cousins but so long the spouses belong to marriageable categories i.e. the opposite moieties, their marriage is recognized to be regular even if they belong to adjacent generations.

Rules of Marriage and Kinship Terminology

The Pagro-Mishing social system is fully reflected in their kinship terminology which classifies their kinship universe into two categories. At the level of the total system they conceptualize their system to be composed of two kinds of people : kinsmen and affines. The kinsmen are collectively referred to as *birrang* (i.e. brothers) and the affines are referred to as *igo-magbo* (i.e. brothers-in-law). Thus the members of one's own moiety are brothers *(birrang)* and the members of the opposite moiety are affines *(igo-magbo*).

The organization of their society into two intermarrying exogamous moieties with symmetrical cross-cousin marriage system is reflected in an extremely simple scheme of kinship terminology. The chief characteristics of their system is the clear lineal differentiation that appears within three generations centred on Ego, with distinction of sex. The kinship terminology of each of these three generations clearly divides both agnates and affines into two categories. The following table gives the kinship terms (Table 9.1) followed by their explanation.

TABLE 9.1
The Kinship Terminology in Pagro-Mishing Society

Kinship Term		*Kin Type*
Tato	=	FaFa, FaFaBr, MoFa
Yoyo	=	FaMo,MoMo
Babu	=	Fa
Babatta	=	FaElBr
Baboi	=	FaYoBr
Yau	=	Mo
Yauatta	=	MoElSi,FaElBrWi

Yauoi	=	MoYoSi,FaYoBrWi
Biro	=	Br, FaBrSo, MoSiSo
Birme	=	Si,FaBrDa, MoSiDa
Awo	=	So, BrSo, SiSo (female speaking)
Ome	=	Da, BrDa (male speaking)SiDa (female speaking),HuBrDa
Eio	=	SiSo(male speaking)BrSo(female speaking)
Eime	=	SiDa(male speaking) BrDa (female speaking)
Uo	=	SoSo (male speaking) BrSoSo (male speaking), HuBrSo
Ume	=	SoDa(male speaking)BrSoDa (males peaking)
Nang	=	Wife
Milbong	=	Husband
Kaki	=	MoBrWi, FaSi, WiMo, HuMo
Magbo	=	MoBrSo, FaSiSo (older than Ego), ElSiHu WiElBr, HuElBr
Igo	=	MobrSo, FaSiSo (younger then Ego) Yo Si Hu, WiYoBrHuYoBr
Mamo	=	MoBrDa, FaSiDa, (older than Ego) ElBrWi, WiElSi, HuElSi
Igne	=	MoBrDe, FaSiDa, (younger than Ego) YoBrWi, YoBrWi, HuYoSi
Yameng	=	SoWi, BrSoWi (male speaking)HuBrSoWi
Kedan	=	SoWiFa, DaHuFa.(occasionally used by Si for her Br).
Kedan	=	SoWiMo, DaHuMo (occasionally used by a Br for his Si)

Analysis of Kinship Terms

The bilateral cross-cousin marriage being the ideal form of exchage of women between the two moieties, the cousin terminology clearly reflects this positive rule of marriage. The parallel cousins who belong to one's consanguineal category are equated with siblings *(biro-birme)* while the cross-cousins are treated as potential spouse. The positive rule of marriage as described above is that a man should marry the daughter of a man and his wife who are related to him as kaki-nyanni and whose daughter is therefore called *mamo* or *igne*. Similarly a woman should marry a man who is the son of a man and his wife whom she addresses as kaki-nyanni and hence that man is related to her as *magbo* or *igo*. The kinship terms for the cross-cousins are *mamo/igne* and *magbo/igo*. These terms are used for FaSiDa, MoBrDa and FaSiSo and MoBrSo respectively. In other words, *igo/magbo* and *mamo/igne* are simultaneously MoBr child and FaSi child. Correspondingly the kinship term *nyanni* is used for FaSi, MoBrWi, WiMo and HuMo and the term *kaki* is used for FaSiHu, MoBr, WiFa and HuFa. Thus the rule of bilateral cross-cousin marriage makes the FaSiHu and MoBr as one and the same man who is also the father of the spouse. Similarly FaSi and MoBrWi is one and the same person. These kinship terms are further extended to include other patrilateral collaterals in the descent group. Thus *kaki* is not only one's real MoBr but also any man whom the MoBr regards as a *biro* (brother) and their wives are referred as *Nyanni*. Similarly the terms for actual cross-cousins are extended to their classificatory *biro* and *birme* (i.e. brother and sister). The Pagro-Mishing, do not necessarily oblige a man to marry the daughter of his real *kaki-nyanni* but any one who falls in the category of *mamo-igne*, that is, any cross-cousin in the classificatory sense is a preferred spouse.

However, the term of address for WiFa(HuFa) is *attode* and for WiMo /HuMo is *ayode*. These terms of address have no extension and are used for real parents-in-law, although the terms of reference for them remain *kaki* and *nyanni*. The reason for individuation of the kinship terms of address is to distinguish the actual relatives from merely potential relatives. Likewise DaHu is addressed as *magbode* and the SoWi as *yameng*.

The rule of symmetrical cross-cousin marriage also makes it redundant to distinguish between FaFa and MoFa and between FaMo and MoMo. Thus the kinship term for the men in the second ascending generation is *Tato* and for the women it is *Yayo*. A person's FaFa is also his MoMoBr and FaMo is MoFaSi, hence both the paternal and maternal grand-parents have common terms. Similarly no distinction is made between the son's children and the daughter's children; both are designated by common kinship terms of *Uo* (males) and *Ume* (female).

The symmetrical cross-cousin marriage system also implies that the children of the brother and sister are the potential spouses and therefore the brother and sister stand as one of the potential parent-in-law of their child. Although relationship between the SoWiFa and DaHuFa is that of *igo* and *magbo* they may address each other as *kedan,* and each other's wife as *kedan-neng*. But a *kedan-neng* actually stands in the relationship of a sister. The terms *kedan* and *kedan-neng* are generally used for actual relatives. However, two men of opposite moiety may address each other as *kedan* though they may not be married at all; similarly a man may address his sister, usually a classificatory one, as *kedang- neng,* though she may not be married yet. These kinship terms of address are not very commonly used, nevertheless, they signify the model of exchange between the children of brother and sister. With dichotomous exogamous division, the Pagro-Mishing have no kinship term for WiSiHu, who is obviously Ego's brother (own or classificatory). But, of late, a new kinship term, borrowed from the Assamese people have become popular among the Pagro-Mishing. This term is *"Salpati"*. This term is used by two young men who may be of the same age and stand as brothers (classificatory) to each other. So the term *Salpati* has become common to identify the man who may be married to one's wife's sister.

From the above analysis of kinship terms and the rules of marriage, it is clear that the Pagro-Mishing have an "elementary structure".[1] The characteristic features of their marriage system is that they prescribe marriage between the individuals who belong to a 'predetermined category of relatives'. The preferred spouse is not a genealogically defined individual but is a member of a class which constitutes the kin type of marriageable relatives. This class of marriageable persons is defined by the kinship terminology. Thus the kinship terms *Kaki* and *Nyanni, Igo* and *Magbo*, and *Mamo* and *Igne* which define the marriageable class should be understood in a classificatory sense and not in the real genealogical sense. That is why the preferred spouse is determined not so much by a demonstrable and precise degree of relationship as by a classificatory relationship which creates an appropriate category of marriageable persons. It is therefore the entire category of the cross-cousins who are the possible spouses. It is also a rule that a man should marry his cross-cousin who is younger than him. So the equation of marriage between the cross-cousins is *Magbo* = *Igne* and not *Igo* = *Mamo,* although the latter are not forbidden to marry.

The bilateral exchange system of the Pagro-Mishing is a'restricted exchange' which according to Levi-Strauss are those systems "which effectively or functionally divide the group into a certain number of pairs of exchange units so that for any pair X-Y there is a reciprocal exchange relationship. The simplest form of restricted exchange is a moiety system" (1969:146). The concept of exchange, however, implies the perpetuation of relationship between the groups rather than individuals and marriages are established between corporate groups and not merely between individuals standing in any particular genealogical relationship (Needham 1962 : 12-14). Among the Pagro-Mishing exchange relationship is, by and large, a perpetual relationship between two subclans as they tend to seek a spouse in the same subclan with which they have pre-existing marriage alliance. The empirical data from Kumarbari clearly demonstrates that the two subclans *Gajera Doley* and *Gūpit Pegu* have a continuous alliance relationship over generations. In exchange relationship between the subclans they do not always emphasize the actual genealogical relationship between the potential spouses; it is the category of kin types which is important and not the actual *Magbo-Ignè* relationship which is sought in perpetuating the marriage alliance between the kin groups. The perpetuation of alliance ties between certain subclans is also reflected in spatial structure of marriage distance. In other words we find that marriage area is determined not by geographical propinquity of the potential affinal groups in the context of the total system but by the existence of those lineages which have perpetual alliance irrespective of their physical distance. This correlation is evident from the empirical data which is presented below.

Correlation Between Alliance Relationship and Marriage Distance

The empirical data consists of 194 marriages that were solemnized in Kumarbari village stretching over a period of three generations. Marriage of 134 men and 60 women belonging to the village took place during this period. Out of 194 marriages 33 persons married within the village and the rest 161 marriages were distributed in 25 villages. These 25 villages are situated at varying distances from Kumarbari---the nearest being about 1.5 Km. and the farthest about 50 Km. (Table 9.2.)

TABLE 9.2
Frequency of Marriage in Relation to Distance

Distance from Kumarbari	Number of Villages	Number of Marriages	Percentage of the Total	Remarks
Below 2 km.	3	53	32.97	27 with Sherpai village 22 with Pamua village
Between 3-5 km.	9	32	19.86	Not more than 9 marriages with any village
Between 5-10 km.	5	61	37.8	28with Ratanpur village 27 with Gajerá village
Above 10 km.	8	15	9.30	Not more than 4 with any village
Total	25	161	100.00	

It is interesting to note that the Kumarbari people have overwhelmingly favoured only four villages viz. Sherpai (2 km.) Barpamua (2 km.), Ratanpur (8 km.) and Gajera (12 km.). These four villages account for 104 (70.84%) marriages out of 161 that were concluded outside Kumarbari village. This fact is important because rest of the 21 villages are also inhabited by those households which belong to the affinal clans with whom marriage relations were possible but the Kumarbari households have shown a definite preference for only a few villages. Further, some of the villages with whom there are relatively few alliances are nearer in distance as compared to Gajera (12 km.) and Ratanpur (8 km.). Thus it is evident that it is not the geographical propinquity that determines thè area of marriage. The reason for concentration of marriage alliances in the few villages has to be sought elsewhere i.e. in the existence of 'subclan connubium'. By 'subclan connubium' I mean that certain subclans of the opposite moieties pair off to have perpetual marriage alliances. These subclans have continuous exchange of spouses, though it may not be done immediately. The ideal, as already mentioned, among the Pagro-Mishing is to seek a spouse only from those households or lineages with whom they already have marriage relationship. Thus if a woman has been married in one lineage, sooner or later, a woman of that lineage is sought by the wife-giver group. This clearly shows that among the Pagro-Mishing, who follow restricted exchange, choice of a spouse is not determined by geographical propinquity but the existing alliance relationships between the subclans.

In order of elucidate this point let me analyse the composition of the 'alliance villages' vis-a-vis the composition of Kumarbari village.

Kumarbari is inhabited by members of three subclans and the total number of households is 43 (Table 9.3). The break up of the 43 households is as follows :--

TABLE 9.3
Composition of Kumarbari Village

Sl.No.	Subclan	Number of Erang
1.	Gupit Pegu	21
2.	Gajera Doley	19
3.	Mili	3
Total		43

The total number of marriage alliances that were established is 194. The marriage alliances of these three subclans of the village were established with a number of affinal clans in the opposite moiety. In the following table (Table 9.4) the frequency of marriage alliances of the three Kumarbari subclans have been shown with different affinal subclans.

TABLE 9.4
Marriage Alliances of Different Subclans of Kumarbari

Subclans in Kumarbari Village	Subclans with alliance relationship	Number of marriage alliances
1. Gupit Pegu	1. Gajera Doley	78
(21 Erang)	2. Ledo Doley	1
	3. Ledang Doley	6
	4. Kumbang	4
	5. Kuli	2
	6. Kutum	2
2. Gajera Doley	1. Gupit Pegu	84

(19 Erang)	2. Gudang Pegu	7
	3. Dumdum Pegu	3
	4. Patir Pegu	3
3. Mili	1. Gupit Pegu	4
(3 Erang)		
Total 3	11	194

It is evident from the above table (Table 9.4) that three subclans of Pagro-Mishing of Kumarbari village have sought spouses for their household members from eleven subclans. The Gupit Pegu have married with persons from six subclans; the Gajera Doley have married from four subclans and the Mili have confined to one subclan only. Kumarbari households are mainly composed of two subclans viz., the Gupit Pegu and the Gajera Doley. Although as many as 11 subclans are involved in affinal relationship with Kumarbari villages, only two subclans, Gupit Pegu and Gajera Doley, are matrimonially linked in as many as 162 marriages. In only 30 cases, the Gupit Pegu and the Gajera Doley have sought the spouse from other subclans.

Thus it is quite evident from the empirical situation that Gupit Pegu and Gajera Doley form a sort of 'subclan connubium' though there is no negative sanction to marry in any other marriageable subclan belonging to the opposite moiety.

The formation of the subclan connubium is the result of the Pagro-Mishing ideology regarding marriage alliance. The Pagro-Mishing ideally negotiate marriage with only those households and lineage who are already joined by marriage alliance. They attach great importance to perpetuate the *'igo-magbo'* (affinal) relationship. Thus most of the negotiated marriages take place between those *erang* which have previous alliance relationship. It is important to note, however, that if the exchange of brides cannot take place in the same generation, it may be done in the next generation. The main idea is to 'return' a girl to the *erang* from which a girl has been 'taken'. This emphasis on the 'return of a girl' keeps the alliance relationship alive over generations. This preference for recreating marriage alliance with the same *erang* or lineage explains the concentration of marriages in only a few villages because these villages are inhabited by those subclans who have existing alliance relationships. It is thus clear that the system of restricted exchange creates perpetual alliance between the subclans and keeps the reciprocal exchange relationship between them alive by establishing new marriage ties. It is, however, not necessary that all marriages should be confined to the subclan connubium.New marriage relationships are created with other lineages which may subsequently develop into reciprocal relationship. These new marital unions are, however, within the prescribed rules since the spouses generally belong to the preferred category of cross-cousins. Thus the system of restricted exchange may create perpetual alliance relationship by forming a subclan or lineage connubium within the wider category of affines that may exist in the society. The continued existence of subclan connubium will, however, depend upon the basic modes of acquiring the spouse. If the marriage is arranged by the parents or elders, they may emphasize the existing alliance relationship in negotiating the marriage of their child. If, however, the choice is independently made by the young people, the existing relationship may be relegated to the background. Since the Pagro-Mishing allow marriage based on romantic love, they cannot be rigid with regard to the ideal of marrying within the fold of the subclan connubium. However, even the self - arranged marriages rigidly follow the rule of marrying a person who belongs to the affinal category, though not necessarily a person who may be related as a cross-cousin.

10

The Marriage System : Ritual, Moral and Jural Content

Marriage and its Ritual Significance

Marriage is a pre-condition for a normal state of life for every man and woman in the Pagro-Mishing society; normal not only biologically but also ritually. The Pagro-Mishing believe, as noted earlier, in the existence of life after death. Every person has a soul (*yalo*) which after being released from the body resides in *sine-mobo* (abode of the dead) from where it visits the descendants. Unless the soul reaches its abode it wanders in great agony and can never attain peace. It may also cause great harm to the living descendants. The soul, in order to be peacefully settled, has to be propitiated by the dead man's legitimate male agnatic descendants. Thus the soul of a bachelor or a man without a son can never attain complete peace, as they leave behind no descendants who would propitiate them. The cult of ancestor, as we have seen is the basis of Pagro-Mishing belief system. The ancestral spirits must be propitiated periodically by one's legitimate descendants to insure the welfare of the living descendants.

Thus, every person desires, first of all to have a son after marriage. Having a son assures continuity of the lineage (i.e. growth of the lineage) and also a legitimate place in the 'abode of the dead'. Therefore, the marriage assumes an extremely important place in the

Pagro-Mishing society, not only for the man who is getting married but also for his father and father's father, because only a son's son is ritually enjoined to offer sacrifices to the ancestral spirits of his deceased grandfather after the death of his father. It is only through marriage that a legitimate son is born and it is this son who propitiates the souls and offers ancestor worship (*Urom-Posum*) to the deceased father's father and father's father's father.

Marriage of the sons and daughters is the responsibility of the parents. Besides the ritual importance of having a son and grandson, marriage has economic importance as well. As discussed earlier, a married son does not establish a separate household after his marriage, so the marriage of a son brings in another member---a daughter-in-law- to the household's manpower. It is, therefore, not unusual to find boys being married in smaller households at a relatively young age. Where the size of a household is relatively large, the boys may be married relatively late.

The position of an unmarried girl in her natal family is transitional. She has to leave her natal family once she is married. A grown up girl is, no doubt, an asset in the family in terms of her economic contributions, but a daughter has some inherent liabilities for her parents. A grown up unmarried daughter, for instance, can become as embarassment to the family if she becomes pregnant. An unmarried mother creates many problems, mainly ritual, as already described. Besides, in the Pagro-Mishing society, the exchange of woman between the affinal groups, also implies that a daughter is exchanged for a daughter-in-law.

The Norms of Legitimisation of Marriage

Marriage among the Pagro-Mishing is both a ritual and social relationship which is ultimately validated by the domestic groups of the bride and the bridegroom by entering into certain transactions.

As we have noted, the Pagro-Mishing marriage involves generally those families which already have alliance relationships. Each marriage, nevertheless, has to be jurally validated. It is true that even in those societies where marriage is based on the prescriptive rules, each marriage alliance between the two affinal groups has to be validated by certain rituals of transactions which legitimize the union. The preexisting ties of affinal relationships are not themselves enough to legitimize the union, though they may be the prerequisites. We must, therefore, make a distinction between affinal ties and conjugal union i.e. marriage. Affinal ties may be a pre-requisite of conjugal ties, but they are not sufficient to validate the union. The distinction explains the presence of the norms that regulate marriage in one form or the other in various societies. If merely 'positive marriage rules' were enough, the institution of marriage would be redundant in such societies and there would be no distinction between sexual cohabitation, either ephemeral or enduring, between the prescribed spouses and a legitimately married couple. A marriage therefore involves socially prescribed norms by which the union is given public recognition. The Pagro-Mishing marriage also involves approval by socially accepted norms to validate it.

Bridewealth as the Basis of Validity

The Pagro-Mishing term for bridewealth is *aalig-murkong* which literally means "exchange silver" (*aalig*=exchange; murkong=silver). *Aalig*, as the term is popularly used, is the most important part of the Pagro-Mishing marriage. The payment of bridewealth is an absolutely essential condition for legitimising the marriage and it must be paid by the father of the boy to the father of the girl. This is a negotiable amount and is paid in cash. Unless the '*aalig*' money is paid, marriage is considered neither jurally nor ritually valid. The payment of and the acceptance of exchange-money, irrespective of the amount, means not only acceptance but also legitimization of the affinal relationship. If *aalig* has not been paid or has not been accepted, the implications are that such a union of a woman with a man is an unlawful union and not a valid marriage and their natal *erangs* have not become legitimate and legal affines. Ritually, it is believed that unless the girl has been formally given by her *erang* after the acceptance of *aalig-murkong*, the ancestral spirits of the man would not accept her as a legitimate affine and some calamity may befall the boy's family. This is the reason that even when the parents of the boy and girl are very keen to establish the marriage relationship, 'exchange money' has to be paid to the girl's parents, although this may be just symbolic and the amount may not be more than Re.1/-. But it must be paid and accepted.

The jural aspect of *aalig-murkong* implies the transfer of girl from her natal *erang* to the *erang* of her husband. In *midang* (arranged marriage) the *aalig* is settled beforehand. In case of an elopement, this is negotiated afterwards. The parents of the boy must make the payment of 'exchange money' to the girl's parents when *aalig* is settled after the elopement, within a reasonable period of time, usually within a month. It is the right of the father of the girl or her agnates to receive the *aalig* money. Even when a girl is married off by her widowed mother, *aalig* money has to be paid to the girl's male agnates and not to her mother. The amount of *aalig* in elopement marriages depends upon the willingness of the girl's family to enter into affinal relationship. If the girl's parents in a case of elopement do not wish to establish the relationship, they would not accept the *aalig*; and unless the *aalig* is accepted the union is not valid either ritually, or legally. So long the *aalig* has not been accepted, the parents of the girl have the right to bring back their daughter from her paramour's family, which has no jural right over her until then. But once the aalig has been paid and accepted, the parents lose their jural right over their daughter and she comes under the jural control of her husband's family. Thus the *de-facto* union of a boy and girl becomes *de-jure* union only after the exchange money has been paid and accepted.

The other essential ceremony connected with marriage is the worship of the bridegroom's ancestors who are propitiated to accept the new bride as part of their descendants' *erang*. This is done in a ceremony in the presence of the lineage elders when the lineage ancestors (*Gomin Bulla*) are invoked and their blessings are sought. This ceremony is conducted in the bridegroom's house. However, this ceremony can be conducted only after the *aalig* has been paid. The aim of the ceremony is to incorporate the bride within the ritual ambit of her husband's *erang*. After this ceremony, a woman becomes part of her husband's ritual group and ceases to be part of her own agnatic ritual group.

In the Pagro-Mishing society there are three ways in which marriage may be concluded. The ideal is represented by marriage which has been arranged by the parents of the bride and bridegroom. This is called *midang.* The second means of marriage is represented by those which fall in the category of 'self-arranged' or 'marriage by elopement'. This type of marriage is known as *dugla lanam.* The third way of marriage is called *solam lanam*, which means 'marriage by capture' or 'kidnapping of the bride'. This type of marriage is neither regular nor favourably approved and has an extremely rare frequency. I will now discuss the social and jural content of these ways of marriage conclusions to show the relationship between the basis of marriage and the role of domestic group, especially the role of the father, and other lineage kins in marriage transactions.

MODALITIES OF MARRIAGE

THE MIDANG MARRIAGE

Midang is the arranged marriage. It is negotiated by either the father or head of the *erang* of the boy and the girl. It is essentially a primary marriage for both boy and girl. Besides being the primary marriage, it is also restricted to only virgins. In other words, a girl who may have become pregnant before marriage, or one who may have eloped but was unable to live with paramour subsequently or the one who may be an unmarried mother, cannot have a *midang* marriage. It was narrated by many informants that in the former days, the bride used to wear a necklace of the flowers called *yamne appum* (bride's flower) a day before the marriage ceremony. If the flowers remained fresh till the marriage time, she was proved to be a virgin, but if the flowers withered away by that time, she was presumed to be unchaste, and her marriage would be unfruitful, and full of misfortunes if performed as *midang*. At present no one, however, seems to know which is the 'bride's flower' nor did I ever come across any midang marriage being solemnized according to this stipulation. This mythical belief only emphasizes that *midang* implies marriage of a chaste girl. As far as the boy is concerned, his premarital acts are not so important, except that he should neither be married nor a widower and nor a divorcee.

The *midang* marriage involves a number of pre-wedding ceremonies. They are as follows :

Betrothal *(Yamne Titkap)*

The search for a spouse is initiated by the boy's family and never by the girl's family, though they are also keen to have a good son-in-law. In the Pagro-Mishing society it is not difficult to find out all about a bride because of the well knit nature of the kinship and affinal ties. When a particular girl has been earmarked and selected, the father or the father's brother of the boy visits her *erang*. They take with them gift of a pitcher of rice beer (*apong*), areca-nuts and betel leaves. In the girl's *erang*, they formally propose to establish the relationship. Since both the families know each other owing to previous relationship, there is not much of searching regarding each other. They may generally talk about *aalig* though in the well acquainted families, this also becomes superfluous, almost a formality.

After *titkap* (betrothal), the prospective son-in-law goes to his fiancee's *erang* for a short spell of 'service'. This is known as *'magbo-dugnam'* (to serve for becoming a son-in-law).

Magbodugnam is an essential part of the *midang*. The traditional importance of this practice was to find out the industriousness of the boy. During his stay, he helps in the fields of his prospective father-in-law, may also go for ploughing, or harvesting or even for felling the trees. He helps the family in its daily chores of the season.

During his stay, which lasts five days, the boy is not treated as an honoured guest, though he is treated well. The boy also carries with him five packets of rice-beer powder. Each packet weighs about two kilogrammes.

During these five days the fiance and the fiancee also get ample opportunity to see each other. This is quite useful if the boy belongs to a different village. The Pagro-Mishing homestead, as we will recollect, is constructed in such a way that the boy and the girl can hardly get any lonely place inside the house for a chat. Moreover, they feel shy to talk openly. Most of my informants, who did a spell of this type of service, told that they felt very much ill at ease, even when they (the boy and the girl) knew each other. No presents are given to the boy at this time. The date of the wedding ceremony may be tentatively decided at this time.

Nowadays when educated Pagro-Mishing boys go for *magbodugnam* they are not required to work in the fields, rather they are treated as guests.

The time between *magbodugnam* and the wedding is mutually settled. If during this period, the betrothed couple meet and have sexual relationship which may result in the pregnancy of the girl, the wedding will not be performed according to *midang* specifications.

When the wedding date has been fixed, invitations from both the bride's and the groom's *erang* are sent to their married sisters and their husbands; married daughters and their husbands; and the mother's brother. In the village every household is invited. The lineage households are invited personally by the head of the *erang*.

All the affines and the kins of the groom who are invited bring at least one large pitcher-full of *apong* as a present. The groom's family needs a very large amount of rice beer, not only for their guests but also for sending it as gift to the bride's family. Therefore, this is in a way contribution to the groom's family towards the expenditure it incurs.

Rituals and Ceremonies in Midang

On the day of the marriage, a new staircase and a new platform is attached to the existing one. The new staircase and platform are not covered by the projecting roof of the house. The new platform and the staircase are used by the groom only when he descends from the platform house to go to the bride's place. The new staircase is known as '*Yame Makrang*' (Groom's staircase).

On the morning of the wedding day, the groom is given a ceremonial bath with water that has been fetched by little girls who have not attained puberty. When they bring water, they are ceremoniously received by the women of the bridegroom's family except his own mother. Marriage ceremonies including the ceremonial bath for the groom which takes place on the rearside of the house. The rearside of the house is regarded sacred; the ancestors are also worshipped here.

The boy is bathed by only married women who are his classificatory mothers. In other words, the wives of the agnates who are his classificatory FaBr may participate in this ceremony. Other women like sisters, sisters-in-law may simply apply a little oil on him. After the bath, he dons new clothes and he is helped in dressing up by only unmarried girls, who may be his real or classificatory sisters.

The bridegroom's sister-in-law do not participate either in bathing or in dressing him. The dress of the groom consists of a shirt, a dhoti, a headgear and some ornaments like necklace and bracelets. These ornaments are made of silver and beads and are used only at the time of marriage.

Once the bridegroom has been dressed, he is provided with two companion youths called '*yamgur*'. One *yamgur* is a male and the other a female. The *yamgurs* must be unmarried and their parents should be alive and they (*yamgurs*) must belong to opposite moieties i.e Doley and Pegu. The *yamgurs* are the constant companions of the bridegroom from this moment till the completion of the last ceremony connected with the marriage. The bridegroom and the *yamgurs* are then blessed by the elderly persons of his lineage and the village. After this they come out of the house, descending from the new platform and staircase. Once again they sit on the ground porch of the house. All the assembled persons also sit. However, the women do not come out of the house. Only menfolk are assembled here. The bridegroom and the *yamgurs* bow before the assembly. The elderly men of the lineage invoke the spirits of the heaven and the ancestral spirit of the groom. After the invocation is over, the beating of the drums start.

The father and the mother of bridegroom also do not come out of the house. They neither accompany their son, nor do they see him off for the bride's place. It is done by the bridegroom's father's elder brother and his wife or in their absence, by any lineage brother of the groom's father.

Throughout the ceremony the bridegroom and his companions (*yamgurs*) look extremely serious; the bridegroom even cries bitterly. The rationale for his crying is that now onwards he would not be a free young man and will not be able to move out at night to see his girl friends. It seems to be a great psychological moment for the boy - a passage from one status to another. The movement is dramatized by his doleful looks, bitter crying etc. which are of course, genuine.

The bridegroom's marriage party consists of his guests from other villages and one man from each household from his village. Unmarried young men and women of the village also join the party. Married women do not accompany the groom.

All along the way, drums and cymbals are played by the youngmen of the village. The drums and cymbals are the village property and are used only on ceremonial occasions.

Marriage Gifts

In *midang*, besides *aalig* some other gifts are given to the family of the bride. The rice-beer powder that is gifted at the time of *magbodugnam* is about 50 Kg. The final gift is made at the time of wedding. These gifts consist of at least one full-size castrated pig. The pig is meant for the sacrifice to the ancestors and for the feast. More than 150 packets of rice-beer powder are also given to them. Other things include a sizeable amount of dried fish along with salt and chillies and a large quantity of areca nuts. In some cases, the bride's family may also demand paddy for use in the marriage feast.

Ceremonies at the Bride's Place

The bride's relatives--- both agnates and affines are invited by her family. The relatives of the bride do not bring rice-beer (*apong*), instead, they bring some other gifts like utensils or clothes etc. for the bride.

The house of the bride is also decorated and a new platform and a staircase is attached to the existing one. If the marriage is intra-village, the persons at the bride's place are mainly her agnates (lineage members) because the villagers are divided on both the bride's and the groom's sides.

The guests at the bride's place arrive a day before the wedding and are entertained with *apong* and fried fish. A temporary thatched shed is made near her house which is meant to house the bridegroom and his party.

On the wedding day, the girl's household is in the grip of feverish activity. Huge quantity of *apong* is prepared for the day. Pork and fish dishes are also prepared. *Apong* is prepared by women and food is cooked by the men.

When the bridegroom's party has arrived near the bride's village they stop there. Then the drummers from the bride's village go there and escort the party to the temporary shed.

No sooner the groom's party reaches the village, than some rough play is enacted between the bride's party and the groom's party. This may include throwing of mud, cowdung and other garbage at the bridegroom's party. This is all in fun and no one seems to mind it. Abusive language is also used. The bride's party say that 'you have come to take the girl, but it will not be an easy thing'. In other words, to a stranger, it may look to be a real brawl, with everyone around inebriated, and shouting at the top of one's voice. But the reality is that it is the nature of relationship (affinity) that is being exploited by everyone. All through the show of hostility and fight, the bridegroom and his *yamgurs* sit quietly in their shed, covering their face with shawls and talking only when pressed to do so. The wedding party is presently entertained with *apong* and some other dishes. The bride herself may serve them. But she avoids to go to the place where the '*yambo*' (bridegroom) is staying.

There is no other ceremony at night. Dinner for the marriage party is not prepared at the bride's place. Instead, the guests are distributed amongst the village households where they dine and stay for the night. It is, in fact, the endeavour of every household to entertain some wedding guests and it would be deemed to be a great insult if no guest is allotted to a certain household. Thus the burden of looking after the guests is shared by the whole village.

The main ceremony is held on the next day in the afternoon. The local guests arrive after taking their lunch and are once again entertained with *apong* and '*pan-tambul*'. The bride, now dressed in new clothes, may herself serve the guests. On this day the bride may also present cotton or silken scarves to her intimate friends, as mementos. These are woven by the bride herself. At this time, the guests also give their presents to the bride's family. After sometime, the drums are played and one can see small girls going in a procession behind the drummers to fetch water to be used to bathe the bride. When they return, they are received by the bride's mother and bride's father's brother's' wives.

As the time passes and evening comes closer, the bride is given the ceremonial bath. For this ceremony she is requested by her brother or a cousin to go inside the house. At this point, the bride, who only a few moments ago was entertaining the guests and chatting to her friends, becomes pensive and starts crying. The aplomb with which she was conducting herself a little while ago, vanishes and she cannot refrain from crying. She talks to her friends and bids them good-bye. The bride cries hoarse if she has an intimate boy friend in the village. If her boy friend happens to be present there, she may go to him, catch hold of him or hold his feet, all the time crying and also muttering all about the good old days which they passed together. This may look a little absurd that a girl about to be married, confessing her youthful relations with her boy friend. But this is customary and may show the sentiments that get better of the person under emotional stress. This type of outbursts is watched by everyone silently and there is a nip of malancholy in the atmosphere, especially among her brothers and sisters.

Inside the house, the bride is bathed by her classifactory mothers (FaBrWi). Then she is dressed in new clothes by her unmarried sisters. After the bride's ceremonial bath, drummers from the bride's side descend the new staircase and proceed to the place where the bridegroom is housed. Lot of dancing is done by bride's people. The groom and the *yamgurs*, who flank on either side of the bridegroom, cover themselves fully and walk very slowly towards the bride's house. At the foot of the new staircase, the bridegroom is received by the bride's FaBrWi. When the bridegroom has arrived there, the bride's FaBrWi moves forward and lifts the veil from his face and then lightly lifts him above the ground, and then places an arecanut and *betel* leaf into his mouth. The *yamgur* are also given betelnuts. Then the bridegroom, followed by*yamgur* climb the new staircase and dip their fingers in the water in the pitcher which are placed on either side of the new platform. They are followed by the drummers.

The main wedding ceremony takes place in the rearside of the house, where the bride is already seated accompanied by her *yamgurs*- a male and a female belonging to opposite moieties. The bridegroom sits on the right side of the bride. They are blessed by the parents of the girl and her lineage kins. After some time a dish prepared of fresh fish, dry fish and rice is brought. Both the groom and the bride partake some morsels from the same plate and also offer apong to each other. Once they finish eating and drinking they bow before the assembled people

--- relatives of both the bride and the bridegroom and are blessed by every one for a happy married life. The ancestors of the girl are invoked and it is then ceremonially pronounced that the girl is now married to the boy.

After the ceremony, which is rather brief, is over, they come out of the house the bride leading the procession. Once again everyone sits on the ground where the other guests are already seated. The drums cease to play. The bridegroom and the bride also sit and then kneel fully, their heads touching the ground and their open palms facing upwards. The assembled people once again bless them. Whenever, the couple is blessed by invoking the ancestors and the Sun and Moon (*Donyi* and *Polo*) it is only the menfolk who utter the words, the women remain quiet.

The wedding ceremony thus consists only of invoking the ancestors; the sun and the moon, and other heavenly powers and eating from a common dish.

The departure of the bride with her husband follows soon after they have been finally blessed by every man present. The mother and grandmother of the bride do not come out of the house to see them off. The bride is also accompanied by two *yamgur* sometimes her younger brother may also accompany her.

If the groom's village is not very far, the marriage party reaches his village the same day. But if the distance is more and it takes two days to reach the bridegroom's village, then they may halt midway in some other village. During this halt, the bride must stay in a house belonging to her own clan. In other words, if she is Doley, she must stay in a Doley house. She is not supposed to stay in a house belonging to an affine till she has been ritually incorporated into her husband's clan.

When the marriage party reaches the bridegroom's village, they are received by the same women who had seen the bridegroom off the previous day. The women who receive them must be married with living husbands and children, that is, widows, divorced or childless women do not receive the couple. Here again, the couple is blessed by the assembled men. The ancestors of the bridegroom are invoked to accept the bride as a daughter-in-law in the house. Immediately upon arrival, the bride is given some light work to do. She may also be asked to serve '*apong*' to the guests. Later on she along with some other girls goes to the water source to fetch a pitcherful of water. At night, there is a feast given by the bridegroom's family for which a castrated pig is slaughtered.

At the bride's house also, after the departure of the marriage party, dinner is/hosted by them for their own guests. The pig which had been brought by the bridegroom is slaughtered for the feast.

The bridegroom and the bride return next day to the bride's house. On this occasion bridegroom's *yamgur* do not accompany him. Instead, he may be accompanied by his sister. This time they are received by the bride's mother. After staying a night, they again go back. The bride is now not accompanied by any of her relatives.

In case of the distant villages, when they make a return journey, the girl stays in the house belonging to her husband's clan. Now she is the wife and hence incorporated in the clan membership.

The bridal night has no special significance. But the cosummation of marriage takes places after the couple have paid a return visit to the bride's people. Since a Mishing house is not partitioned, the newly-wed couple also start their married life in the same long house where they are provided their *ope soar*.

Marriage Gifts to the Daughter

Thr bridegroom does not bring any clothes or jewellery for the bride or for any other relative. They pay only '*aalig*'; bring '*apong*', a pig and sometimes paddy besides dried fish and areca nuts.

The gifts to the daughter consist of a thick cotton woven mattress *(Gadu),* a pillow and a wooden box, filled with the bride's trousseau. In fact, the bride herself makes her trousseau which consists mainly of many pairs of silk dresses. Besides these many utensils are also given. The presents given by the guests also belong to the bride and are sent along with her.

The Post -Wedding Ceremony

There is a post-wedding ceremony which is known as *dune-gilaknam* and is performed shortly after the wedding. This ceremony is essential when it is a primary marriage for both the spouses. In this ceremony, the husband and wife together visit the wife's *erang* and take with them *apong* and a castrated male pig as a sacrificial gift which is offered to the wife's ancestors as the last offering from her. This ceremony is performed to mark the final break of the ritual ties of the bride from her natal *erang* after which she is no more under her ancestors. During their stay the visiting couple is entertained by the father-in-law and other *erangs* of the bride's 'lineage'. They stay in the bride's village for four to five days. This ceremony is performed either in the months of Bhado (August-September) or *Magh* (January-February) whichever follows immediatly after the wedding.

THE MARRIAGE BY ELOPEMENT (DUGLA LANAM)

Marriage by elopement is called '*Dugla Lanam*', which literally means to "marry by stealing". The Pagro-Mishing society fully recognizes a marriage by self-arrangement. Elopement is a regular form of getting one's beloved as the life partner. There is no opprobrium on elopement marriages and once it has taken place there is no distinction maintained either on the recognition of the status of the couple or the status of children born out of such marriages.

In elopement marriage the active part is obviously played by the principals viz. the boy and the girl themselves. Usually elopement marriages are confined to the same village or to the nearby villages. The spatial propinquity gives the boys and girls enough opportunity in their daily life to know each other and develop romantic friendship. But sometimes such elopements may take place even when the boy's and the girl's respective villages are quite far from each other.

Although apparently it seems that the boy and girl arrange their elopement independently, actually it is not so. However, the decision to get married is theirs. An elopement is possible only when both the parties viz., the boy and the girl are willing to cooperate. The initiative is taken by the boy. He proposes to marry the girl and if she too is willing then he goes ahead with his plan. As soon as he comes to know of the girl's consent he starts arranging for the elopement.

Jural Obligations of the Domestic Group in Elopement Marriage

However, elopement also implies an implicit consent of the boy's parents and the *erang* because ultimately it is the responsibility of the boy's parents, especially the father, to settle the concomitant formalities of elopement and to legalize the conjugal relationship. If the boy's parents are reluctant or unwilling to support the boy's plan then it is next to impossible for the boy to elope with the girl, because the legitimization of the marriage is possible only upon the two *erangs*---that of the boy and the girl ---on agreeing on the payment of *aalig*. The responsibility of the act is deemed to be on the boy's *erang* and not on the boy alone.

However, the boy may not tell his intentions to his parents directly. He may let them know it through his sister-in-law or may confide in his mother. When the parents come to know about their son's intentions and give their approval it becomes their responsibility to negotiate with the girl's father after the elopement.

Nevertheless, the whole affair from planning to execution, is kept a complete secret. It is known to the principal actors, and the boy's parents and only a few of his friends' the girl's *erang* must not know about the elopement, otherwise they can foil their daughter's efforts. Elopement by a girl is considered an infringement of the rights of the parents over her.

When the whole plan has been finalized, the boy picks out one of his relations living in some distant village as a secret hideout immediately after the elopement. A distant place is usually chosen so that they may not be caught. The boy does not bring his girl friend directly to his own house. Sometimes his friend may also help him in his adventure. On the appointed day the boy and girl slip away to their premeditated rendezvous.

Within a short time, the news of elopement becomes well known throughout the village. Of course, it does not create a great commotion except in the *erang* of the girl. When the news has spread, it is the obligation of the boy's *erang* to inform the girl's *erang* about the elopement. The father of the boy and one or two other close lineage kins visit the girl's family and formally request her parents to give their daughter as his daughter-in-law. The girl's family is apparently much perturbed because the girl has gone against the wishes of her parents. This is not treated so if the girl's parents also approve of the boy. But if they do not like the boy or his family, they will not feel happy about it. They do not like to be ignored by their daughter, and therefore usually the boy's father may be curtly treated. Despite the resentment and anger of the girl's parents, the boy's father,and his *erang* insist on taking her as their son's wife. In the meantime, girl's brothers and cousins may go to all the suspected places in search of the run-away couple. If both the parties are adamant on their respective stand, it can result in a stalemate. The boy's side, which is genuinely inclined for this marriage and the relationship and yet not being acceptable to the girl's family, may also feel insulted, because the boy's family thinks that by not accepting the relationship their social status is being looked down. They argue with the girl's party that they too stand in the category of affinal-relationship (*igo-magbo*) and if the relationship is formalized there would be no harm done to either party. 'The girl has to be married, then why not in our own family? they ask.

If personal negotiations fail then a council of village elders is called. This assembly is known as *'Orai-binam'*. The *orai-binam* takes place at the girl's house. In this gathering both boy's and girl's side speak and request the assembled men to decide the matter.

In the *'orai-binam'* the girl's side, if agrees to the relationship, speaks out the amount of money they would take as 'exchange money' (*aalig*). This may be any amount. The amount depends on the willingness or resentment of the girl's side. If her *erang* is adamant, only two courses are open for the boy's father---either to return the girl, or to keep her against her parents' wishes and to agree to pay *aalig* which may be exorbitantly high. Despite the show of hot tempers on both the sides, such cases rarely turn into physical quarrels. Of course, for sometime the relationship may remain strained, but ultimately they are all smoothened out.

Let me cite some cases of elopement in order to illustrate the process of the negotiations and their resolutions.Gorya, son of Bapi Ram Pegu, eloped with his girl friend, the daughter of Pagum Doley. Both belonged to Kumarbari. Their families were not on good terms for some time due to certain reasons and when the elopement took place, the girl's family was very much annoyed with Bapi Ram's *erang*. This boy had already attempted to elope with this girl thrice before he was finally successful. Since the boy is not considered handsome and he is quite lazy and belongs to a relatively poorer *erang*, the girl's father never wanted to establish any relationship with his family. When the boy ultimately eloped with her, negotiations were started. But the girl's father firmly told them that under no circumstances would they make them their actual affines. The matter lingered on for many days. In *orai-binam* no decision could be taken, because girl's parents were not willing to validate the affinal ties at all. So ultimately the boy's father was advised by the assembly to ask his son to return the girl, and much against his wishes, Gorya persuaded her to go back to her parents. This happened after 15 days of the elopement. When she returned to her family she was severely beaten by her brothers.

In another case from Kumarbari village again, great resentment was shown by the parents of a girl when she eloped with her friend. Phaguni, the daughter of Pakkali's deceased brother eloped with Togun, son of Aki Ram Pegu. In this case the girl was already betrothed to a man from Kekuri village and the date of her wedding was also fixed. But a few weeks before the *midang*, the girl and her boy friend eloped. This caused great resentment in her family. The boy's father Aki Ram was keen to have her (Phaguni) as his daughter-in-law, so he approached the girl's *erang*, but they gave him cold shoulder and curtly told him to return their daughter. They even threatened Aki Ram with confiscation of his land and cattle. But as father of Togun, he told them that his son would not return the girl and he himself would be pleased to have her as his daughter-in-law, come what may. In the meantime, the girl's prospective father-in-law in Kekuri was informed about the elopement. He was still willing to marry his son to Phaguni, although she had eloped with another man.

The economic position of Phaguni's *erang* is quite sound but Togun's *erang* is not so well of. Therefore, the girl's *erang* thought it below their prestige to let their daughter marry Togun, because they wanted to marry her in a good erang and at the same time through '*midang*' which is considered more respectable.

In the *orai binam* ,village elders met and hot words were exchanged. Both the sides were equally adamant. But in such cases if the boy's family does not wish to return the girl, there is no other recourse for her family but to find her and bring her back forcibly. When Aki Ram said that his son would not like to part with her, the girl's father asked him (Aki Ram) to disown [1] his son so that they may deal with him directly. But this, he said, was impossible. He told them that once his son had done it, he would pay whatever they demanded. On hearing this in the assembly, the girl's uncle, as head of the *erang*, said that he would accept no less than Rs. 500/- and that too within five days, otherwise there would be no legitimization of the relationship. The assembly agreed to it. The sum of Rs. 500/- was rather on the higher side for Aki Ram, but he told them that he would pay it. Further, he was warned that if he failed to pay the specified amount, he would be turned out of the village. In order to raise the money, Aki Ram sold his bullocks, took some loan and finally paid Rs. 400/-. The girl's *erang* ultimately agreed to the reduced amount.

Yet in another case, a married man Lakhi Ram (35 years) tried to elope with a girl but both of them were apprehended before they could escape. In this case too the assembly met and they decided that the young man was in the wrong and so the girl should not be married to him. His father paid some fine on behalf of his son to the assembly.

Such cases of elopement are quite common. Some cases of elopement may cause great resentment whereas the others may be settled amicably. The resentment is too much when the families concerned are not on good terms. The girl's erang shows indignation specially if the boy belongs to a poor erang. As far as the girl's *erang* is concerned, its status is already known to the parents of the boy, otherwise they would not give their consent to their son to elope with the girl. Sometimes elopement marriage is the most convenient and also expedient for the concerned *erangs*.

In one such case, Noor, a young man of Pamua village eloped with Bhadon of Kumarbari. Both the families were of equal economic position and therefore there was no opposition from the family of the girl. However, Noor's mother did not feel happy because she wanted to perform *midang* for her son. But the boy did not want it and was able to convince his mother. Bhadon's father asked exchange money of Re. 1/only. The boy's father knew of his son's intention about a week before and he had given his consent to this effect.

In the elopement marriage, once the girl's parents give their consent to establish the relationship, boy's father or grandfather or any other elder male member of his lineage goes to the girl's house and present a pitcher full of *apong* and betal nuts to the girl's father or the head of the erang. Thereafter they settle the amount of *aalig* that is to be paid. The *aalig* may be paid immediately. or shortly afterwards.

The payment of *aalig* is the most essential act in the elopement marriages as well. Unless the payment is made, marriage can neither be legal nor ritual. The acceptance of money, irrespective of amount, means acceptance of the relationship also. If *aalig* has not been paid and the girl is kept against the wishes of her parents, it is believed that the ancestral spirits of the lineage may harm the boy's family. Therefore *aalig* must be paid. That is why, when the girl's family is also keen to establish the relationship, they have to accept the *aalig* money, however small it may be. It validates the relationship.

Rituals and Ceremonies in *Dugla Lanam*

There are no elaborate ceremonies when the marriage is by elopement. Once the '*aalig*' has been paid, the couple comes out of their hideout and goes to the boy's place. There, the boy's father invites all the heads of the *erang* of his lineage, who invoke lineage ancestors to accept the girl as a daughter-in-law of the *erang*. No sacrifices are offered. The guests are entertained with *apong* only.

Here it may be pointed out that the expenditure involved in the elopement marriage is minimal and if *aalig* money is also low then there is hardly any burden on the *erangs* of either the boy or the girl. Thus the economic aspect is the most important incentive that prompts even the parents to tacitly approve of their children's marriage by elopement.

A delayed ceremony, after a year or two may, however, be performed in these types of marriages. This ceremony is called *Gadung Kunam*. This ceremony is usually performed when the couple has fully settled and the girl has also become a mother. In this ceremony the boy's *erang* sends a pig and some *apong* to their daughter-in-law's father. Reciprocating, the father invites his daughter and the son-in-law and some of their relations to his place. They are entertained with *apong*. At this time, if the girl's parents wish, they may also give marriage gifts to their daughter. The purpose of the ceremony is to smoothen the '*igo-magbo*' relationship, which might have been strained due to this marriage.

Domestic Group and the Marriage of Unmarried Mothers and Pregnant Girls

In the Pagro-Mishing society where the institutionalized courtship is a common phenomenon, the frequency of unmarried mothers, pregnant but unwed girls or the 'caught-while-eloping girls' is not insignificant. Such girls cannot be married by *midang*. It is also rare that an unmarried mother would be befriended by a boy to elope for marriage. Such girls thus become a burden on their own domestic groups. It is, however, the duty of their domestic groups to arrange their marriage. The marriage of such women is performed quite distinctly from other types of marriages. The choice of a spouse for such a girl is very limited for it is generally men belonging to the economically poor *erangs* who would be marrying women of this category.

Midang is an expensive affair, so if an erang is poor, it cannot afford a *midang* marriage for its sons and daughters. In elopement *marriage*, firstly both the girl and the boy should be friends and willing to elope. But a boy can think of eloping with his girl friend only if his family has agreed to this. So if a boy from a poor *erang* wants to elope with a girl from a well off erang, the boy's father may not approve of it, because usually the girl's *erang* will not be willing to establish its affinal relationship with them and consequently it may demand a high *aalig* which may be beyond his capacity to pay. So in a poor *erang* the usual way to arrange the marriage of a son is by exchanging a daughter of the *erang* for a daughter-in-law or to utilise the daughter's aalig money for the marriage of a son. The exchange of a daughter implies that the *erang* has to accept a daughter-in-law without exercising any choice.

Therefore, the economic condition of a household is an important criterion in the Pagro-Mishing society for determining the mode of marriage they would choose for the sons and daughters of the erang.

A boy, belonging to a very poor *erang* may not be able to marry a girl of his choice if she hails from a better off family because the payment of higher aalig is a deterrent for such unions. Similarly if a girl is not good looking, or suffers from some disease or physical deformity or has lost her virginity, she too loses a chance of getting a good husband. All she can hope to get is a widower or a boy of a poor family or a physically disabled man, for her husband.

Such women are not married ceremoniously. It is the moral duty of the parents or *erang* to marry their daughters when a girl has conceived and her lover has refused to marry her. Although the parents may demand compensation for the crime in the form of money from the boy's parents, they cannot compel the boy's parents to marry their son with their daughter. Under these circumstances, the parents of the girl may have no alternative but to marry her to any man who is willing to marry her. Such a man may be a widower or a man from a poor family. The following case study will bring out some of the modalities in this type of marriage.

Lapchan's *erang* was not very well off. His household was small, comprising himself, wife, four sons, two daughters, and his widowed mother. Neither did he have any lineage kins in the village. There were only four adults to support the whole *erang*. The economic conditions of a household in the Pagro-Mishing society as has been discussed earlier is very much dependent upon the number of adults in the household.

Lapchan's son who was 23 years, was young enough to be married but the boy, according to young women of the village, did not have a good bearing and was generally lazy. He was therefore unable to find any girl friend. His father was also not in a position to arrange *midang* for him due to his poor economic condition. One day he got a message from someone in another village that he had a daughter, an unwed mother, and he would be glad to marry his daughter to Lapchan's son provided, of course, he was also willing. Lapchan and his son agreed and the girl was taken as a daughter-in-law by Lapchan. The *aalig* had to be paid which was obviously nominal.

Lapchan's own daughter wanted to marry a slightly elderly man and eloped with him. But they were caught. The girl thus forfeited her right to be married ceremoniously. Later on she was married to a boy of Pamua village.

In another case, Pagu Ram's daughter had eloped with a boy, Goryan but her father did not approve of the union, even after 15 days of elopement. She was brought back by her father and later on was married to another man of Kekuri village.

The incidence of such marriage is, however, very low. There seems to be no particular term for such marriage. In this type of marriage, one point that emerges is that neither the boy nor the girl, nor even their families seem to be happy with the union. The girl is married against her choice; the boy has to be content with any type of woman she may be as a wife; and the parents are not happy because if they have a daughter, they lose not only '*aalig*' but also do not get affines of their choice; and the boy's parents also become affines due to extraneous reasons which may not really be the formal perpetuation of the alliance ties which is their ideal. Thus any lapse on the part of a girl brings unhappiness not only to her but to all concerned. The plight of such a girl is a positive deterrent for any girl to become indiscreet during her days of a maidenhood.

In the wedding ceremony of such marriages, only the boy, his parents and a few agnates go to the girl's house. They carry a pitcher of *apong*, one pig and some areca nuts as gifts. They are entertained with apong at the bride's house. In the presence of the elders of the lineage, the man and the woman are united as husband and wife. There is no ritual ceremony. On the same day the bride accompanies the groom to his house, where the lineage ancestors are propitiated by the lineage elders. In this type of marriage, drums are not played and the marriage party also goes most inconspicuously to the bride's place. The *yamgurs* are also dispensed with. In the evening, the boy's household may invite some village elders and entertain them with *apong*. The overall expenditure is very low.

The Jural Basis of Marriage Relationship : Marriage Stability and Divorce

Among the Pagro-Mishing, marriage creates almost permanent ties between a man and woman. Though marriage has a ritual basis yet divorce is recognized in the society. However, the frequency of divorce is almost nil, and is conspicuous by its absence. The frequency of divorce is an aspect of the instability of marriage and the absence of divorce is the manifestation of the durability of marriage. Owing to the non-existence of divorce in their society, there is no clarity as to determine the basis of seeking divorce. However, most of them thought that if one of the spouses is suffering from a disease like leprosy, marriage would be dissolved. A man may also divorce his wife if she is infidel and a woman would be justified in divorcing her husband if he is incapable of/consummating the marriage.

A woman in the Pagro-Mishing society, however, has no right to divorce her husband. The right to divorce a wife is exclusively a male prerogative. A woman may not even desert her husband.

In case a woman is divorced by her husband, she has no right in her husband's property nor does she have any right on her children. Although, as I have mentioned earlier, a woman ceases to have any right in her natal *erang* after her marriage, she may temporarily go back to her natal *erang* after being divorced. Her father or other agnates are morally bound to help her during this time. However a husband has no claim on the *aalig* money he might have paid at the time of marriage nor is it the duty of the woman's *erang* to take cudgels on her behalf with her husband or his *erang*. Even when a woman is not willing to stay with husband for any reason, her parents or any of her other agnates have no right to bring her back. Jurally a woman is under the control of her husband's *erang* and unless the domestic group (i.e. the effective lineage) agrees to release her, she cannot go to her natal *erang*. For the remarriage of divorced woman, the ex-husband's *erang*'s concurrence is essential. Thus, to all intents and purposes, a woman and her natal *erang* have no right to decide either the divorce or the remarriage of the divorced woman. The major determinants of marriage stability among the *Pagro-Mishing* lie in their kinship system which is also true of many other tribal societies. Gluckman (1971) strongly feels that the general stability of marriage is to be sought in the system of kinship relationship. Similarly Mitchell (1971) puts foward a hypothesis that in patrilineal societies with corporate groups, marriage duration is long. However, it is not merely the existence of corporate groups that ensure the durability of marriage but is the function of the total social system within which its operation takes place. The norms, values and religious sanctions are important factors which contribute towards the stability of marriage union in the society.

Marriage Stability and the Domestic Group

In order to understand the stability of marriage in the Pagro-Mishing society it is imperative to see it in the context of their social system. It has been already discussed that the domestic group is the corporate jural unit through which the position of a person is defined in the Pagro-Mishing society. A marriage becomes legal only when the bridegroom's household has paid the stipulated amount of *aalig*. The role of the individual actors (the bride and the bridegroom) in the negotiations regarding the *aalig* amount is none. It is the concern of the respective domestic groups of the bride and the bridegroom. So it is the domestic group (the effective minimal lineage) which has the jural responsibility to legitimise a marriage. This is so even for those marriages which are contracted on the basis of romantic love.

A marriage entails establishment of certain rights and obligations involving not only the husband and wife but also their domestic groups and lineage. Looking from the point of view of a man and his kingroup, two types of rights are acquired over a woman through marriage. One pertains to the domestic and sexual services of a woman which have been called *rights in uxorem,* and the other pertains to rights over her procreative powers, called *rights in genetricem.* Uxorial rights are held in the woman as a wife and genetrical rights are held in the woman as a mother. In the societies with corporate descent groups the partilineage as a whole acquires the genetrical rights in the woman whereas the uxorial rights are held by one of their members (Mitchell 1971 : 251). Marriage is, thus, acquisition of the rights over the woman.

Marriage among the Pagro-Mishing also involves a transfer of these rights over a woman from her domestic groups to that of her husband and his lineage group. The rights in *uxorem* and the rights *in genetricem* are transferred along with the ritual incorporation of the woman in her husband's lineage. The transfer of a woman to her husband's *erang* and lineage after marriage is complete and absolute.

The sexual rights of a husband are absolute over his wife along with the rights over her reproductive powers. After the husband's death these rights are inherited by his younger brothers or his classificatory younger brothers in the lineage. The Pagro-Mishing marriage thus not only gives rise to a union of man and a woman, but involves a total transfer of a woman in her individual, jural and ritual capacity from her lineage to her husband's lineage. A widow, therefore, has no right to leave her deceased husband's group. Her husband's younger brother, even if he is married, has right over her. She may be asked to become his wife or she may be kept only as a sexual partner by him. If there is no younger brother of her deceased husband, any one of his lineage brother, who is '*igo*' in relationship to her, may remarry her, with the concurrence of her husband's *erang.* Under no circumstance the woman or her *erang* has any right to break the affinal relationship thus established. The husband's *erang* has full rights over her during her life time.

Ritually too, after marriage, a woman comes under the protection of her husband's agnatic ancestors and does not have to propitiate her own ancestors any more. She is not even allowed to participate in the ancestral rituals performed in her natal *erang*. However, if she had committed knowingly or unknowingly any sinful act before marriage, the misfortune may follow her even after her marriage if proper ceremony to propitiate the ancestors has not been performed. In such case, the woman must offer sacrifice to her agnatic ancestors and not to her husband's ancestors. But her agnatic ancestors can neither be worshipped by her husband nor it is permissible to propitiate them at his place. They must be worshipped by her father or any other close agnate, if her father is not alive in his house. For example, the elder sister of Gapong of Kumarbari was married in a nearby village. One day she visited her brother and told him that the persistent bad health of her children was due to the ancestral wrath. This was divinated by the *Mibu* (diviner) who was consulted and had told her that it was not her children's agnatic ancestors, but her own ancestors who were giving them the trouble. This might be because of some breach of taboo which might have taken place involving her, prior to her marriage. Since they were her agnatic ancestors, they had to be worshipped only in the house of one of their male agnatic descendants. Therefore, she had come to her brother, the eldest male descendant, to arrange for the performance of the ritual called *yakti'* This case clearly brings out the distinction between the premarital and the postmarital ritual status of a woman with respect to her natal *erang* and the conjugal *erang*. Marriage is, thus the turning point in a woman's life with regard to her jural and ritual position.

Alliance and Stability of Marriage

Another important structural feature of the Pagro-Mishing society is the dichotomization of the society into two categories namely kins and affines and also the existence of the positive rules of marriage, which as we have seen, result in the formation of alliance between two lineages. This type of alliance relationship creates greater cohesiveness between the domestic groups. A daughter-in-law is not a total stranger in the domestic group because of the preexisting ties of affinity between the two *erangs* which also contribute greatly towards making the conjugal union more successful and enduring.

Moreover, the norms associated with the kinship morality preclude the possibility of divorce. The Pagro-Mishing themselves point out that a divorced woman is inherently a bad woman and therefore her notoriety itself would be a handicap on her getting a new husband. Of course, the menfolk never think that instead of a wife the husband could be at fault. A divorced woman might remarry only a widower or physically handicapped man or become a second wife of an old man. A man's primary marriage is usually with a maiden and that too either with a girl whom he has chosen himself or with one selected by his parents from one of the domestic groups with which they have alliance relationship. A divorced woman has therefore remote chances of getting a good husband because she carries the stigma of divorce. Besides, the men with whom she can remarry would be already familiar with her ex-husband's *erang* and would not like to offend them by taking her as a wife or daughter-in-law. It is, therefore, extremely difficult for a divorced woman to remarry anyone. The parents and other agnatic kin also do not view a divorced daughter or any such female kin with any sympathy. Divorce, as the Pagro-Mishing point out, is the manifestation of the shortcomings of a woman's morality and her lack of adjustability with her affines. Such woman would hardly be acceptable in any domestic group.

Thus, the stability of marriage in the Pagro-Mishing society is the function of several factors amongst which their kinship structure, including the system of marriage alliance, and ideals and values regarding the position of a wife in the domestic family, have important bearing. The negative values associated with divorce and the divorced woman, render the institution of divorce redundant in their society.

Rights of Women and Secondary Marriage Widow Inheritance

It may be mentioned once again that among the Pagro-Mishing, marriage involves a transfer of the jural control over a woman from her patrilineage to that of her husband's patrilineage. Therefore after the death of her husband, a woman is not free to plan for her own future. She remains under the control of her husband's domestic group. A widow, along with her children, continues to live with other members of the *erang*. If she is still young enough to be remarried, her deceased husband's younger brother may marry her. But a woman may not be ever taken as wife by her husband's elder brother. If the younger brother of the husband happens to be married, the next younger brother may be asked to take her as his wife. If the deceased husband has no brother, his classificatory brother (FaBrSo), who would be younger than the deceased man may remarry her. In the absence of any cousin within the *erang*, a lineage brother who is younger than the deceased man may be asked to marry the widow. Only when a widow is not taken as a wife by her deceased husband's younger brother (own or classificatory) the widow may be allowed to marry any man willing to take her as his wife. However, the widow has no claim either on her husband's property or on her male children. They live in their late father's *erang*. The daughters may, however, go with their mother.

The practice of a widow remarrying her husband's younger brother (real or classificatory) among the Pagro Mishing, is technically widow inheritance and not true levirate[2] because the husband's younger brother becomes her husband and acquires full rights over her person as well as the children born subsequently. The widow is not treated as wife of the dead man, but of the man who remarried her.

The widow inheritance is fully recognized by the society, and as such does not entail any opprobrium either on the position of the man or the children born subsequently. If a widow is young and also good looking, there is absolutely no difficulty in her getting a second husband. In some cases, the opinion of the widow may also be taken into consideration by her husband's family. If she shows interest in a person other than her own '*igo*' they may allow her to marry him. But this is not done as a matter of right but only out of sympathy and compassion for the widow.

When the widow becomes her husband's younger brother's wife, kinship terms are also appropriately changed. Before her remarriage HuYoBr was addressed as' *igo*' and she was addressed by him as *mamo*. But after marriage they do not address each other as such. The children of the widow by her first husband continue to address their mother's second husband as *baboi* (FaYoBr), but if they are too young they may address him as *babu* (father) when they grow up.

Widow Concubinage

In some cases the age of a widow may not be in the marriageable category, but at the same time, she may be sexually active. In such a situation, it becomes difficult for the widow to be remarried though she may be tacitly allowed to have sexual relations with her HuYoBr. In case she does not have a HuYoBr she may cohabit with another man of her husband's lineage who may be in the relationship of a HuYoBr to her. Although the latter type of relationship is not common, it is accepted and also tolerated by the society. But if the deceased husband's domestic group does not approve of such relationships, she may be asked to leave the family house (*akum*) if she continues in her illicit relationship. But, generally, a middle aged woman does not leave the husband's *erang* if she has grown up children.

A widow is remarried in a simple ceremony, which takes place only after the funeral ceremony of her husband has been performed. In this marriage ceremony only the elders of the prospective husband's lineage participate; woman's own lineage kin have no ceremonial function. The ceremony is held at the prospective husband's place.

Adultery : Jural and Moral Aspects

A husband has exclusive rights over his wife's sexuality. But the position is not the same for a wife who may have to tolerate her husband's extra-marital relations, which are not approved by the society, but are nevertheless, tolerated. A woman before her marriage may have indulged in the sexual intercourse with someone but after the marriage, she would not even think of infidelity, like divorce; adultery is also very rare, and if a wife is even suspected of adultery, she is severely beaten by her husband and should it become a persistent affair, she may be turned out of the house.

After the marriagc, the position of a woman changes greatly in terms of her activities . A young, unmarried girl may move about freely with her friends in the village. She has little or no participation in the household chores, like cooking or washing utensils. She only helps in the harvesting and fetching water etc. But as soon as she is married, the same young girl, bears a serious countenance and is generally busy in the household chores that start early in the morning. Even if a married woman has time to spare, she cannot participate in dancing and singing with the unmarried girls. In this way, the freedom of mobility of a married woman is greatly restricted and she is very much bound down by her domestic chores. On the other hand, the position of an unmarried man and a married man are not vastly different in terms of their household chores and extra-domestic activities. There is definitely a change in a married man's activity, but if he wants to, he can still move about amongst his friends. From this disparity in the work schedule of married man and woman, one may surmise that a married man has greater opportunities of befriending the girls than a woman has for befriending the men.

A married man may develop illicit relations with an unmarried woman, especially one of those women who are unable to find a husband due to their physical or social stigma. A man may also have sexual relations with a widow who may be unable to remarry. A Pagro-Mishing husband seldom brothers to hide his appreciation of other women, even in the presence of his wife and thereby he may deliberately try to tease the wife either seriously or jocularly. But a wife, on the other hand, would not even jocularly hint at such relationship about herself. A man, if he wants, may always marry a second woman. Being the husband he has a superior position vis-a-vis his wife. A wife has neither the right to divorce her husband nor would she be allowed to remarry without being released by her late husband's *erang*. These basic differences between the rights of the husband and wife are manifested in various spheres of the Pagro-Mishing conjugal life,

Polygyny

Polygyny among the Pagro-Mishing is an exception, the norm being monogamy. Polygyny is neither a status symbol nor a desirable status for a man in the Pagro-Mishing society.

The Pagro-Mishing marriage system is basically against encouraging polygyny. A man may take a second wife. but not in the normal ceremonial way. He may either elope with a maiden or marry an unwed mother or a pregnant woman who is not acceptable to her lover. The first method i.e. of marrying a maiden by elopement is very rare, though not non-existent. It may happen when a man, not very old, becomes friendly with an unmarried girl and the girl is convinced of his sincerity that he would take her as his wife. The man, of course, must confide this in his parents, if alive, otherwise to other members of the household. Unless they agree to his second marriage as was described earlier it is almost impossible for a man to marry a maiden. In case of elopement, it is usually a girl of a poor family or someone who is unable to find a young unmarried man due to some reason, who agrees to elope. However, there is generally a tremendous opposition from the girl's family, in spite of all the handicaps that the girl has. The village elders may also oppose such union. In case such a union is acceptable, the *aalig* money is invariably high.

The freedom to choose one's own spouse in the Pagro-Mishing society is a positive impediment in securing a maiden as a second wife. It is rather a rare phenomenon when a maiden would like to become the second wife, who has an inferior status in relation to the first wife. The chances of an unmarried woman eloping with a married man are rather rare. However, the women who suffer from some physical defects or are not attractive enough to make friendship with the village young men may remain unmarried for a long time. Such a woman may become someone's second wife who may be either a widower or a monogamist. The parents of such girls also do not have objection if their daughter becomes a second wife of an older man. For instance in Kumarbari, Takila, a woman of 30 years was placed in such a situation. She was not good looking and was also alleged to be suffering from leprosy. She lived in her brothers' *erang*. However, Pakkali, a married man of 55 years of age, got interested in her and one night brought her to his own house and declared her to be his second wife. The elopement was enacted with full connivance of the girl's brother. In this case, he paid a nominal *aalig* of Rs. 1/- only.

Polygyny may also be an outcome of the widow inheritance among the Pagro-Mishing. This may happen when a man is already married but is prepared to keep his elder brother's widow as a second wife.

The legality of polygynous marriage is not disputed among the Pagro-Mishing, but the moral constraints definitely go against it. However, the jural position of the second wife and her children is in no way different from the first wife and her children. In the process of the growth of an *erang*, however, matrifiliation becomes the focal point of fission in the domestic group.

11

Summary and Conclusion

The Pagro-Mishing are primarily organized on the basis of kinship. Their social system is characterized by the existence of dual organization which divides the society into two exogamous moieties; by strong patrilineal descent system which provides the structural framework of the society; and by the system of restricted exchange which regulates marriage between the members of the opposite moieties.

The Pagro-Mishing conceptualize their society as comprising only two kinds of people who are both related to each other. One category of the members of the society is recognized as consanguineal kins and the other category is regarded as affines. The kins belong to one's own moiety, whereas the affines belong to the opposite moiety. Every person in the society is related to every other person, either by the bonds of consanguinity or by the bonds of affinity. The totality of social interactions in the Pagro-Mishing society is, therefore, comprehensible within the framework of kinship and affinity.

The Pagro-Mishing follow the principle of patrilineal descent which is determined strictly by the biological ties of fatherhood, consequently the membership of the descent group (*ope*) is acquired only on biological basis of fatherhood and not simply by social recognition of the fatherhood of a child. An individual acquires the membership of a descent group (*ope*) at birth through his genitor who except in some rare cases, is also the father. The implication of this rule is that even an illegitimate or adulterine child becomes member of his genitor's *ope* because such a child cannot be incorporated into his mother's *ope* or in the *ope* of the man who may subsequently marry the mother of such a child. The strict adherence to the rule of patrilineal descent based on biological relationship is reflected in the formation of clearly defined and well demarcated descent groups with exclusive membership. The Pagro-Mishing clans (*ope*) are thus marked off and counterposed to like groups in the total society by a uniform descent boundary that strictly defines the membership.

The principle of patrifiliation, defined strictly in biological terms, creates the descent groups. Since the Pagro-Mishing recognize only the members of one's descent group as the consanguineal kins (*ope birrang*), the basis of kinship among them is patrifiliation. Hence for the Pagro-Mishing, patrilineal descent is coterminous with consanguinity. Those persons who are not related agnatically are therefore not recognized as consanguineal kins. The Pagro-Mishing, nonetheless, recognize bilateral ties of filiation, but it is only the ties of successive patrifiliation which create the ties of consanguineal kinship whereas the ties of successive matrifiliation do not create kinship. In other words, relatives of a person through the mother are not recognized as consanguineal kins (*birrang*) but they are recognized as '*igo-magbo*' (*affines*) and hence marriageable. Thus they make a clear distinction between the patrilineal ties, which are consanguineal, and the ties through the mother, which are affinal. The symmetrical cross-cousin marriage which is the basic form of marriage relations in this society presupposes a model of genealogical connections between the inter-marrying persons. Affinity in the Pagro-Mishing society is, therefore, based on the preexisting ties of genealogical kinship between the intermarrying individuals. However, the Pagro-Mishing conceptually make a distinction between the patrilineal relatives who are regarded as consanguineal kins and the mother's kins who are regarded as affines. This dichotomy of the kins and affines is reflected in the terminological cat gorization, as well as in the behaviour pattern and interpersonal relationships among the Pagro-Mishing. A mother's brother is, thus, not recognized a *birrang* i.e. a consanguineal kin, but he is recognized as an *igo-magbo* which means that he is an affinal relative and so are the children of the mother's brother. Though the genealogical basis of these relationships is not denied, yet it is the genealogical model itself which creates kinship and affinity through the father's and the mother's kin respectively by placing them in the dichotomous divisions of the society. Through the genealogical model itself the Pagro-Mishing recognize the kin who are patrilineally defined and are non-marriageable; and the affines, who are defined matrilaterally and belong to the category of marriageable relatives. And these two categories of the kins and affines constitute the permanent and continuing categories of a person's bilateral relatives in the Pagro-Mishing society---kinship continues from the father's side, and affinity continues from the mother's side.

The Pagro-Mishing are organized on the basis of patrilineal descent into a number of descent groups. The clan is the widest unilineally constituted group. Though clans, in some cases, are divided into subclans, yet the subclans do not emerge on the basis of regular genealogical proliferation. Consequently, the subclans of a clan are not of the same genealogical depth. The Pagro-Mishing clans and subclans are dispersed groups and have neither economic nor political functions. And yet, the clans are the most important structural units of the Pagro-Mishing society. A clan is the widest social group which defines the limit of incest taboo. Any breach of the sexual taboo within the clan is the most serious offence which is punished by the ancestral spirits as well as by the community itself. Although a clan is widely dispersed and the genealogical connectedness are not demonstrable between its constituents, the relationships between the clan members are governed by kinship and moral values i.e cultural basis of kinship norms shared by the members. Thus, the genealogical distance between the members of a clan in no way diminishes the values of clanship. A clan, in the Pagro-Mishing society is a permanent, ongoing structural unit of consanguineal kins between whom the relationship is defined by the observance of shared culture norms, and immutable kinship ties manifested in incest taboo, which is regarded inviolate in the Pagro-Mishing society. The normative behaviour of the members of clan is a manifestation of the kinship values which are sanctioned by the belief in the cult of ancestors.

As a social group, the most important segment of a clan is an effective lineage which has a definite genealogical span and it is also corporate group since it manifests as a 'unit' of action unlike a clan. A corporate lineage is founded by an apical ancestor in the fourth ascending generation, counted from the seniormost living descendant of the ancestor. This is the 'effective maximal lineage' in the Pagro-Mishing society, and it also provides the core of a local group. An effective maximal lineage is a ritual unit. It is segmented into major and minor segments. The structure of the effective maximal lineage and its segments are defined by the ancestor worship. Each segment is enjoined to perform a separate ritual of ancestor worship to that ancestor which defines the genealogical basis of the segment. All the segments also join in the worship of the common ancestor. However, the effective maximal lineage is not a permanent group in the society. It is internally split into two or more units with the death of the members of the senior generation. In this way, the genealogical span of the effective maximal lineage always remains constant and hence the process of segmentation is intrinsic to the Pagro-Mishing lineage structure.

The minor segment of a lineage defines the structure of the domestic group. Thus, the core of the Pagro-Mishing residential group is provided by the male agnates who belong to the minor segment of a lineage. The minor segment of a lineage, as a residential group, is the most significant corporate group of the society which has economic, jural and ritual functions.

A domestic group -- the *erang* -- is the most important organized social group of the Pagro-Mishing society. An *erang* is both the family and home of a Pagro-Mishing. It is a family group which also is a householding group. The composition of an *erang* is based on the principles of kinship and marriage. The male agnates who are the descendants of a common father's father constitute the senior generation of a domestic group. Thus a group of male parallel cousins having a common grandfather may constitute a domestic group along with their wives and children. This is the structural boundary of the maximum growth of a domestic group which is explicitly defined by the cult of ancestor worship.

The agnatic ancestors of a man are watchful guardians and hence the welfare of the living descendants depends on the benevolence of the ancestors. The norms of kinship behaviour and the sanctions reinforcing them, derive their coercive power from the cult of ancestors who are both feared and venerated by their living descendants.

The male core of a domestic group is thus defined by the worship of a genealogically specified ancestor. Hence, any person who is not an agnate within the ritual unit, comprising the minor lineage, cannot become a member of the domestic group. For this reason, a son-in-law or a daughter's or a sister's son cannot be incorporated in one's domestic group. They are non-agnates and, therefore, do not belong to the same ritual unit around which a domestic group must be composed.

The Pagro-Mishing strictly follow the rule of patrilocal-virilocal residence. Their household is organized on strict agnatic *ideology* and manifest strong ties between the brothers. The strict adherence to the patri-virilocal rule contributes towards the formation of the joint family as the normative form of the Pagro-Mishing household. The strong agnatic ties are also reflected in the structure of relationship within the domestic group which functions as an economic, jural and ritual unit under the headship of the seniormost male member. The relationship in the domestic group are hierarchic, being determined by generation, age and sex. The jural status of an individual in the society is determined by his membership of his domestic group. A person's rights and duties, privileges and responsibilities are all derived from his membership of the domestic group. In other words, the acts of an individual obtain their legitimacy on the basis of his membership of the domestic group and hence their accountability is familial and not individual in the Pagro-Mishing society.

In the Pagro-Mishing economy, which is a household economy, the domestic group is the unit of production and consumption and there is a total correspondence between the unit of production and the unit of consumption. Although the married sons and brothers have the option to establish their own households, yet this tendency is almost non-existent. However, when a domestic group has grown to the extent where it ceases to be economically viable, a joint family may undergo the process of fission. The constraints of kinship values, however, inhibit the sons to secede from the natal *erang*. It is not the non-availability of land or purely economic considerations which compel the father and sons, and subsequently also the brothers to live in a single domestic group, but it is the kinship norms and values sanctioned by the ancestor worship that create cohesiveness in the Pagro-Mishing domestic group,

Thus the kinship and descent rules and the social norms and values provide the structural basis of the organized groups and their functioning in the Pagro-Mishing society. The principle of descent provides the basis for the formation of ongoing and permanent kin groups namely the clans, which constitute the structural framework of the Pagro-Mishing society. The clan remains a permanent group, without undergoing any change in its structure. A clan also provides the framework of unity among its members on the basis of kinship values sanctioned by the cult of ancestors. For the members of clan,the sanctity of the moral kinship and ritual values is permanent and immutable. Although the various clans that comprise a moiety are not consanguineally related with one another they are, nevertheless, regarded as *birrang* and the rule of exogamy and incest taboo are scrupulously followed by the entire moiety.

The Pagro-Mishing have *elementary structure* of kinship. They follow the positive rule of marriage which enjoins a man to marry either his mother's brother's daughter or his father's sister's daughter. This rule of bilateral cross-cousin marriage is crystallized in the form of the dual organization among them. The two moieties are Doley and Pegu.

The Doley and Pegu moieties are affines of each other. The ideal rule of marriage stipulates marriage between a man and a woman who are simultaneously matrilateral and patrilateral cross-cousins of each other. The positive rule of marriage is reflected in the Pagro-Mishing kinship terminology which may be labelled as belonging to the Dravidian sub-type, which is marked by a terminological equivalence of in-laws (affines) with those consanguineal relatives who would be identical because of consistent cross-cousin marriage.

The Pagro-Mishing, however, do not strictly follow the rule of marrying the actual MoBrDa or FaSiDa. In fact the kinship terms *magbo-igne* (the marriageable cousins) are extended to include the children of the classificatory *Kaki* (MoBr) and *Nyanni* (FaSi). Thus, it is not the genealogically determined individual but anyone belonging to the same kin type who is regarded as the prescribed spouse. The kin terms *magbo-igne* refer to a class of marriageable cross-cousins, these terms are used in a classificatory sense and not only for the actual bilateral cross-cousins.

At the empirical level marriage alliances are generally confined between the subclans. This is reflected in the actual distribution of marriage alliances among those domestic groups which are structurally proximate due to alliance relationship, though geographically they are widespread. Marriage alliances are not determined by geographical proximity but by existing ties of alliance.

The Pagro-Mishing have restricted exchange or direct exchange with patrilineal descent and patri-virilocal residence. The restricted exchange (bilateral cross-cousin marriage) implies the division of the group into two sections, or a multiple of two, "but these are always limited in their integration capacities to linking pairs of symmetrically placed groups" (Jenkins 1979 : 84). It has also been argued that direct exchange is confined to small populations or it suits small isolated populations but breaks down in large and complex ones (Fox 1970 : 219). The corollary of this argument is that system of direct exchange "can only grow by splitting into four, eight, sixteen etc. groups and by continuing to exchange directly" (*Idem*).

The Pagro-Mishing provide us with a different situation. The dual organization among them have developed due to historical necessity when they were forced to emigrate to the plains of Assam. This fact, as I have shown, is fully reflected in their myths and legends, and it is also corroborated by the historical events that took place in the recent past

Initially there were only two clans, Doley and Pegu, that constituted the dual organization. Subsequently many other cognate clans emigrated and joined them. The addition of new clans to the initial Doley-Pegu dual organization resulted in the formation of multiclan moieties but which continued to be known as Doley and Pegu. The relationship between the Pegu and Doley clans was initially based on the rule of bilateral cross-cousin marriage. They were affines of each other in dichotomous division and the relationship between them was based exclusively on matrimonial exchange. The Pagro-Mishing dual organization does not entail either symbolic or ritual or economic interdependence between the moieties. The dual organization, it may be inferred, was created out of necessity because the ties of clanship or consanguinity among the Pagro-Mishing are immutable and norms of clan brotherhood, sanctioned by the cult of ancestor worship, have a timeless validity. Thus the emigrating clans had to create affinal relationship with other clans because a clan could never become a viable and self-perpetuating group by a process of divison into two or more intermarrying subclan units among the Pagro-Mishing. The initial Doley-Pegu moieties, therefore, provided the structural base to the later emigrants to the plains of Assam. This resulted in augmenting the size of the moieties and of the Pagro-Mishing society itself. However, the system of dual organization could continue only by following the rule of moiety exogamy. Hence the clans that became part of any one of the moieties, followed the rule of moiety exogamy and created marriage alliances in the opposite moiety. The incorporation of a new clan in the moiety was socially legitimized by, according them, the status of *birrang* (kins). This automatically put them in the status of affines in relation to the other moiety. The process of accretion has been thus a major factor in the growth of the dual organization of the Pagro- Mishing. One such case of incorporation of a clan is reported to have occurred only about five or six decades ago. However, the majority of the clans which became part of the Pagro-Mishing (Doley-Pegu) dual organization subsequently are numerically small in size and are also localized only in a few villages.

Thus the structural relationship between the Doley and Pegu have provided the model for the continuity of the dual organization in spite of additions of small clans to it in the later stages. The total system is therefore conceptualized by the contemporary Pagro-Mishing to be made up of kins and affines. The norm of bilateral cross-cousin marriage is held to be the ideal rule. With the additions of new clans, however, the size of the affinal moieties increased and new alliances were also created. But this did not alter the norm of repetitive alliances between the subclans and lineages.

It may, therefore, be surmised that the dual organization in the Pagro-Mishing society is an adaptive mechanism which provided the basis of an integrated and viable social system to the emigrating clans which now constitute the Pagro-Mishing society. However, after several generations of adjustment within the system of dual organization, the ties of alliance have been created and recreated between the clans of the opposite moieties, and hence the principle of affinity and alliance provide the integrating factor between the clans of the opposite moieties. Moreover, the absence of the rule of prescriptive marriage with the actual bilateral cross-cousin has also facilitated in creating greater solidarity between the moieties by the machanism of classificatory kinship terminology which defines the potential category of the affinal kin types. Thus the system of direct exchange that enjoins marriage between the kintypes which are classed as bilateral cross-cousin in the classificatory sense has ultimately resulted in greater degree of integration in the Pagro-Mishing society. This is so because the clans of one moiety may create alliance relations with all the clans of other moiety, and they do not necessarily confine alliances between the pairs of affinal clans. The rule of direct exchange has thus, created a societal solidarity in the Pagro-Mishing society and it has not caused split into groups of two or four sections. On the contrary, the various clans have become integral part of the Pagro-Mishing social system.

Marriage in the Pagro-Mishing society also involves complete severance of a woman's jural and ritual relationship with her natal family and lineage, and correspondingly her incorporation into her husband's family and lineage. A marriage union is legitimized only after the payment of the bridewealth by the man's family. The marriage union among the Pagro-Mishing is almost indissoluble. The factors that contribute in making the marriage union stable are the jural and ritual norms by which a woman is fully incorporated in her husband's lineage. The Pagro-Mishing woman forfeits her filial rights after her marriage and consequently the bonds of daughterhood and sisterhood are jurally and ritually severed, though her affective bonds remain unaffected. My analysis thus supports the hypothesis put forward by Fortes who wrote that, "a woman who has no status by complementary filiation, even if she has a descent status, is undivorceable" (1970 : 117).

From the analysis of the Pagro-Mishing kinship system, it clearly emerges that the dominant principle in the articulation of the Pagro-Mishing society is provided by kinship and marriage. These are the two axes around which the total social system of the Pagro-Mishing society is woven. The Pagro-Mishing have no social groups except the kin groups. In the absence of any other formal groupings, kinship and affinity provide the norms of social interaction and interpersonal relationships. Kinship also serves in politico-jural functions at the lineage level. The cognitive view of the Pagro-Mishing about their own society is also based on the idiom of kinship; the entire society comprised the relatives who are either kin or affines.

Summarizing the analysis, thus, we have seen that the basic structural form of the society is provided by the principle of descent. The organized groups of the Pagro-Mishing society, namely the clan, subclan, lineage and the domestic group are all structured on the patrilineal descent and sanctioned by the cult of ancestor worship. The descent groups unite the persons for common social purposes and interests by identifying them exlusively with one another through common patrilineal descent. The descent principle thus determines not only the familial domain of kinship but also the jural aspects of kinship. In other words, it provides the rules that lie behind the kinship institutions and kinship relations. The domestic group, as we have noticed, is not only a householding unit composed strictly on the basis of kinship and affinal relationship but it also serves as jural, ritual and economic interests of the individual within the total system. The relation between the clans belonging to the same moiety are reinforced by extension of kinship ideology metaphor to incorporate them within the category of *'birrang'*. The rule of exogamy which, prescribes marriage in the opposite moiety defines the social norm which is sanctioned by the external relationship between the clans. Exogamy enforces the moral principles of social kinship. And it is the system of direct exchange or symmetrical exchange between the two exogamous moieties which provides the integration between various discrete corporate groups that constitute each moiety. The alliance principle thus integrates the descent groups of the opposite moieties through the concept of perpetual affinity. This is also reflected in the categorization of the moieties as *igo-magbo.* The integration of the social divisions of the society on the basis of the rules of marriage and the principles of affinity takes place between the social units i.e. clans which already are integrated by descent. In other words, marriage provides the integrating link between the social divisions viz. the moieties composed of various clans, which are already integrated by the principles of kinship and descent.

The integration in the Pagro-Mishing society is thus based on the principles of kinship, descent and affinity. The principle of affinity provides integration between the exogamous moieties which embrace the entire society; the principle of descent provides structural basis of the descent groups; and the principle of kinship and descent provide the structural basis of the organization of domestic groups. Though the stability and continuity of the structural relation between the units of the dual organization is the function of the rules of marriage, yet the ongoing structure of the society is provided by the organized groups which are the units of exchange in the system. In other words, the continuity of the structural groups in the society is based on kinship and descent and the continuity of the structural relationship between them are based on the principle of affinity. The structural form of the Pagro-Mishing society is thus maintained by the principles of kinship, descent and affinity.

Among the Pagro-Mishing thus, kinship system provides the articulating principle. It is the basis of the membership of the social groups; it is the basis of the inter-personal relationship within the domestic group; and it is the basis of conferring the status of an individual in the society. The principle of kinship also provides the basis of religious units and the focus of religious rituals through the cult of ancestors. The framework of economic activities in the society is also organized on the basis of kinship through the domestic groups which are the units of production and consumption. And finally, it is kinship that prescribes the basis of marriage by predetermining the category of the affinal relatives. So it is kinship and descent that provide the articulation within the organized social groups and it is the affinity that provides the articulation between the organized groups, thereby interlocking the Pagro-Mishing society in a network of kinship and affinity.

Appendix 1

The term Miri has caused some confusion in the proper identification of the Mishing who regard it to be a misnomer. The Mishing firmly believe that the term was coined by the people of the plains to designate them. Initially the term Miri was not used exclusively to identify the Mishing alone; it was also used to designate some other tribal communities inhabiting the hills of the northeast frontier regions between the Subansiri and the Siyang rivers in Arunachal Pradesh which was regarded as the original abode of the Mishing. This region was referred to by the plains people of Assam as Miri Pahar (Miri Hills). This is situated to the north of the Brahamputra valley between the Subansiri river in the west and Dibong river in the east. All the ethnic groups inhabiting this region were identified by the Assamese under one broad term, Miri. This popular misconception was carried forward by these early British administrators who explored this region for the first time, who failed to distinguish clearly different hill tribes. For example, Dalton (1845 : 423) did not make any distinction between the various ethnic groups like the Sarak, Panibotia, Tarbotia, Ghasi and the Gahghasi and designed all of them as Hill Miris. These communities are closely related to the Daflas rather than to the Mishing who, according to their traditions, are closer to the Adi group of tribes. However, Hamilton (1912 : 84) did not agree with Dalton and wrote that though "the term Miri is officially used to designate them, it is undoubtedly a misnomer. It is of interest to note that the names of various tribes have been arbitrarily given by the people of Assam and the tribesmen concerned never identify themselves as such". Thus, writing about the Apa Tani and their neighbours, the Daphla and Hill Miri, Haimendorf (1962 : 10) wrote that the names "Miri and Daphla are given by the Assamese and the tribes so-called do not identify themselves as such", and he further added that "the distinction between Daphlas and Miris (Hill) is entirely arbitrary, the two names are used by Assamese Plainsmen". In other words, the ethnic groups identified as the Hill Miri are, in fact, subgroups of the Daphlas. On the other hand, the Mishing of Assam claim to be closely related to the Bor-Abor or the Adi groups of tribesmen. It was only in the recent past that these two i.e. the Hill Miri and the Plains Mishing, were clearly distinguished.

It would be relevant to discuss the reasons why the Mishing were called Miri by the plains people who coined it and which never was used by the people themselves.

Some historians of the region and administrators scholars are of the opinion that the term 'miri' means 'go-between'. According to them since the Mishing originally inhabited the area which was situated between the Abor hills and the Assam plains, the Mishing became the medium of communication between the Abors and the Assamese. Thus Dalton (1845 : 426), Mackenzie (1884:3) and Gait (1905 : 317) were convinced that due to their role of 'middle man', they were named as the Miri. The interpretation of acting as the 'go-between' the Abors and the Assam plainsmen, and thus being designated as Miri, is not convincing linguistically. Grierson (1909 : 586) does not agree with this interpretation either and has given a linguistic explanation. He is of the opinion that the word is "Mi-ri", (of which only the first syllable is Tibetan, which means 'man') may possibly means 'nobleman' or 'gentleman'. However, Crooks (1927 : 33) does not agree with this interpretation. He thinks that the first syllable 'mi' does mean 'man' in the Abor-Miri languages, but the latter syllable 'ri' does not quite clearly show how the whole compound would mean 'gentleman' or 'nobleman'. According to Waddel (1911) also the term Miri is of Tibetan origin, which is equivalent to 'hill man'. He writes "The Miri are a typically Mongoloid people and call themselves Mi-zhing or Mishing, that is to say 'man of the soil or land', with the sense of native of the soil. They are in turn termed Miri by the more Hinduized settlers in the Assam valley, which means Hill men. Doubtless they are so-called because they have retained the customs of their ancestors in the upper Himalayas and South-East Tibet, the Hill Miris and Daflas with whom the Miri in fact claim kinship" (Waddell 1911 : 58). This explanation seems to be equally obscure, because if the term is of Tibetan origin one fails to understand why did the Assamese use this term whose language is not Tibetan. Besides, the people for whom this term is used express their ignorance about the meaning of the term.

A plausible explanation about the origin of the term Miri may be discovered within the Mishing society itself. According to this view, the term Miri may be a derivative form of *Mieureu* or Mirui which is a religious ceremony among the hill tribes viz. the Padam, Minyong, Galon and also in some subtribes of the Mishing of the Plains. The chief functionary of this ritual is also called *'Mirui'* Miri or Mibu. The mirui is a very important functionary in the life of the hill tribesmen. "He keeps the mythical legends alive in the community, conducts the rites of sacrifice, takes the more important omens ... visits the sick and conducts the various rites and semi-religious dances that take place on these and other occasions" (Dunbar 1916:68). He is also credited with exceptional powers and can cause the death of an enemy. Besides, it is the business of the *mirui* to propitiate various types of spirits who are intimately connected with the lives of the people."

It emerges from the above discussion that the term Miri connotes among the Padam-Minyong a religious functionary like the diviner, the medicine man, the spirit curer, the sorcerer and the like. But this term is *not* used to designate an entire community. It is therefore quite plausible that the hill people were identified as coming from or belonging to the land of the Miri, whose feats of divine or supernatural power might have spread far and wide. Thus, the Mishing who were emigrants from Padam-Minyong land were named as the Miri and their abode as the Miri Hills. Gradually it became popular, and for the plains people the Mishing became the Miri. Nevertheless, the Mishing would like the term Miri to be dropped in favour of the Mishing. The Mishing also identify themselves as 'Tani'. Tani means 'man'. When a Mishing meets someone not known to him, he would ask the stranger, "Tani e' Mipak?" meaning "are you a Mishing or a stranger"? though literally it means "a man or a stranger?".

Appendix 2

The Ethno-history of Mishing Political Relationships : The Mishing and Padam-Minyong Political Relationship

It is believed by the Mishing that they orginally occupied the area upstream of the Dihong river, the Minyong inhabited the area north of the Dihong up to the eastern bank of the Dikari river and the Padam lived between the Dibong river in the east and the Dihong river in the west. According to the Mishing folk history the relationship among the three communities could not remain brotherly and peaceful, in spite of the belief in common origin and following a common cult of Donyl-Polo. Although they occupied different though contiguous mountain terrain, they began fighting over the possession of the valleys and hill slopes for practising the shifting cultivation which was the major subsistence activity of the hill tribes. Thus with the increasing need for cultivable land, the days of internecine feuds began which finally took the shape of regular war among these communities living in the Dihong Valley.

The Mishing folklore has a rich repository of folktales which vividly bring out the nature of social relationship that existed between the Mishing and Padam-Minyong' communities when they lived together in the same vicinity in the hills. Some of the folktales also describe the important socio-political events that occurred in the hoary past which eventually forced the Mishing to migrate from the hills in search of a new home where they could live in greater peace. Of course, we need not accept the Mishing folktales as relating historically true events, but they are also not necessarily untrue in every detail. These folktales are part of their tradition which brings to recapture some unforgettable events by knitting a tale around them and then reflecting on them. They probably reflect actual historical events that took place in not too distant past. Besides, they also reflect the folk view of their historical connections with their original home and relations with the communities that were their neighbours there. One such folktale, described below, recapitulates the hostility between the Mishing and the Padam-Minyong tribes:[1]

A segment of the Minyong tribe inhabited the village called Kebang situated on the north bank of the river Siyang. The Padam also inhabited the same vicinity and occupied the south bank of the river. The Mishing migrated later to this place and settled in the neighbourhood of the Padam. For sometime all the three communities lived peacefully and also celebrated many feasts together. One day the Minyong men were invited to a feast hosted by the Padam. The Minyong attended the feast led by their *Gam*. The Minyong Gam was short in stature and had a potbelly. While the feast was on, a Padam young man injudiciously joked about the physique of the Minyong *Gam*. This was taken as very insulting by the Minyong and they resolved to avenge their insult. A few days later, the Minyong also hosted a communal feast and invited the Padam. The Padam went and enjoyed themselves thoroughly. The Padam did not know anything about the plot which had been hatched by the Minyong people. When the Padam *Gam* was quite inebriated a young Minyong suddenly attacked him and slit his throat. As soon as other Padam came to know about the treacherous murder of their *Gam*, they panicked and fled away to their village. The Minyong pursued them up to the bridge (*ayam*) and afterwards destroyed the bridge thus making the river Siyang uncrossable.

The murder of the Padam *Gam* infuriated all the Padam and they resolved to destroy the whole Kebang village. But as the bridge had been destroyed by the Kebang men, it was impossible to cross the river. The Padam did not know how to construct boats.The Mishing, however, were deft in boat making. The Padam, therefore, requested the Mishing to help them by constructing some boats. The Mishing built two big boats, and one day the Padam went to their war mission. The boats were steered by two Mishing men by the name of Lebang and Tumsik. At midnight, the Padams attached the Kebang village and destroyed it completely. In the morning, when the victorious Padams were returning to their village, their boats were again being steered by the same Mishing men. When the boats were in the midstream, Lebang intentionally crashed it against the trunk of a big tree that was floating there. The impact was so sudden and terrific that the boat capsized and all the Padams sitting in it were drowned except Lebang who swam across the river safely. Lebang's reason in capsizing the boat was due to the belief that if he did not sacrifice some Padams, the *Piyangs* [1] of the Kebang people would not spare his own life. Tumsik, who was steering the other boat, managed to guide it safely to the other bank, but while going to his village Tumsik was killed by the piyangs of the Kebang men.

The Padams, who came to know of the deceitful action of Lebang, were very much infuriated with the Mishing. This episode resulted in the estrangement of the two communities. At the same time, Kebang people, the Minyong, were also extremely annoyed with the Mishing because soon they also came to know that it was the Mishing who had built and steered the boats which helped the Padams. The Minyong too, thus, became enemy of the Mishing giving rise to internecine wars.

Consequently after some time, the Mishing were forced to move away from the vicinity of the Padam and the Minyong, the Mishing first moved to a place near the confluence of the Lohit with the Dibong river. But this place was also not safe from the raids of the Padams and the Minyongs. Therefore they were once again forced to move away to a safer place. This time the Mishing sailed on their boats in the Dibong, down the stream until they finally reached the plains of upper Assam and settled on the banks of the Brahmaputra and the Subansiri and some of their tributaries.

The basic theme in these folktales and legends is the emphasis that is laid firstly on the close ethnic and mythical relationships between the Mishing and the Padam-Minyong communities and subsequently on the gradual deterioration of their relationship, forcing the Mishing ultimately to emigrate to the safer haven. These folktales, however, do not give any hint that the relationship between the Padam-Minyong and the Mishing were akin to those of feudal lords and vassals respectively, although their history reveals that such relationship did exist between them as described below.

The Mishing during the Ahom Rule

The Mishing had developed relations with people of Assam during the pre-British period. Brief historical references are found regarding their relationship with the rulers of Assam during the reign of Ahom king, Pratap Singh (1603-1614) and later, during the reign of Chakradhwaj Singh (Gait, 1905 : 85).

During the reign of the Ahom Kings (1228 A.D. to 1826 A.D.), the hill tribes of the northeastern hills lived in complete independence. In the earlier part of their rule, the Ahom subjugated the Chutia[5] king, who ruled the easternmost part of the Subansiri adjoining the Sadia area. The Ahom King Suhunmug annexed the Chutia Kingdom in 1523. During this period, the Mishing lived beyond the jurisdiction of the Ahom administration and several hill tribes like the Mishing, the Dafla and the Abor used to raid the Ahom subjects. According to Gait (1905 : 85), in 1615 the Mishing and the Daphla raided the Ahom villages and a force was sent to report them, but the Ahom force could not subjugate them. In 1655, the Mishing again made a raid on the Ahom subjects. A force was sent against them. In this encounter the

Mishing lost and many of their villages were burnt. Consequently the Mishing agreed to pay an annual tribute to the Ahom King. The Mishing also surrendered twelve of their men to the Ahom rulers as a compensation for two Ahom subjects whom they had killed (*Ibid* : 124). However, it was only by 1685 that the Mishing were fully subjugated by the Ahom. Later on during the long reign of the Ahom Kings, some Mishing were given responsible position in the administration. The Mishing had thus relatively crossed longer exposure to culture contacts with the people of Assam as compared to the Padam, Minyong and other hill tribes.

The Mishing during the Post Ahom and Early British Period

After almost six hundred years of unbroken reign, towards the end of the 18th century, the Ahom rule in Assam began to disintegrate. Due to internal strife, the Ahom Governor of Gauhati invited the Burmese who plundered Assam thrice and virtually ruled over entire Assam from 1819 to 1824. In 1826, the British were invited by the Ahom King and the Burmese were finally crushed leading to the treaty of Yandabu in 1826 and Assam was finally annexed by the British East India Company (Gait : 1905). However, it took more than sixty years to consolidate the British rule in Assam, which has been totally devastated by the retreating Burmese and committed the most atrocious barbarities. An official report states that, "when we assumed the charge of Assam...the people had been so harassed and oppressed by the long civil and internal wars that had followed the accesion of Rajah Gourinath Singh in 1780 down to 1826, that they had almost given up cultivation and lived on jungle roots and plants and famine and postilence. They (the Burmese) - carried off thousands that had escaped the sword and captivity... (nearly) half of the country or the divisions of Sibsagar and Luckimpoor, only came under our management in 1839" (Mills 1853: Appendix I).

This brief historical account of the annexation of Assam by the British East India Company makes it amply clear that the condition that prevailed in the north-eastern region of Assam were far from smooth. The region was scantily treated even by the British administrators long after they had annexed it, therefore the only historical material that is available on this region is in the form of few government reports and narratives of the military and survey expeditions that were undertaken by the British officers soon after the annexation of upper Assam from the last Ahom King, Poorunder Singh, in 1839. However, the British had neither the time nor the interest to introduce any sort of administration in the northeast frontier region. For about a century since the annexation, the British were content with protecting the plains area from the occasional raids by the tribal people from the hills and taking out a few punitive expeditions. These expeditions were either intended to put down the tribal uprisings or to induce the tribal to lead a peaceful life with a show of force (Reid, 1942).

The Mishing and the Relation with the Bor-Abors

As already mentioned the British were not unduly interested in the hill people bordering their annexed territories, consequently there are hardly any exhaustive accounts of the hill people for this time. Whatever scanty information we have is based on exploratory surveys undertaken by them from time to time. One of the earliest mention of the Mishing (who were then called Miris or Meerees) is found in R.B. Pemberton's book *The Eastern Frontier of India* (1835). Pemberton (1835 : 78) wrote that, "The Abors occupy the lower ranges extending from the Dihong river to Soobunsiri and the Meeries principally, the plains stretching from the foot of the Abor hills up to the right or northern bank of the Brahampooter (sic)". This description is based on the reports of Captains Bedford and Wilcox, the two officers who were first Britishers to have gone into this territory in 1831-32. Pemberton further added that the "Bor Abors occupy the more lofty and retired ranges and appear to be held in great dread both by the Meerees and Abors below them..."*(ibid).*

Most of the administrative reports of the time are mainly concerned with the relationship between the hill tribes, especially the Bor-Abors, the Daphals and the Mishmi on the one hand and the British administration on the other. Besides this, they were also directed to find out the inter-tribal relationship in the northeastern frontier regions.

One of the earliest British administrator to have visited the hills in the neighbourhood of the Subansiri river was E.T. Dalton. After a survey of this area, he observed that, "there was no material difference between the Abors and Miris. They are of the same race. The Miris (of the plains) from their intercourse with the plains are, in some respects, more civilized" (Dalton,1845 : 426).

Hunter (1879 : 228) in his *Statistical Account of Assam* also wrote that the Mishing of the plains were an offshoot from the Padam-Minyong. Similarly the *Census of Assam,* conducted for the first time in 1881, described that the "Miri, Daphla and Abor are names which have been given by the Assamese to three sections of one and the same race" (Stack, 1883 : 86). Mackenzie (1884) in a comprehensive historical account of the hill tribes of north-eastern frontier which is based on all the available accounts of the time also came to the same conclusion. He wrote :

> Abors and Miris undoubtedly came from the same habitat and they are so alike in all material respects as to warrant calling them earlier and later migrants of the same tribe, though the Miris have been to some extent influenced by their association with the plain and the settled habitat of civilization. (Mackenzie, 1884 : 33).

Another valuable historical work is the *History of Upper Assam* (1914) by Col. Shakespeare wherein he writes about the Mishing as follows :

> The Mirris (sic) dwelling between the Daphla and Abors are allied to the latter and are so alike that it seems evident they both came from the same original home-wherever that was. The Mirris (sic) migrating first and having been longer influenced by association with the plains folks, have lost their savagery and hardihood which the late arrivals of the Abors have retained. Intercourse between these tribes is intimate which does not seem to exist between the others who live entirely independent of each other, (1914 : 109).

The Linguistic Survey of India (1909) includes the Mishing language in the North Assam group of Tibet-Burman branch of the Sino-Tibetan family of languages. The report points out that the dialects spoken by the Miris and Daflas are so clearly connected that they may be considered as one and the same language, and the language spoken by the Abor is not different from the Dafla-Miri language. The report clearly mentions that the Abor dialect is almost identical with the Miris (Grierson, 1909 : 584).

From the preceding accounts, both legendary and historical, it becomes amply clear that the Mishing of the plains and the Padam and Minyong of the hills have had close ethnic, linguistic and cultural relationship. They shared not only the same geographical region but also claimed a common mythical origin from the creator Sedi and shared a belief in the cult of Donyi-Polo. After the annexation of Assam by the British, many military and Survey excursions went up to the hill which also confirmed that there was no sigificant difference between the Mishing and the Padam-Minyong communities. Thus, it is not only the Mishing traditions and their ethno-history but also the impression of the various British observers which emphasizes the close proximity, both ethnic and cultural, between the Mishing and the Padam and Minyong. However, the political relationships between the various groups that inhabited a contiguous region of the Miri Hills were far from peaceful. The various tribal groups lived in a state of perpetual hostility, the consequence of which was the migration of the Mishing to the plains of Assam. In order to understand the cause of the Mishing migration to the plains of Assam, we have once again to look upon the political nature of relationship between the various tribal groups during the times of the Ahom rule and later on, in the early phase of the British occupation of upper Assam.

The Emigration of the Mishing:
The Mishing and Bor-Abor Hostility

Historically it is difficult to pinpoint a definite time when the Mishing began their downward journey to the plains of Assam. It is, however, not difficult to reconstruct the conditions that prevailed in the hills on the basis of the administrative history of the 19th century. Besides, the Mishing folktales also allude to internecine feuds that characterized their relationship with the Abors. The main source of conflict among the various tribal groups seems to be converging on a single factor, namely the possession of the cultivable land. The internecine conflicts among the various tribal groups in the rugged north-east frontier were due primarily to the ecological conditions that prevailed there. The entire region is a mountainous terrain. The high hills and mountains tower the sides of the river and streams. These narrow river valleys are the only places fit for cultivation. Since the entire tribal population of this region was dependent upon shifting cultivation, the value of cultivable land, which was scarce, was enormous. The relationship between various tribal groups was therefore basically determined by their access to the cultivable land and the control over it. This resulted in constant wars to control land between various tribes. The smaller and weaker tribes were kept under constant pressure by the more powerful groups and consequently it was the weaker groups that had to migrate to the safer places. In fact, migration was a way of life due to political and economic conditions, which were themselves shaped by ecological factors.

This relationship between the Mishing and the Bor-Abor form part of this general political and economic situation that prevailed in their frontier home. Under this pattern the stronger tribes wielded a great power over their less powerful neighbours resulting in formation of exploitative relations. Thus the history of tribal groups of the north-east frontier region is the history of internecine feuds and extraction, of predatory movements of the powerful tribes, and of constant migration of the smaller and weaker communities.

As already mentioned, the neighbours of the Mishing in the hills were the Padam and Minyoung (the Bor-Abor)[2]. They were one of the most querrelsome and next to independent of all the tribes of the Subansiri region. According to Hamilton :

> For a longtime past the Abors have been cocks of Assam. Very independent and quarrelsome, they had come to regard themselves as the rulers of this far distant corner of India from the fact so many Miri and Mishmi tribes have submitted to their exaction (1912 : 18).

Due to these oppressive relations, the Mishing were forced to migrate to the plains of Assam. Many groups of the Mishing had already settled in the plains, much before the annexation of upper Assam by the British in 1839. But there too the Padam-Minyong did not spare them from their exactions. Mackenzie has elaborately discussed the status of the Mishing in relation to the Padam-Minyong. According to him :

> The Miris of the plains are here claimed by the Abors as their runaway slaves. The Miris for many years acknowledged Abors as their masters. They readily agreed to be go-between the Assamese and the rude hill people. The Assamese Government (Native) (Ahom) anxious to conciliate their highland neighbors, *had long since relieved Miris of all revenue charges, acknowledging thereby the subjection of that tribe to the Abors.* During the Burmese invasion and after the British assimilation of Assam, more than one community of the Miris moved away from the vicinity of their Abor lords, and one of the earliest notices of the Abors outside of the geographical memoirs is an account of the demand made by the *Duba* tribe of Bor-Abor in February, 1830, that the British authorities would send back a village of the Miris who had moved away to the detriment of the Abor trade. The Government of course could not coerce the Miris in returning, *but it sanctioned certain expenditure by the Political Agent with a view to induce them and kindred tribes to settle where they could minister to the wants of the Abors in the way of trade.* (Mackenzie 1884 : 37) (emphasis added)

The Padam-Minyong exercised a great power over the natural resources in their highland abode and all the tribes of that area had to submit to their oppressions. "By claiming an inalienable right to all the fish and gold found in the streams which flowed from the Miri lands, the Abors exercised almost feudal powers over many sections of the Miris. The oppressive effect of this power by 1826 had caused an exodus of the Miris from their tribal lands to Sadiya where they placed themselves under the protection of the old Assam Government, who refused to assist the Abors to get them to return... and when efforts were made in 1847 when we had taken the possession of Assam, to establish trading posts on the Dihing, the Abors objected and emphasized their objection by kidnapping a numb r of Miri" (Hamilton, 1912 : 31). The regular exodus of the Mishing in the Pre-British and during the British raj was mainly to escape from the oppressive behaviour of the Abors. But the Abors to show their displeasure continued to raid the Mishing, even as late as 1888 when Pasi-Minyong decoyed four Miris over the *'inner line'*[3] and killed all of them. In 1892 this action was raided by Pasi-Minyong. Abors and captives were carried off" (Shakespeare, 1914 : 16). The supremacy of the Padam and Minyong people over the Mishing was so conspicuous that Stack went to the extent of saying that "The Assamese word *abor* means independent (*bori* means 'subject' or 'dependent ' and bor is the root of the verb meaning 'to submit or' own allegiance') and the Abors may have been so-called by way of contrast with the vassal Miri" (Stack, 1883 : 86).

In the initial days of consolidation of the British empire, the British administration was not in a position to challenge the Bor-Abors in their periodic raids on the villages in their jurisdiction. On the contrary, they also wanted to appease them. In 1827, Captain Neufville, the then Political Agent: collected all the Miris he could find, who had migrated into Assam and *endeavoured to compel them to resume the land from which they had fled in consequence of the Abors...*This endeavour to resettle the Miris failed" (Michell, 1883 : 54) (emphasis added). Another report of the Political Officer in 1879, when the British were supposedly well entrenched in Assam, also speaks about the incompetence of the British administration against the Abor raids which went on all within the British territory. According to this report, 'on the land which we have left uncared for between our present outpost and the Abors, many Miri colonists had settled and their villages were scattered from the Dihong to the north of Dibrugarh but in the year 1877 and 1888 most of the villages had to be abandoned in consequence of the exaction of the Abors who yearly visited them to levy tribute and live at free quarters claiming the people as their slaves..." (Michell, 1883 : 64).

The exodus of the Mishing from their hill abode was thus a great economic loss to the Abors because they treated the Mishing as their slaves and dependents toiling for their masters, the Abors. In this connection Robinson (1841 : 55) has pointed out that; "some Abors have lately settled at the foot of the hills in the district of Sudia (sic) where they have been apparently driven to the necessity of cultivating the fields by the desertion of the Miris, who formerly inhabited that tract of country and were looked upon by the Abors as their slaves and dependents". The Abor economy was almost shattered due to the emigration of the Mishing. In the report of the then Political Officer of Assam, it is reported that in 1835 an Abor Chief with 200 followers wanted to settle in British territory, but they were refused the permission because the Abor Chief refused to pay any taxes to the Government. "Scarcity of the means of subsistence was, it is supposed, the cause of their visits, and they evidently mediated replacing the Miris, who formerly laboured for the Abors in the Dihong quarters but have since emigrated to Upper and Lower Assam to escape the exaction of that tribe (Michell 1883 : 56).

All these accounts exemplify beyond doubt that the Mishing had only a subordinate political status and were subject to payments of tribute to the Padam and Minyongs. Once the exactions became more taxing, the only recourse left for the Mishing was to move to a safer haven, which was the plains area of upper Assam. However, the emigration of the Mishing was not in the interest, especially economic, of the Padam and Minyong tribes and hence they continued to attack and plunder the Mishing villages even when their villages were well within the British territory. But with the consolidation of the British administration in the frontier area, and signing of the peace treaties with the Abors, the raids of the Bor-Abors became less frequent and consequently more Mishing moved down to the safer places.

The oppressive relationship between the Abor and the Mishing was thus the main cause of the emigration of the Mishing to the plains of Assam in search of peace, protection and land. Though the exodus of the Mishing became very conspicuous after the establishment of the British administration in upper Assam in 1838, the Mishing had been emigrating to the plains of Assam from much earlier times as is evident from some of the Mishing legends which described the days of the Burmese invasion. The Burmese invasion of Assam took place in 1816 and there was great plunder and destruction all around. In one of the folktales of the Mishing, for example, it is narrated that a company of the Burmese soldiers was ambushed by a Mishing village situated on the north bank of the Brahmaputra. This implies that the Mishing had been well established, much before the Burmese invasion of the plains of Assam.

The Mishing emigration to the plains of Assam is thus spread over a very long period of time. The oldest historical account of the Mishing that we find is during the reign of the Ahom Kings when they (Mishing) were still independent and were causing some concern at the frontiers of the Ahom Kingdom that stretched up to the foothills. As already mentioned duruing the reign of the Ahom King Pratap Singh (1603-1614) and later on, in 1665, in the reign of King Chakradhwaj Singh, the Mishing created border problems. But the Ahom King subjugated them with his mighty force. The important point that may be inferred from the above account is that till the middle of the 17th century, the Mishing remained confined to the hills and only later on did their emigration begin. The Mishing exodus was initially small but gradually it became more and more conspicuous, and continued right up to the beginning of the present century. This phenomenon was recorded by the 1911 decennial census of Assam wherein it was pointed out that each successive census report shows a very substantive increase in the number of the Mishing which makes it evident that there must be continued emigration from the hills (McSwiney1912).

Notes

Chapter II

1. A serious effort to study the ethnography of the north-east region was, made in 1903 when the then Government of Assam established a directorate of ethnography. The aim of the directorate was to bring out series of monographic studies on the tribes of this region. The scope of the monographic studies was predetermined which was to give a systematic account of manners and customs, ethnological affinities, laws and institutions, religious beliefs, folk lore, theories of religion and language, and of the material culture etc. (Majumdar 1980 : 137). Under this scheme, a number of monographs were published which, by and large, followed the prescribed guidelines. These monographs were written by the British civil servants who were posted in different parts of the region. However, these monographic studies were not based on intensive anthropological fieldwork, obviously because the authors were not professional anthropologists. Many tribes were covered by these monographic studies. Among them, the more notable ones are about the Khasi (Gurdon:1907), Garo (Playfair:1909) Sema Nagas (Hutton:1921), Angami Nagas (Hutton:1921), Lhota Naga (Mills:1922), Ao Nagas (Mills:1926) and the Rangma Nagas (Mills:1937). During this period, only few tribes were studied by the non-administrators, namely by the missionaries or the academic scholars. Among them one was Rev. Sydney Endle, a missionary, who wrote a monograph on the Kacharis (1911) who were under his parish at that time. The other monographic study was done by W.C. Smith, a professional sociologist, of the Ao Nagas (1925). Furer-Haimendorf (1939), published a monograph on the Konyak Naga and later on, brought out a study of the Apa Tani (1962) of Arunachal Pradesh. After Independence, the administration of North East Frontier Agency (NEFA now Arunachal Pradesh) also initiated ethnographic

studies of some of the important tribes inhabiting the region because the tribes of NEFA had not been studied systematically by the British administrators. Thus the tribes like the Dafla, Idu Mishmi (Barua 1960), Gallong (Srivastava 1962) , Aka (Sinha 1963) and the Padam Minyong (Roy 1960) *etc.* were studied by the research personnel of the NEFA administration. However, the focus of all these monographs was to present a rounded ethnographic account of the tribe it described.

All these monographic studies are thus primarily a simple descriptive account of the customs, institutions and the material culture of the tribes. In all these studies kinship forms only a routine part of the descriptive account. Kinship as the major focus, has not been made the basis of any full-length monographic study. However, in the last few decades, a few analytical studies of kinship systems of the region have been made by professional anthropologists. Notable among them are the studies of Robbins Burling (1963) and Chie Nakane (1968). Burling has devoted his study to the analysis of the family and kinship system of the Garo. Although his study is based on an intensive study of a Garo village, the study is representative of the Garo society. Chie Nakane's study is a comparative study of two matrilineal kinship systems, namely of the Garo and the Khasi of Meghalaya.

Thus it is noticed that none of the studies conducted by the administrators or even by the professional anthropologists in the north-east region focussed on a full-length analytical study of the kinship system of a tribe, except the studies done by Burling and Nakane and few others. Other noticeable point that emerges from this brief survey is that mainly the hill tribes were the primary focus of ethnographic studies and a full-length study of any plain's tribe of Assam was rarely undertaken during the colonial period. Endle's study of Kachari is perhaps the only exception, although there are as many as nine tribes in Assam, out of which seven tribes, namely Boro (Borokachari) Sonowal, Rabha, Lalung, Deori, Hojai and Mishing inhabit the plains area of Assam and only two tribes, Dimase and Mikir (now also known as Karbi Anglong) inhabit the hills of Assam. None of these plains tribe was studied either by the social anthropologists or by the administrators during the British Raj. Only recently, some anthropologists have shown interest in the plains tribe of the region.

2. I have used 'Discussion' (amongst the actors) as a technique of data collection. The researcher may or may not participate with the actors in their discussion. As a non-participant the researcher is a witness to the entire verbal interation in a group of actors and hence able to perceive the meaning attributed by the actors to the subject of discussion. As a participant the researcher may interject his views on the subject of discussion and may be able to elicit more information from the participants or actors. In a prolonged field work "discussion situation" become more and more meaningful in providing diversified views of the actors within a given context.

3. Padam and Minyong were called Abor or Bor (great Abor by the Assames. "The term Abor signifying barbarous,rude independent, i.e., by the Assamese, applied very indiscriminately to all the independent hill clan on both sides of the valley of Assam...but it's more peculiarly the appellation of the hill races on the southern slopes of that portion of the great Himalayan range between the Dihong and Soobunsheri (sic) rivers" (Dalton1855 :151). The term Abor has been replaced now by Adi.

4. Gam connotes the chief. Gam could be chief of a clan or a community.

5. The Ahom ruled Assam from 1228 to 1826 A.D. They had come to Assam from South China and preferred to describe themselves as Tai (Gait 1905).

6. The Chutiya, a Hinduised tribe and speaking a Bodo tongue, once ruled the north-estern part of Assam king in 1523 A.D. (Ibid)

CHAPTER III

1.. After the establishment of Vaishnavism in 16th century A.D. by Sri Sankardev, a number of Satras i.e. Vaishnava religious institutions were started in various parts of Assam. Each Satras is under a spiritual head who is known as *Gossain* or *Satradhikar* who has a number of disciples. The Satras have an extremely important place in the religious and cultural life of Vaishnavite Hindus of Assam. In Majuli, the Satras were established when the then Ahom King started persecuting the Satradhikar and their followers. Since Majuli island offered a safer place many persecuted Satradhikar fled to Majuli and gradually established the Satras.

2. The system of land tenure in the Sibsagar plains is Ryotwari where each individual holder of land is made directly responsible for payment of land revenue. Land for ordinary cultivation is held under the State in three different systems
1. *Lakheraj* - Revenue free estate;
2. *Nisf-Khehraj* - Half revenue paying estate, and
3. *Kheraj* - full revenue paying estates.

The holders of Kheraj are given settlement extending for a term of years at a time (period Kheraj or from year to year (Annual Kheraj.) The annual kheraj is normally renewed. Anunal kharaj are granted mostly in fluctuating areas where uninterrupted relation of land is not customary (Sharma 1952 : 23)

3. Considering by village groups the Miri village are seen to have the highest proportion (97.26 percent) of wholly agricultural families and the ex-tea labour village have the least (50.43 percent), the corresponding figure for Assamese and Ahom villages are 57.88 percent and 66. 26 percent respectively. The percentage of families having large holdings (above 30 bighas)

is comparatively low in all cases expect in the Miri villages where it is as high as 41.1 percent which is almost equal to the percentage in the small holding group (42.46 percent). In large holding groups the variation in the average size of holding is rather large ranging from 44.92 bighas in the Ahom village to 75.33 bighas in the Miri Village while the Assamese and ex-tea labour village have an intermediate size of the average holding (Sharma 1952 :17)

4. According to 1971 census, out of a total number of 259,551 Mishing in Assam,258,294 followed Hinduism. The rest of the population is professing either Buddhism or Christianity. None of them, according to the census, professes animism.

Chapter IX

1. Levi-Strauss defines elementary structure of kinship as follows.

"These system in which the nomenclature permits the immediate determination of the circle of kin and that of affines, that is these systems which prescribe marriage with a certain type of relative, or alternatively, those which while defining all members of the society as possible spouses and prohibited spouses" 1969 : XXIII) 'Since the term prescription' generated a lot of controversy, in the preface to the second French edition of Elementary Structures, Levi Strauss states that an elementary structure can be equally preferential or prescriptive.. neither prescription nor preference is the test of an elementary stucture. It's one and only one criterion rests in the fact that preferred or prescribed, the spouse is the spouse solely because she belongs to an alliance category or stands in a certain kinship relationship to Ego. In other words, the imperative or desirable relationship is a function of the social stucture'. (1969: XXXIII-XXXIV) (Emphasis is added).

Chapter X

1. Disowning the son would imply that father has forsaken his jural rights over the son which would make the son a full legal

person with whom one can deal directly, both legally and jurally.

2. True levirate is "when a man dies and his wife has not passed the age of child-bearing, it is the duty of the man's brother to cohabit with the widow in order to raise children, which will be counted, not as his, but as children of the deceased whom the brother is surrogate and not strictly speaking her husband" (Radcliffe-Brown 1950:64)

APPENDIX-II

1. Piyangs are spirit of those persons who are killed by drowning or who are murdered. These spirits take revenge on the culprits, unless propitiated by sacrifice.

2. Until 1912 Bor-Abor was the common term to designate the Padam and Minyong tribes.

3. In 1873 the Inner Line Regulation was enacted to bring under more stringent control the commercial relations of British subjects with the frontier tribes. According to this enactment no British subject or foreigner could pass beyond a certain part without a licence (Mackenzie 1894 : 395).

Bibliography

Allen, B.C.(1905). *District Gazetter of Sibsager.* Shillong : Government of Assam.

Barnes, J.A. (1973). Genetrix: Genitor:: Nature:Culture? In *The Character of Kinship* . (Ed). Jack Goody. Cambridge :Cambridge University Press.

Barua, T.K. (1960). *The Idu Mishmi*, Shillong :Adviser's Secretariat. NEFA.

Beverley, H. (1872). *Census of Bengal*, 1872. Bengal Census Report.

Boudillon, J.A. (1883). *Census of India, 1881. Assam Census Report and Tables*. Calcutta :Government of India.

Burling, Robbins. (1963). *Rengsanggri : Family and Kinship in a Garo Village* . Philadelphia :University of Pennsylvania Press.

Choudhary, N.K. and Das M.M. (1973). *The Lalung Society*. Calcutta : Anthropological Survey of India.

Clammer, John.(1985). Power, Descent and Reproduction : A critique of the concept of 'Lineage Mode of Production' in Chinese Society. In *Anthropology and Political Economy* by John Clammer. London :Macmillan.

Crooks, W. (1908). Abor, Abor-Miri. *In Hasting's Encyclopeadia of Religion and Ethics*. (Vol.1)London.

Dalton, E.T. (1845). Correspondence and Journal of Capt. Dalton Principal Assistant at Luckimpore of his progress in a late visit to clan of Abors in the Dihong river. *Selections from the Records of the Bengal Government,* No. XXIII. Calcutta.

Dalton, E.T. (1872). *Descriptive Ethnology of Bengal,* Calcutta : Office of the Superintendent of Government Printing.

Das, Tarak Chandra. (1945). *The Purums : An Old Kuki Tribe of Manipur.* Calcutta :University of Calcutta Press.

Dumont, L. (1957). *Hierarchy and Marriage Alliance in South Indian Kinship*. London :Royal Anthropological Institute Occasional Papers, No.12.

Dunbar,G.Duff-Sutherland.(1916). *Abors and Gallongs*.Memoirs of the Asiatic Society of Bengal. V, Pt.III

Dupre, Georges and P.P. Rey. (1973). Reflections of the pertinence of a theory of the history of exchange. *Economy and Society* 145.

Endle, Rev.S.(1911). *The Kacharis*. London:Macmillan and Co.

Evans-Pritchard,E.E. (1945). *Some aspects of marriage and family among the Nuer*. Rhodes-Livingstone Paper No.11. (Republished).

Fortes, Meyer. (1945). *The Dynamics of Clanship among the Tallensi* London : Oxford University Press.

Fortes, Meyer. (1949). *The Web of Kinship among the Tallensi* . London :Oxford University Press.

Fortes, Meyer. (1953). 'The structure of unilineal descent group. *American Anthropologist*. 55, 17-41

Fortes, Meyer.(1958). Introduction. In *The Developmental Cycle in Domestic Groups*. (Ed) Jack Goody. Cambridge University Press.

Fortes, Meyer. (1959). Descent, filiation and affinity : a rejoinder to Dr.Leach, (2 parts) *Man*, 59(309): 193-197, and (331)-206-212.

Fortes, Meyer. (1969). *Kinship and the Social Order* . London : Routledge and Kegan Paul.

Fortes, Meyer. (1970). *Time and Social Structure and other Essays*. London : The Athlone Press.

Fox,Robin.(1967). *Kinship and Marriage*. Hammondsworth : Penguin Books Ltd.

Furer-Haimendorf, C.von. (1939). *The Naked Nagas*. London: Methuen Co. Ltd.

Furer-Haimendorf,C.von. (1962). *The Apa Tanis and their Neighbours*. London :Routledge and Kegan Paul.

Gait,E.A. (1892). *Census of India 1891 : Assam-Census Report and Tables*. Vol. 1 & 2. Shillong. Assam Secretariat Printing Office.

Gait, E.A. (1905). *A History of Assam*. Calcutta :Thacker Spink & Co. (Revised 1926).

Gellner, Ernest (1987). The concept of kinship. In *The Concept of Kinship and other Essays*. Ernest Gellner. London :Basil Blackwell.

Gluckman, Max. (1950). Kinship and marriage among the Lozi of Northern Rhodesia and Zulu of Natal. In *African System of Kinship and Marriage*. (Ed) A.R. Radcliffe-Brown and Daryll Forde 166-206. London : Oxford University Press.

Gluckman, Max. (1971). Marriage Payments and social structure among the Lozi and Zulu. In *Kinship*, (Ed) Jack Goody, Hammondsworth: Penguin Books.

Godelier, Maurice. (1972). *Rationality and irrationality in Economics*. London: The New Left Books.

Godelier, Maurice, (1979). The Appropriation of Nature. *Critique of Anthropology*. 4 (13 & 14)

Goody, Jack. (Ed.) (1958). *The Developmental Cycle in Domestic Groups*. Cambridge Papers in Social anthropology, No. 1. Cambridge : Cambridge University Press.

Goody, Jack, and Tambiah, S.J.(1973). *Bridewealth and Dowry*. Cambridge Papers in Social Anthropology. Cambridge : Cambridge University Press.

Gurdon, P.R.T. (1907). *The Khasis*. London : Macmillan & Co.

Grierson, G.A. (1909). *Linguistic Survey of India*. Vol. III, Tibeto Burman Family, Part-I. Calcutta :Government Press.

Hamilton, Angus. (1912). *In Abor Jungles 1912*. London: Eveleigh Nash.

Harris, C.C. (1990). *Kinship*. Buckingham : Open University Press.

Hindess, B. and Hirst, P.Q. (1975). *Pre-capitalist Modes of Production*. London : Routledge and Kegan Paul.

Hunter, W.W. (1879). *A Statistical Account of Assam*. London.

Hutton, J.H. (1921a). *The Angami Nagas*. London. Macmillan and Co.

Hutton, J.H. (1921b). *The Sema Nagas*. London : Macmillan and Company.

Jenkin, Alan, (1979). *The Social Theory of Claude Levi-Strauss*. London : The Macmillan Press Ltd.

Kahn, Joel S. (1981). Marxist Anthropology and Segementary Societies: A Review of the literature. In *The Anthropology of Pre-Capitalist Societies* (Ed) Joel S.Kahn and Joseph R.Liobera. London : MacMillan.

Leach, E.R. (1951). The structural implications of matrilateral cross cousin marriage. *Journal of Royal Anthropological Institute*. 81, 23-55.

Leach, E.R. (1957). Aspects of bridewealth and marriage stability among the Kachin and Lakher. *Man*, 57(59) : 50-55.

Leach, E.R. (1961). *Rethinking Anthropology*. London: University of London, Athlone Press.

Levi-Strauss, C. (1956). The Family. In *Man, Culture and Society*, (Ed) Harry L. Shapiro, 261-285. New York : Oxford University Press.

Levi-Strauss, C. (1963). *Structural Anthropology*. New York : Basic Books.

Levi-Strauss, C. (1969). *The Elementary Structures of Kinship* .Translated by J.H. Bell, J.R. von Sturmer and Rodney Needham. Boston : Beacon Press.

Lloyd, G.T. (1923). *Census of India*, 1921. Vol.III, Part I. Assam Reports and Tables, Shillong :Government Press.

Mackenzie, A. (1884). *History of the Relations of the Hill Tribes of the North-East Frontier of Bengal*. Calcutta :Government Press.

Majumdar, D.N. (1980). North-East India : A Profile. In *Eastern Himalayas*, (Ed). T.C. Sharma and D.N. Majumdar, Delhi : Cosmo Publications.

Marar, K.W.P. (1942). *Census of India*, 1941. Vol. IX, Part I & II Assam-Reports and Tables. Delhi : Manager of Publications.

Meillasoux, Claude. (1986). *Maidens, Meal and Money*. Cambridge : Cambridge University Press.

McSwiney, J.(1912). *Census of India*, (1911) Vol. III Part I & II Assam-Reports and Tables. Shillong:Assam Secretariat Printing Office.

Meggit, M.J. (1965). *The Lineage System of the Mae-Enga of the New Guinea* . London : Oliver and Boyd.

Michell, Capt. St. J.F. (1883). *Report (Topographical, political and Military) on the North Eastern Frontier of India*. Calcutta : Government of India.

Middleton, John, and David Tait.(Eds.)(1958). *Tribes Without Rulers Studies in African Segmentary System.* London : Routledge and Kegan Paul.

Mills, A.J. Moffat. (1853). *Report on the Province of Assam* . Report submitted to the Government of Bengal (Reprint 1980) Delhi : Gian Publication.

Mills, J.P. (1922). *The Lhota Nagas*. London :Macmillan & Co.

Mills, J.P. (1926). *Ao Nagas*. London : Macmillan & Co.

Mills, J.P. (1937). *The Rengma Nagas.* London :Macmillan & Co.

Mitchell, J.C.(1971). Social Change and the Stability of Marraige in Northern Rhodesia, In *Kinship*, (Ed). Jack Goody. Hammondsworth :Penguin Books.

Mullan, C.S. (1932). *Census of India* . 1931. Vol. III, Part I & II Assam-Reports and Tables, Calcutta :Govenment of India, Central Publications Branch.

Nakane, Chie. (1968). *Garo and Khasi* : *Comparative Study in Matrilineal Systems* . Paris :Mouton and Co.

Needham, Rodney. (1962). *Sturcture and Sentiment*: *a test case in social anthropology* . Chicago : University of Chicago Press.

Needham, Rodney. (1971). Remarks on the Analysis of Kinship and Marriage, In *Rethinking Kinship and Marriage*, (Ed). Rodney Needham. London : Tavistock.

Pakyntein, E.G. (1965). *Census of India*, 1961. Vol. III. Part V-A, Assam-Special Tables for Scheduled Caste and Scheduled Tribes. Delhi : Manager of Publications.

Pegu, N.C. (1956). *The Miris*. Dibrugarh.

Pemberton, R.B. (1835). *The Eastern Frontier of India*. Calcutta : Government Press. (Reprinted 1979, Delhi : Mittal Publications.)

Playfair, A. (1909). *The Garos*. London : David and Nutt.

Plowden, W.C. (1883). *Reports on the Census of British India*, 1883, Vol. 1. London.

Radcliffe-Brown, A.R. (1950). Introduction. In *African Systems of Kinship and Marriage*, (Ed). A.R. Radcliffe-Brown and Daryll Forde pp.1-85. London : Oxford University Press.

Radcliffe-Brown, A.R. and Forde, Daryll. (Eds). (1950). *African Systems of Kinship and Marriage.* London : Oxford University Press.

Reid, R. (1942). *History of Frontier Areas Bordering on Assam, from 1883-1941*. Shillong : Government of Assam.

Rey, P.P.(1975). The Lineage Mode of Production. *Critique of Anthropology* No. 3 Spring.

Rivers, W.H.R. (1906). *The Todas*. London :Macmillan & Co.

Robinson, W.M.(1841). *Descriptive Account of Assam*, London.

Roy, Sachin. (1960). *Aspects of Padam Minyong Culture*. Shillong : On Behalf of the Adviser, NEFA.

Saikia, A.K. n.d. *Census of India, (1971), Series 3, Part II-c(i)*, Assam Social and Cultural Tables. Delhi: Controller of Publications.

Shakespeare, Col. L.W. (1914). *History of Upper Assam, Upper Berma and North Eastern Frontier.* London : Macmillan and Company.

Shapiro, H.L. (Ed.)(1956). *Man, Culture and Society*. New York : Oxford University Press.

Sharma, S.C. (1952). *A Survey of Rural Economic Condition of Sibsagar*. Shillong : Government Press.

Sharma, T.C. and Majumdar, D.N. (Eds.)(1980). *Eastern Himalayas*. New Delhi :Cosmo Publications.

Sinha, R.(1963). *The Akas*. Shillong : Adviser's Secretariat, NEFA.

Smith, W.C. (1925). *The Ao Naga Tribe of Assam; a study in Ethnology and Sociology*. London : Macmillan & Co.

Srivastava, L.R.N. (1962). *The Gallong*. Shillong :Adviser's secretariat, NEFA.

Stack, E.(1883). Miris, Daphlas and Abors. *In Report on the Census of India 1881, Assam* Calcutta Government Press.

Statistical Handbook of Assam. (1980). Gauhati: Government of Assam.

Terray, Emmanuel. (1972). Historical Materialism and Segmentary Lineage Based Societies, In *Marxism and Primitive Societies*. (Ed). Maurice Bloch. New York : Monthly Review Press

Terray, Emmanuel. (1979). On Exploitation : Elements of an autocritique. *Critique of Anthropology.* 4(13-19), 37.

Vaghaiwalla, R.B. (1953). *Census of India. (1953). Vol. Part II-A. Assam, Manipur and Tripura-General Population and Social Tables (A.D. and E Series).* Shillong : Office of Census Superintendent.

Waddell, L.A. (1900). The tribes of Brahmputra valley. *Journal of Asiatic Society of Bengal.* LXIX, 1-III: 127.

Waddell, L.A. (1911). A note on the derivation of Miri. *Man.*11 (56) : 86.

INDEX